Table of Contents

Presented to Carla
on this 17th Day of
June, 2005.

Wayne Cox

Getting Well

Four Basic Principles for "Getting Well"

By

Wayne Cox, Patient
Dale Guyer, M. D.

authorHOUSE™

1663 LIBERTY DRIVE, SUITE 200
BLOOMINGTON, INDIANA 47403
(800) 839-8640
WWW.AUTHORHOUSE.COM

First published by AuthorHouse 11/04/04

ISBN: 1-4184-9329-5 (e)
ISBN: 1-4184-9328-7 (sc)
ISBN: 1-4184-9327-9 (dj)

Library of Congress Control Number: 2004096385

Printed in the United States of America
Bloomington, Indiana

This book is printed on acid-free paper.

Important Reader Information

Names

The majority of people's names presented in this book are real. However, others have been changed to protect their privacy.

Disclaimer #1

Wayne Cox has no formal medical training and, in writing this book, has shared with you, the reader, his interpretation of the medical information he has collected for his personal use in his process for "Getting Well." You should be aware that some of Wayne's opinions and treatments used to get well are not accepted by or are viewed as highly controversial by the conventional medical community. You should not assume that what turned out to be best for Wayne will be best for you. Instead, you should do your own investigation by consulting with your medical doctors to determine what is best for you. Cox Limited Publishing, LLC, owner of this book, *disclaims any responsibility to anyone who misinterprets the contents of this book as medical advice.*

Disclaimer #2

The doctor's commentary in this book is not intended to provide medical advice or to take the place of medical advice and treatment from your physician. Readers are advised to consult their doctors or other qualified health professionals regarding the treatment of their medical problems. Neither the publisher nor the authors take any responsibility for any possible consequences resulting from any treatment, action, or application of medicine, supplement, herb, or preparation to any person reading or following the information in this book. If readers are taking prescription medications, they should consult with their physicians and not take themselves off of medicines to start supplementation without the proper supervision of a physician.

Opinions and Beliefs

Getting Well is not intended to be a statement of facts and conditions concerning the practice of medicine in the United States. Instead it is based on a true story, written through the eyes of the author Wayne Cox, as to why he became so seriously ill. It is a journal of his opinions and beliefs he developed during the past twelve years that he struggled to regain his health.

Reserved Rights

To contact the authors, mail to or email to:

Advanced Medical Center
836 East 86th Street
Indianapolis, Indiana 46240
www.daleguyermd.com
317-580-9355

Cox Limited Publishing, LLC
P.O. Box 253
Brownsburg, Indiana 46112
wbcox@msn.com

Dedications

I dedicate this book to my lovely and faithful wife for the past fifty-two years, Betty (Chalfant) Cox. This book would not have been possible without her willing support of my writing effort. In my eyes, Betty is a professional reader. During the thirty months it took me to write *Getting Well*, Betty occupied herself by reading over 285 books. But anytime I handed her a draft of my work, she would, without complaint, quietly lay down her book and edit my work with a critical red ink pen. Words cannot express my gratitude to her for her loving care and support.

—Wayne Cox

As a youth, I remember an episode of *Leave It to Beaver* in which June advised her husband Ward that "If everything were left to men, we would still be crossing the country in covered wagons!" I have at this point in my life acquired enough wisdom to understand that message. Likewise I dedicate this book to my wife, Lisa, for inspiring a healing vision beyond the "HMO covered wagon." Additionally, her faithful love and support created a "better me" than I could have developed on my own. Also, my children, Skip, Lydia, Jake, Jimmy, Katie, and Abigayle, are my continuous source of inspiration and enjoyment. They always help me see things anew. Finally, I offer a dedication to my mother, father, and grandparents who long ago planted the seeds of holistic understanding and always saw in me more than I may have seen in myself.

—Dale Guyer, M.D.

Acknowledgments

This book required more assistance and time than I had anticipated. I am particularly grateful to the following wonderful people, who helped make this book possible. Thank you one and all!

- **Pat Blackwell, Content Advisor:** Before I created each chapter, Pat, my youngest sister and a professional dental hygienist, advised me on what an ill patient wanted to learn from a particular chapter about "Getting Well." Pat's special talent is thoroughly entwined in *Getting Well*.
- **Jackie Burgess, Content Editor:** After Pat reviewed my first draft of each chapter, Jackie, also a professional dental hygienist with newsletter writing experience, marked up changes to improve the clarity and flow.
- **Lillie Britton, Reader/Critic:** Ms. Lillie paid particular attention and offered advice as to what I wrote about my relationship with the Lord during the period of my "Getting Well."
- **Dawn Kinney, Reader/Critic:** I was introduced to Dawn when she called and asked how to get well. I agreed to tell her if she would agree to be a reader/critic for *Getting Well*. Her encouragement, advice, and support for this book have proven precious to me.
- **Nadine McCracken, Reader/Critic:** Nadine, her husband Greg, and her mother Analee live directly across the street from our home in Brownsburg, Indiana. Their combined honest comments made about my first-draft manuscripts created sizable improvements.
- **Wanda Reddick, Reader/Critic:** Wanda and I attended school together from the first grade to the twelfth. Fifty years later when I learned she wrote poetry, I asked that she be a reader/critic for *Getting Well*. Wanda's first bit of advice was "Wayne, don't tell me how to get well, show me." Each time I outlined a new chapter, I remembered Wanda's advice.
- **Robert Wade, Reader/Critic:** Robert is a professional engineer who became very ill from mercury that leeched into his body from his silver amalgam tooth fillings. We met at Dr. Guyer's clinic. Since then, he has become a valuable advisor to *Getting Well*.
- **Ron Viehe, Reader/Critic:** I became acquainted with Ron on the telephone, discussing both the book I was writing and how he could beat heart disease. Ron's expertise was to cross-out

anything I wrote that did not directly apply to "Getting Well." As a result, *Getting Well* developed into a better book.

- **Ellen Williams, Reader/Critic:** Ellen has a small clinic that provides a therapy for the ill. As a result, she has become very sensitive to the needs of chronically ill people. Her comments on first-draft manuscripts made *Getting Well* more sensitive to the needs of the chronically ill.

- **Paul Wilson, Copy Editor:** Paul is a professional copy editor with the talent to retain the "voice" of the main author of *Getting Well*, while at the same time composing the changes needed to make the book acceptable to the readers' high literary expectations.

- **Scot A. O'Farrell, Esq., Legal Advisor:** Scot has coached me on how to take full advantage of my First Amendment rights to free speech as a writer, but has advised me not to cross the line of needless insult or bad taste.

- **Mark Sullivan, Esq., Legal Counsel:** Mark maintains a legal office in Indianapolis and is a media lawyer representing several writers and authors.

Foreword

Being well, full of healthy vitality, is the most precious gift. If you or a loved one has been robbed of this gift, there may be no more important issue for you than to experience "Getting Well." No matter whom the thief may be—an unhealthy lifestyle, aberrant genetics, a polluted environment, misguided medical advice, or just inexplicable fate—you can either succumb to defeat or battle courageously to restore the treasure trove of wellness of spirit~mind~body wholeness.

If you decide to take on the battle, you are not alone. The authors of this book have joined forces to equip you to regain as much of the stolen assets in your wellness as is humanly possible and divinely granted.

The remarkable person who discovered The Four Basic Principles for "Getting Well" is Wayne Cox. His amazing and unforgettable story will inspire and educate you. Dr. Dale Guyer, his physician and the creator of The Advanced Medicine Center, will provide valuable knowledge that should be the heart of all treatment plans to restore the wealth of health.

Wayne and Dr. Guyer will use the forum of this book to inspire, educate, and challenge you or a loved one not to settle for an empty wellness bank account. Greater than the accumulation of money is the wealth of wellness and the richness of vitality. Your resources to restore your assets of healthy living are amazing and are probably underused.

Your part in "Getting Well" is to choose to be committed to a vision of new possibilities of wellness, so you can live a greater richness of health courageously, no matter what condition you are facing, or how long you may live. Together, we can ask for help from the Physician Within, the source of the power behind "Getting Well," so that the maximum possible restoration can take place.

—Dr. Craig Overmyer
Author, *Dynamic Health* and *Success Is a Decision of the Mind*
National Speakers Association Professional Member
Offering keynote speaking, training, and coaching
CanterburyCoach.com, covermyer@canterburygroup.com
317-506-5788

Introduction

This book is written for people who are tired of being sick and who want to learn a new approach to "Getting Well." *Getting Well* is not another book of sermons dictating what "you must do" to get well. Instead, this true story invites you on a journey with me to explore why we were so healthy while growing up and what went wrong that caused us to become so very ill. We learn on this journey that there are logical reasons for our illness that we can identify. Some reasons for getting ill are easy to understand and are within our control, while other causes for illness seem out of reach, but we find ways to control them along the way in our journey through these twenty chapters.

First, allow me to introduce myself. My name is Wayne Cox. I have been assigned as your guide throughout this journey. Some of the roads we will travel will seem a little gloomy at times when we realize that at any moment in our lives there are people dying prematurely from the same serious illnesses that have invaded our bodies and restricted our lives. But, do not despair, for you will soon find yourself traveling with me down a new road lined with bright lights of hope. Your hope will turn to great excitement as you learn to apply *The Four Basic Principles for "Getting Well"* and begin to realize that, regardless of your illness, you, too, have a good chance of regaining your active lifestyle by getting completely well.

I have qualified as your guide and relate to your situation because twelve years ago I was so ill that most of my family and friends felt I was not going to live very long, and my doctors seemed to agree. Today, at age seventy-two, I enjoy excellent health without aches or pains or physical restrictions. Recently, two physicians commented, "Wayne, I see no reason why you should not live to age ninety or beyond."

My goal while we are on this journey is for you to develop into an "exceptional patient." An exceptional patient is a seriously ill patient who refuses to be a victim. Instead, he or she learns and becomes a specialist in self-care with a goal to find *the cause of his or her illness* and participate in *a complete cure*. Exceptional patients are the twenty percent of the seriously ill who get completely well and often go on to enjoy a healthy life to age ninety years and beyond. Unfortunately, another twenty percent of the seriously ill will die before their fifty-ninth birthday, and the remaining sixty percent will die within a few years of age seventy. Not many of this majority group will reach a full, expected lifespan of seventy-seven years.

Exceptional patients have what psychologists call "an inner focus of control." Bernie S. Siegel, M.D., in his book *Love, Medicine & Miracles,* says that exceptional patients are guided by their own standards rather than by what others may think. I believe that The Spirit of God usually supports that inner focus within us. Both Dr. Guyer and I recognize the spiritual side of healing. I have experienced it, and Dr. Guyer has witnessed it. On this journey, you, too, will be exposed to it.

In Chapter 3, "Discovering My Illness," I have listed and will discuss with you the twenty physical and mental symptoms of illness I battled during my first two years of trying to get well. Before we can get completely well, we must first determine, and then eliminate, the many causes of our illness. By learning what caused each of my illness symptoms, you can learn to make your own list.

Although I have always made it a practice to take my illness symptoms to my primary-care physician first, I have found that many of our conventional medical doctors today lack skills for treating illnesses caused by toxins we contact in our environment and our lack of complete nutrition from the highly processed food we eat. I found it necessary, to get completely well, that I add medical treatments not available from conventional modern-day doctors. To assist you in your determined search for wellness, I have added Chapter 15, "Selecting a New-Type Medical Doctor," who can provide those additional medical treatments that can help you get completely well.

Why I Wrote This Book

After my first full year (1994) of weekly conventional medical treatments at my local hospital, I did not make much progress with most of my illness symptoms. In fact, I was worse off than when I started treatment. Realizing that changes must take place if I was to survive, I selected a new primary-care physician. After a complete review of my past and present health problems, this young family-practice M.D. referred me to an "environmental medical doctor" to determine the contribution toxins in my body were making to my health problems. My body tested high on toxins and low on nutrition. My environmental medical doctor immediately began treating me with chelation therapy to remove the toxins from my body and nutritional therapy to rebuild my weak immune system. Combined with the three-day-per-week exercise rehab program I was receiving at my local hospital, I soon began to show visible signs of "Getting Well."

After about six months of these additional treatments, my nurses at the local hospital who had treated or monitored me for the past eighteen months began to notice a big change in the way I looked and began to ask what I was doing to make such big improvements. After finding it necessary to reduce my high blood pressure medicine twice in six months, the head nurse called me into her office and demanded that I tell her every detail of the recent changes I had made. She said, "I know from your medical records you have been taking blood pressure medicine for the past twenty-four years, and now suddenly you don't need any; what's going on?" So, I shared with her that I was having the toxins removed from my body, and that I was taking a large assortment of vitamins and minerals prescribed by a medical doctor. This nurse wrote everything I said into my hospital medical record.

Soon, the word circulated among the nursing staff, and from that day on, while I was on an exercise bicycle or treadmill, a flow of nurses began visiting me and asking detailed questions about the additional treatments I was receiving at the environmental doctor's clinic.

It was not long before some of these nurses began asking for advice about nutrition or requesting that I talk with a person they knew who had been very ill for a long time, but not improving. Their requests often involved a loved-one like a father, aunt, or neighbor. Soon, I became very busy at home talking on the telephone to chronically ill patients who were trying to get well.

Each chronically ill caller usually started talking by saying, "I understand you know how to get well!" Because they always expressed their strong desire in terms of "Getting Well," that became the reason I called this book *Getting Well*, implying that, with hope, you, too, can get well.

As a result of these telephone calls, I began developing a strong desire to share information that might help chronically ill people find a way to get well. Often, after I hung up the telephone, I would write a personal letter in longhand and include articles and sometimes a book that might help them. Although I was making good improvements, I continued weekly medical treatments. Interestingly, I found that helping others was not a burden, but instead was good therapy for me.

In 1997, when I announced that I was completely well, my wife Betty and I began to do a lot of traveling, including exercising the freedom of leaving the Indianapolis area in our motor home and not knowing for sure when we would return. This made it almost impossible for me to help the steady flow of chronically ill people who called for help.

I continued to harbor a strong desire to help the chronically ill who were often desperately seeking help, so I came up with the idea to find a book that would tell an ill person how to get well. My idea was to buy, say, a hundred copies and send a free copy to those who continued to call me. While we traveled in our motor home, Betty and I spent a lot of time in bookstores trying to find that exact best book for "Getting Well." We struck-out. We could not find the book.

The next time we returned to Indianapolis, I asked Dr. Guyer, my new-type medical doctor, for the name of a book that would guide a chronically ill patient, like I used to be, to complete wellness. Dr. Guyer looked everywhere and struck-out, too. He said, "Wayne, the book you want does not exist, and if you want to buy a book like that, then my opinion is that you are going to have to write it yourself." He then recommended that I write my own story of "Getting Well" and said that he would help me with the book in any way he could.

I spent part of the year 2001 practicing my writing by learning to transfer my thoughts from my brain directly into MS Word on my computer. I continued to hone my writing skills in 2002 but spent most of my time sunning myself at the big Olympic-size swimming pool at the Sun-N-Fun RV Resort, in Sarasota, Florida. While in these relaxed surroundings, I began to encourage my mind to plan what I should say to the reader and to develop an outline of the book I had already named *Getting Well*.

Why Does This Book Have Two Authors?

In December 2002, I sat down at my computer and created a book outline with an overview for each chapter. I quickly realized that this book called *Getting Well* might appear to be a medical book. To address this possibility, I contacted Dr. Guyer, who suggested that I write this book in the first place, and requested that he join me as a co-author by writing medical commentary at the end of each of the twenty chapters.

Dr. Guyer agreed. As a result, it is now my pleasure to present to you my co-author and personal physician, Dale Guyer, M.D. He has written his own introduction to *Getting Well,* just for you.

Introduction to Medical Commentary for *Getting Well*

Getting Well emphasizes a pivotal consideration—*the individual perception of victim versus activist.* In this context, the average medical consumer, or should we say the consumer of life experience, tends to take the side of the victim. All problems that arise happen to be those that are outside of one's control. Therefore, it is easy to blame the government, the medical system, the insurance companies, family, friends, or other perceived inadequacies. Certainly, these perceptions may be correct, but the tendency to become an activist is seldom done in our society. Wayne is clearly an activist. He is an individual medical consumer, who has chosen not to take with absolute certainty everything pontificated to him by medical experts. Wayne looks beyond what is being said and thinks out of the medical box at adjunctive therapies that might contribute to his overall health.

An existing problem within standard medical practice falls within the mechanics of its evolution. As medicine is currently practiced in our country, doctors are obligated to bow to the dictates of large insurance corporations. While the situation is gradually changing, it remains the status quo for the average medical consumer. Under this system when a patient visits his or her doctor's office, often the doctor is seeing 50 to 60 patients a day, so the encounter typically lasts less than three to four minutes. He or she is generally ushered out of the room with a gift in hand of a few scribbles on a prescription pad designed to alleviate symptoms.

The doctors themselves are very limited by insurance dictates as to what laboratory analyses can be ordered, what diagnostic avenues may be pursued, and even what suggestions or prescriptions can be offered therapeutically. Insurance companies continue to maintain a death grip on medical practice. It would be incorrect, however, to point the finger solely at the insurance world, as doctors themselves are often woefully complacent and allow the predictive comfort of their medical practices to lull them into a sense of disconnected security.

Candidates for medical schools are selected not based on their capacity to think outside the box or to possess great insight, but generally on how accurately they can reproduce information given in a classroom lecture setting and, therefore, achieve a very high grade point average. In *Getting Well*, Wayne points out the often glaring inconsistencies from the perspective of the consumer and offers an invitation to the reader to move from a state of mechanization to activization and to pursue this relationship by working with a physician who will operate as a selective partner in one's healthcare, rather than as an antagonist to one's health. In the following chapters, these conceptions will be refined and amplified, and a path will be created such that, if the reader so chooses, he or she can move to a more activated state in his or her healthcare.

—Dale Guyer, M.D.

Chapter One
Just Like Me

Most of you, just like me, were born very healthy with an excellent set of genes. Less than five percent of us received a disease or a defective life-limiting gene from our parents. Although no combination of genes is perfect, we received from our young, dynamic, healthy parents an assortment of the very best genes their bodies had to offer. Our parents retained their weaker genes and sent forward to us their very best.

The preformatted design of the exciting human conception process guaranteed that only the single best egg available from your mother survived the complex trip from her ovaries through her fallopian tubes, just in time to receive from your father his single strongest sperm, which just beat out more than 300,000 other sperm that were also determined to swim the difficult upstream race to your mother's egg and become your proud father. The winning sperm arrived first, knocked gently on your mother's egg, and was invited to enter. She then shut out all others. Just like me, you received from this wonderful mating process the combination of delicate ingredients needed to begin a healthy life.

After birth, most of you, just like me, began receiving the world's most perfect food, breast milk. Our healthy mother's milk was not only perfect nourishment, but it also contained a balance of protective natural antibodies designed to fight off the undesirable bacteria, viruses, and parasites that surrounded us in our new environment outside our mother's womb.

As you approached age nine months, your mother began preparing your digestive system for adult food by mashing, then straining, fruits and vegetables from the table or by using prepared baby food from the grocery store. Wise mothers, just like yours, worried during this conversion period that the small amounts of table food were not supplying the ultimate nourishment needed for a rapidly developing child. As a result, most of our mothers began supplementing our diet with doses of cod-liver oil, fruit juices, vegetable juices, and even children's vitamins and minerals at about age one year. Our mothers were determined to raise a healthy child, and most of them did.

Growing Up

Just like many of you, I was born into a middle-class family with a low-class income, the first of four children. My mother was only eighteen, and my father had just turned twenty-one. They had not yet learned to earn much money.

But, when it came to "quality of life," we were rich. We lived on three acres of high-quality farmland in a four-room house on a gravel road. The fact that we didn't have much money to spend was the primary reason we were so healthy. We could not afford to buy processed food or eat at restaurants. Instead, we developed our three acres into a family production operation that provided nearly 100 percent of our nutritional needs. Looking back, based on present-day knowledge of nutrition, our diet was nearly perfect.

We had no choice but to drink raw, whole un-pasteurized milk directly from our Guernsey cow, which my dad hand milked each morning and I each evening. My mother and two sisters converted some of the cream into butter, buttermilk, and cottage cheese. Our Guernsey was always pregnant and produced a healthy young calf each year that we fattened out with whole grain and clover, then butchered into choice veal. The surplus milk was mixed with ground-up whole grain bran and table scraps that provided slop-food for three little pigs that we were preparing for fresh pork and high quality breakfast meat.

Each year we would buy from the hatchery 100 baby chicks that quickly grew into tender delicious fryers. Some chickens were saved as layers that produced dozens of fresh eggs. But, the centerpiece of our rich life was our being forced to eat large volumes of fruits and vegetables from our "organic garden." We were so short of cash that we could not afford commercial fertilizer, so we had no choice but to use composted cow manure. Instead of shrubbery in our lawn, we planted apple, pear, and cherry trees along with grape vines, strawberry plants, raspberry bushes, gooseberries, and a family favorite, rhubarb.

During the summer and fall months, our family was always busy canning and preserving a twelve-month supply of the fresh fruits and vegetables we had grown. We canned volumes of fresh fruit juices and vegetable juices that served as our soft drinks. We also made and bottled our own catsup. During the winter months, we butchered our yearling calf, butchered the three grown-up pigs, and canned the meats into various-sized glass containers. Bacon, ham, and sausage were processed with a hand-rubbed curing method called "sugar curing" after which the delicious meat did not require refrigeration.

Each spring a new calf would be born, three little pigs were selected from a local farmer's litter, 100 baby chicks were purchased, fruit trees were trimmed, and a new organic garden was prepared and then planted. Our family's self-contained food factory began a new cycle.

Staying Healthy

My mother prepared each meal from scratch. She served meat as a protein centerpiece, surrounded by a minimum of one fresh fruit and two or more large servings of nutritious vegetables that provided our vitamins, accompanied by a glass of fresh whole milk, canned juice, and a pitcher of mineral water, hand pumped cold from our own well just moments before the meal was served. Five days a week, our mother hand packed my dad's work lunch and our school lunch with the same nutritional balance as the meals she served at home. She furnished dad with a large thermos of hot coffee and us kids with a small thermos of fresh whole milk or cold fruit juice.

Daily exercise was considered necessary for good health. Our local school required a one-hour gym period three days a week. We played volleyball and basketball and learned floor exercises. I could easily climb hand-over-hand a thirty-foot, two-inch diameter rope to the ceiling of the gymnasium or wrap my legs around the fifty-foot flagpole in the front school lawn and work my way to the top. However, our family experienced plenty of exercise keeping our self-contained food factory going. Hand pumping water for our animals and our drinking, bathing, and laundry was real exercise. Keeping our animals fed and clean, processing meat in the winter time, and working in the garden in the summer, then canning the harvest in the fall, was routine but great physical exercise for the entire family.

You may have grown up in the city, but just like me, your school provided exercise for health reasons. Also, your mother was so concerned about your future health that she carefully shopped for the very best food available at the highest quality local markets. She made every effort to provide you with three highly nutritional, well-balanced meals each and every day. That is why when you grew up and left home, you were so healthy, just like me!

Slowly, It Began to Change

Change from this perfect diet I grew up with first surfaced while I was still at home at age eighteen. Indiana passed a law that all milk must be pasteurized. We could no longer drink whole milk fresh from our Guernsey cow. We tried boiling it, but it tasted terrible. Our family sold our cow and converted to factory-pasteurized milk, but we began drinking much less because, when compared to un-pasteurized, it tasted watered down and flat. We began buying commercial meat. We continued to provide most fruits and vegetables from our three acres, however, after converting to commercial fertilizers, the vegetables were noticeably less tasteful and, we suspected, less nutritious.

Today we know this to be true. Fruits and vegetables, grown with commercial fertilizers in nearly barren soils, lack a long list of essential vitamins and minerals necessary for good health. We also know that the meat tissue of our commercially grown beef, pork, and poultry contains animal growth hormones used to shorten the time needed to prepare an animal for market. Steroids and antibiotics are also used, which, along with animal-type growth hormones, accumulate in our body causing chemical imbalances resulting in immune system dysfunction that contributes to actual disease.

I remained home for the next two years, and, while most of my nutrition continued to come from my mother's good cooking, I began eating some meals at restaurants. At age twenty, I was drafted from college into the Army during the Korean War. That same year my sister Betty married, and one year later my sister Pat left home for college. With only mom, dad, and my kid brother Ed at home, our family's cash flow increased immediately. Organic gardening was no longer the centerpiece of our meal planning. My family began to have enough money to buy foods more convenient to prepare, commercially processed by large food companies.

The nutritional value of the food my family members began eating was reduced, and as we know today, traces of food additives used in commercially processed foods began to accumulate in the tissues of our bodies. Combined with the toxic, polluted air we breathe, this can cause a chemical imbalance in our body and chronic illness.

My sister Betty was the least affected by the change in eating habits. She was married at age eighteen and two years later began a family of three children. She and her husband Lanier started a new dry cleaning business and, like our mom and dad when they were first married, had little extra money to buy factory-processed food. Instead, they continued to grow and home process fresh meat, fruit, and vegetables from Lanier's family farm. Over the years, Betty has continued to prepare meals from basic fresh natural ingredients, and as she approaches seventy years is very healthy and continues to work with a high energy level in their family business.

After graduating from Indiana University School of Dental Hygiene, my second sister Pat married and began practice in the Cleveland area. She and her husband Bronson, a high school business teacher, raised two daughters. Both Pat and Bronson developed into the most dedicated, health-conscious organic cooks in our family. Unfortunately for Pat, her health was challenged by mercury vapors she breathed from cleaning and polishing the silver fillings in her patient's teeth. She had to retire early because mercury accumulated in her body and began causing chronic illnesses. Fortunately, Pat met a young Harvard Medical School graduate who recognized the problem, directed the removal of the mercury from her body, and treated her immune system. Today as she approaches sixty-eight years, she is once again very healthy.

Sadly, I cannot report a happy ending for my kid brother Ed. When my family sold our Guernsey cow, converted to commercial fertilizer for gardening, and then began consuming factory-processed milk and meat, Ed was only eight years old. We now know that his immune system was not fully developed. Two years later, we three older kids left home. Ed along with mom and dad began eating fewer meals prepared at home. Ed ate a commercially prepared lunch at school. Dad began having lunch at restaurants. They introduced luncheon meats to the family table, and started a tradition of Sunday dinner at restaurants. After eight years of this type food, Ed was off to Purdue for four more years of typical college food. After graduation as a professional engineer, he began working for the Highway Department of the State of Indiana, designing bridges, traveling, and holding meetings with outlying communities. Meetings in Washington, D.C., and travels throughout the United States and Europe all caused Ed, year after year, to eat over half his meals at restaurants.

Ed was a handsome man, physically trim, who exercised daily, had a full head of wavy hair, and always maintained his cholesterol level below 200. He was very gentle and always presented a warm, friendly smile. But, at age fifty-three, a virus entered his body and began attacking his heart. His heart slowly weakened and enlarged trying to keep blood supplied to his body. Ed's immune system was not strong enough to kill the virus, and doctor-prescribed drugs were not effective. Ed never missed a single day of work due to his illness, but three days before Christmas at age fifty-six he passed away on a treadmill doing his very best to get well. Knowledge available today indicates that incomplete nutrition over several years could have been involved with his weakened immune system.

By now, you are hopefully thinking back over your own family and the well-balanced meals your mother provided during the growing-up period of your life, resulting in outstanding good health. If, instead of from-scratch, well-balanced, nutritious meals, your family relied on food from tin cans, high-carbohydrate snacks, frozen dinners, and carryout fast foods, there is a very good chance that at middle age you are now chronically ill. Do not despair; by the time you finish this book, you will have learned *The Four Basic Principles for "Getting Well."* Regardless of age, it is never too late to return to complete wellness, experiencing life's exciting days waiting for you!

Doctor's Commentary

A model of human health often presented is that soon after conception everything starts to decline. While we tend to think of the developing embryo in its purified state with cellular energy as at an all-time high in terms of efficiency, replication, and energy production, we are often not able to see a potential dark side of how a dynamic biological process, while unraveling in its most dramatic fashion, is also afforded with the noxious agents of biological decline, i.e., toxin interference from the environment.

From conception, we are exposed to many pollutants. Tobacco smoke—either primary or secondary—alcohol, numerous environmental toxins, and persistent nutritional deficiencies on all levels start to wreak biological havoc. At an early stage in life, the damage is much less likely to be evident except on the molecular level and, therefore, would not be detected even on a standardized blood test. I am confident that in the future we will have defined this enigma so precisely and organized our thoughts around this challenge that we will be able to offer standardized testing of all newborns. Through blood and urine analysis, we will be able to determine from a genetic and biochemical basis exactly what types of diets, environments, and important nutritional elements an individual is going to need to function optimally.

Once a child is born, even before the immune system is mature, he or she is ordinarily met with an onslaught of immune system-modifying vaccinations, often containing preservatives known to be toxic, e.g., mercury, and we are just starting to understand that, in select individuals, these approaches may not confer the best health benefits. Also, our diets have declined substantially through the years, imposing secondary nutritional deficiencies, while the level of toxin exposure in our industrialized society continues to increase. Therefore, our health and basic biological destiny have become products of how our unique genetic system is bathed in the fabric of our environment. For some like Wayne and fortunately even me, our lives started with access to an optimal, mostly organic food supply with all food commodities generally farm fresh and of much higher nutritional value. Luckily, some of us were born into a health-conscious family that encouraged the consumption of antioxidant vitamins and nutrients that later clinical research has proven to be very beneficial.

However, this is not usually the case in modern society. Recently, I took my son to a basketball game. While sitting on the stands watching the game, I observed what the average youth was snacking on during the game. It may not come as any surprise that I could not find one healthy item being consumed by any of the many children present. Caffeinated, high-sugar sodas with high-fat corn chips, hot dogs laden with nitrates and processed meats, and high-sugar Slushies with synthetic chemicals, dyes, and coloring agents were typical fare. Just stroll down the aisles of a modern supermarket. Rarely will you discover an option that one would categorize as truly healthy or nutritionally dense. As a matter of fact, the products are high calorie, high fat, or simple carbohydrate-dense.

Collective activity in our society has declined as well. The farm life that Wayne experienced is now non-existent. Physical activity was replaced by hours in front of video games. As a result, the average weight of America's youth has increased dramatically, creating an environmental and populational predisposition to developing insulin resistance, Syndrome-X, lipid abnormalities, immune system deficits, and nutritional deficiencies. The greatest surprise is not so much that we are unwell, as that we can actually function at all.

—Dale Guyer, M.D.

Chapter Two
On Your Own

When most of us grew up and left home, we were in excellent health. Being the oldest sibling, I ate more perfect organic high-nutrition meals than my sisters or brother during our growing-up years, so I had the very best chance for good health as an adult. Just before entering the Army, I also made a very smart move health-wise. I married my teenage sweetheart Betty Chalfant. Betty grew up in a family of twelve children. With fourteen mouths to feed, more people than just Mrs. Chalfant were involved in meal preparation. All meals, for cost reasons, were prepared from basic organically grown produce raised in their garden or purchased from local truck-patch gardeners. As a result of her childhood eating habits, Betty developed a natural instinct to prepare all meals from basic fresh produce instead of factory-processed foods.

When I married Betty fifty-two years ago, she had already discovered the need for food supplements. She was using vitamin C to improve her complexion and ward off the common cold. She soon began taking calcium and magnesium, which improved her energy levels. She added vitamin E when an older brother developed heart disease. Over the years, Betty has experimented with various natural health recommendations she has read about. "Not all of them work," she says, "but I have never been hurt by any of them either."

Betty has learned to listen to her body and become attuned to its needs, accepts the responsibility for her own health, and educates herself about the relationship of good nutrition with good health. As a result, she has not found it necessary to contact a medical doctor for a medical illness during the past thirty-two years and has not had a drug prescription filled for the past forty-two years. We do, however, perform at-home basic tests like blood pressure (typically 110/70) and blood glucose (typically 80), and then annually, being a natural blond, Betty has her fair skin examined by a dermatologist. Occasionally she has some lab tests done for peace of mind.

At Age Twenty, I Was Drafted into the Army

They gave me a physical exam and two days of written tests. My I.Q. scored above 110, which qualified me for Commission Officer's School. My physical condition scored in the top one percent, and this qualified me to apply for pilot training. It was obvious that my parent's good genes and their dedication to raising a healthy child were the reasons that I was presented with these exciting opportunities.

During my first year in the Army, I was separated from Betty while I completed, as a Private, sixteen weeks of Basic Infantry Training followed by twenty-two weeks of Officer's Candidate School. I was awarded a Commission, rank of 2nd Lieutenant, along with a set of orders to Gary Air Force Base, San Marcos, Texas, for a year of pilot training.

Off to Pilot Training

Back in Indiana, Betty and I hooked up our twenty-seven-foot house trailer to an eight-cylinder Pontiac and headed for Texas. In the back seat of our Pontiac was a bed for our first little baby, Cynthia. Down a country road from the Air Force Base, under a huge pecan tree along the San Marcos River, we set up our house trailer in the fresh clean air of the wide-open spaces. During the day while I was learning to fly airplanes, Betty and Cindy explored the surrounding area looking for locally grown fresh fruits, vegetables, fresh eggs, and a variety of meats raised on the open range of Texas.

Betty, who supplemented her own diet, placed Cindy on vitamin and mineral supplements within a few days of being born. I did not take supplements because our Flight Surgeon, a specially trained medical doctor who directed the health of military pilots, said that vitamin and mineral supplements are not needed for good health. I was very healthy and believed him. Betty, however, was not impressed with his knowledge.

Healthy and Very Happy

Upon graduation from pilot school, I received my silver Army Aviator Wings, and we moved our little house trailer to Fort Rucker, Alabama. I completed four months of tactical flight training after which I was assigned to Fort Benning, Georgia, as a pilot in support of the 3rd Infantry Division ground troop training. Shortly after arriving at Fort Benning, our second daughter, Shirlee, was born. We sold our house trailer and moved into a nice three-bedroom double located on the military post. We remained at Fort Benning for almost three years to complete my five-year commitment of active duty. Because of Betty's strict attention to family nutritional needs, we all returned to Indiana very healthy, but slowly over time things began to change for me.

A Gift from a Major Manufacturing Corporation

I was released at age twenty-five from military active duty, and we moved back to Indiana. I accepted a job at a large—fifty-three acres under one roof—major manufacturing plant because I qualified for its four-year training program, learning machine shop operation, involving the highly technical process of designing and building the dies that stamp out from flat sheet metal the various complex parts making up an automobile. I received on-the-job training during the day in the plant and attended college level classes at night for the first four years. My employer paid me good wages and all educational expenses while training.

During this period, Betty and I had two more children, Greg, our third child, and Julie, our fourth. We lived on four acres of very rich farmland where Betty had a successful gardening operation from which she and the kids earned extra money selling fresh fruits and vegetables to the local supermarket. Our land, as explained in our land deed, was formerly part of the Miami Indian Reservation. The black loam soil was so rich that no fertilizer of any kind was required to grow prize produce. The supermarket sold Betty's fruits and vegetables at a premium price because of superb taste. The high content of natural minerals in the soil provided a taste of nutrition far superior to produce grown with commercial fertilizers.

After the four years of training, I became a supervisor for sixty to one hundred machinists, toolmakers, die makers, and welders doing the same work on which I had trained. The salary and family benefits were excellent, but I believed the working conditions were terrible. Three acres of the plant were two stories of office space, but the remaining fifty acres contained nearly 3,000 employees, some at work creating clouds of toxic polluted air hovering continually at floor level along with a constant barrage of nerve-ravaging noise. Conditions included:

- smoke from burning machine cutting oils
- toxic fumes created by thousands of spot-welders in a twenty-acre automobile body sub-assembly area
- large clouds of metallic dust created by giant machines down to workmen with hand-held grinders
- large semi trucks driving into the plant delivering supplies, belching smoke from their diesel engines
- a diesel switch engine spotting a hundred railroad freight cars each day inside the plant for shipping finished body parts from the production lines

Employees' on-the-job illnesses and job related injuries were so numerous that this modern plant had a full-time medical doctor and a large staff of nurses to attend the workmen's medical needs created during working hours.

After about five years, being thirty years old, I began to develop sinus problems and developed a tendency to gain weight. I also began to take notice that supervisors, like me, were having a lot of heart attacks and strokes around ages forty-five to fifty-five. This concerned me. Then one day at a management, health, and safety meeting, I looked up my job classification and was horrified to discover that my life expectancy was only fifty-three years.

Betty and I discussed it and decided I must find a new job. It took five years, but finally we were offered the *American Dream,* an opportunity to be part owner of the business I worked for. After ten years with automobile manufacturing, at age thirty-five, with four children, Betty and I sold our beloved four acres and moved to Brownsburg, Indiana, a small community west of Indianapolis, to help organize this new startup business in Indianapolis.

Out of the Frying Pan and into the Fire

During my last eight years while working at the automobile plant, the Vietnam War escalated, and the Army required me to maintain combat readiness as a Reserve Pilot flying on weekends with the Indiana Army National Guard. I met a former Navy Fighter Pilot, Jim Graham, flying to meet his requirements like me. Jim was a Purdue graduate and did research for the Eli Lilly Pharmaceutical Company. As we flew together on weekends, we became good friends and shared a common dream of having our own little business instead of working for the giant corporations. After about five years of dreaming went by, in the summer of 1968 we resigned from the respective corporations and began forming our own company.

Because the trucking industry was forecasted to grow very fast over the next ten years, we decided to get involved. We organized a mobile service company that performed oil changing, lubrication, engine tune-up, and general repair of commercial trucks at the customer's location, seven days a week, during the night hours when the trucks were not in use.

Jim worked during the day and was responsible for sales and making the company grow. I worked at night supervising the service mechanics. The business was an instant success. At the end of the first year, Jim had contracted over 2,000 commercial vehicles for our scheduled service, and

I trained several crews of mechanics for servicing and repairing trucks at various customer garage locations in Indianapolis.

Just like the automobile industry, the money was good but the working conditions were terrible! Imagine the polluted air we created by starting up the engines of fifty utility company trucks in a parking garage, in the middle of the night, warming up engines in preparation for an oil and filter change, and then after the service, again starting the fifty engines checking for leaks. Of course we always opened the garage doors for maximum fresh air and turned on exhaust fans, but that did not erase the fact that the air my service crews and I breathed was very toxic. Because this was the nature of our business, we breathed these leaded gasoline exhaust fumes night after night.

After being in this business for about six years, my partner Jim made an unannounced visit to me at around midnight at a customer's garage during a truck service work period. He was concerned about the detrimental effect our service business might be having on our mechanics' and my health. Just a few weeks before, I had been rushed by ambulance to the hospital emergency with heart attack symptoms. It turned out to be an anxiety attack, but this did not satisfy Jim. He was aware of my big weight gain and the fact that I no longer looked healthy, and he wanted to discuss it.

Jim suggested we sell the service business and then start up a truck parts warehouse business and get away from what he called "the greasy fingernail business." With just two hours of discussion at 2:00 A.M. in that service garage, we agreed to change the entire direction of our business, for health reasons.

The very next day Jim began making sales calls and selling truck parts from our own large parts inventory to other service garages. At the end of the first year, Jim had contracted for a 10,000 square-foot warehouse and hired two additional outside salesman. We found a buyer for our service business, and I joined Jim in our new truck parts business.

For the first time in sixteen years, I was away from the terribly polluted working conditions. Since I was now working days, Betty insisted I eat only her cooking. She purchased about twenty-four ten-inch diameter plastic food plates with covers. She would make up about six different well-balanced, nutritious meals, carefully weighing out the calories, and then place the attractive meals on the twenty-four plastic food plates, attaching the covers and freezing them.

Each morning after breakfast, she selected a different frozen meal I would heat up for lunch. If I were going to work late, she would send two frozen meals. Following Betty's simple plan, I lost forty-five pounds over the next four years, but I was still twenty pounds overweight. Although I was eating correctly, I continued to look ill and age faster than I should have. Betty suggested I take vitamins and minerals like she and the kids. I asked at least ten medical doctors for advice, all of whom stated that I did not need vitamin and mineral supplements, that I was getting everything I needed from eating a large variety of good food. Betty strongly disagreed and began demanding I take at least vitamin C twice daily.

Over the next fifteen years, Jim and I built a successful business of four truck parts stores with thirty-six employees. During these years, my health continued slowly down hill. I required regular contact with doctors and two surgical operations and continued to look older than my age. A voice inside me warned that something was not right with my health, although doctors could not find much wrong, except high blood pressure and being overweight.

At age fifty-four, I informed Jim that I wanted to sell my share of the business. Jim understood why and decided to sell his share, too. We sold our business to a much larger truck parts company after which we both continued to work for the new company for five years, and then both of us retired. My concerns about my health proved to be accurate. I retired at age fifty-nine, and at age sixty, I was seriously ill and unable to work.

Just between You and Me

The detailed information you have read in Chapters 1 and 2 about my life is the same type of information your doctor should know about your life if you are going to get completely well. Your doctor will be looking for and should treat the cause of your illness. To find that cause, he or she will begin by matching your symptoms with the details of your life. For example, after reading my life's history, my new-type doctor whom I selected responded that he believed that the polluted toxic air I breathed for sixteen years at my workplace had something to do with my illness. But, if my doctor had not invested the two hours interviewing me about the details of my life, he would have known about my symptoms only. With nothing but symptom knowledge, doctors usually say, "I don't know what caused your illness, but here are some drug prescriptions that should take care of the problem."

As you read the next chapter, please keep a notepad and pencil handy. I will expose how my twenty symptoms of illness began to slowly develop in my body and eventually caused "A Rude Awakening" in my life. If you note a symptom I had that you now have, write it down because, in chapters that follow, I will reveal the cause of my symptoms and what treatment cured them. Then you may get well, too, just like me.

Doctor's Commentary

As previously observed, Wayne and many others had the luxury of growing up in an environment that provided the healthiest foundation from which to launch their life experience. Historically in the United States, that was the norm, with people consuming foods locally grown and organically produced without chemicals, pesticides, synthetic fertilizers, or herbicides. In addition, the nutritional content and antioxidant levels were higher. All that changed with the advent of modern agricultural techniques and processed, prepared foods, which provide a much narrower niche of healthy consumables. As often is the case, Wayne's spouse Betty was years ahead of conventional understanding. She was already taking multivitamins and insisting on good healthy meals for her husband and family.

Men, I have experienced, tend to be less focused on overall health to the point of ignoring it. They are also less focused on the overall body in general, at least until they experience the first symptoms of chest pain. I have often joked with male patients that I insist that they should bring their spouses or significant others to an office visit with them, so that we could get to the real truth of the matter. Even though years ago Betty and many other well-informed members of society were aware of the health benefits of nutritional supplementation and a healthy diet, the medical profession then and now levels disclaimers at any statement that people can benefit from nutritional supplements, or that organically grown foods are superior. At this point in our clinical and scientific understanding, it seems to be almost unconscionable, but one must remember that opinions rendered by experts are often couched in biases, emotional attitudes, and paradigms, as opposed to basic science.

Sometimes, as Wayne has attested, many of the healthier patients I have encountered in my practice are those who stayed away from medical intervention, prescription medicines, and diagnostic procedures. I would be the first to state that a balanced approach is best, but our medical profession tends to overindulge on the side of invasive procedures and multiple prescription drugs, all of which can make the patient feel worse.

I will always remember an encounter I had as a medical student in the emergency room. A seemingly very healthy, 80-plus-year-old woman came into the emergency room with nausea and stomach pain. While the problem turned out to be minor, I will always recall my interesting conversation with her. Since it is the medical student's job to acquire the basic medical history from each patient, I discovered that she had no previous medical history. When asked who her family doctor was, she had none. When asked what other surgeries or prescription medicines she was currently using, she had none. As a matter of fact, the last time she said that she saw a doctor was when her last son was born when she was 25. I was shocked, because from a medical student's perspective, when everyone you see is sick, you get used to the fact that all have extensive histories. I shared this information with the staff ER physician. He jokingly said, "That is probably why she has done so well; she has chosen to stay away from doctors her whole life." While given in a jestful way, the statement did contain ironic truth, in that we later find that many of the treatments and therapies offered probably contribute to unraveling of the quality of a person's health. Then, the only agencies that benefit are the pharmaceutical companies.

For Wayne, however, and many others, despite having a good foundation, he found himself immersed in a highly toxic environment, requiring an extensive commitment of time, effort, and energy, which invariably places extensive stress on the body and can be maintained only so long. Quite likely, if Wayne had not been so healthy to begin with, he never would have lasted so long. He would have invariably become a matching statistic to the ones presented to him at the plant where he was employed, where the average lifespan of someone in his position was only 53. It does not take much of a rocket scientist to understand how that environment could gradually contribute to a downward spiral of that person's overall health. The constant barrage of toxic vapors, fumes, and metallic dust, all of which are known toxins to the body, would eventually start to usurp its overall health, and it was really the sequence of Wayne's work experience that gradually stripped away what little he had left remaining of a healthy foundation. That is also the reason why he and others find themselves somehow holding on to a retirement (or early retirement), only to experience that the years that they worked toward and looked forward to are often met with medical tribulation, poor health, and a new full-time job of attending doctor visits and medical procedures.

—Dale Guyer, M.D.

Chapter Three
Discovering My Illness

We don't get ill suddenly. Our body sends out little indicators of change when cells begin reacting abnormally. Often we ignore these little changes in our body because there is no pain or discomfort. If they don't go away, we often dismiss it as normal, a part of aging we say. When some of the little indicators begin creating discomfort and pain, we go to our doctor. Usually our primary-care physician listens sympathetically, writes a drug prescription, and advises us to come back if the medicine does not take care of the problem. Should we ask the doctor what caused the problem, he or she usually gives us about two or three possibilities and then often ends up saying, "In your case we don't know." What the doctor may be thinking:

- *It's a lot of work to find out the cause of an illness!*
- *Let's wait and see if the patient gets sicker; then it should be easier to spot the cause.*

If the medicine stops the discomfort, we usually say we have a good doctor. We do not realize that the cause of our medical problem may be covered up and that our body's natural alarm that illness is on the way has been turned off by the medicine.

Being aware of even a slight change in our body is important. If we can determine the cause of the little changes in our body and make corrections, we can often prevent serious chronic illness from developing. As I list in this chapter the series of body-change indicators and symptoms I experienced, make your own list. If you are seriously ill, you will need your list, along with a history of your life as detailed in Chapters 1 and 2; then, when combined with extensive laboratory testing, your doctor should be able to diagnose the cause or causes of your illness, and treat them, and you can get completely well, just like me.

My Health Indicators and Illness Symptoms

Age twenty-nine, sinus problems—an early indicator of serious illness developing. Remember that I was working in a large manufacturing plant during the 1960s, breathing that terribly polluted air. When it overpowered and infected the filtering system in my nose and head, toxic particles flowed freely to my lungs. They transferred the toxins directly to my bloodstream, which circulated them to all areas of my body. Toxin buildup eventually causes a variety of diseases. If you have chronic sinus problems, toxins from the polluted air around you are being circulated throughout your body.

Age thirty, weight gain—an early indicator that my absorbed nutrition was inadequate. My weight gain was being caused by my diet lacking all the nutrients needed for good health. My hunger pangs and food cravings were signals that my body lacked some of the essential vitamins or minerals. As a result, I continued to overeat, trying to satisfy the food cravings, resulting in weight gain. I found thirty-five years later that my food cravings stopped when I began taking vitamins and minerals at levels prescribed by a medical doctor skilled in nutrition. I then discovered that weight control is a function of adequate nutrition, not willpower.

Age thirty-four, skin rash—began developing on my chest, underarms, groin, and feet. This is a good indicator that the heavy metal toxins from my work environment were accumulating in my body. My healthy body was attempting to expel toxins through my sweat glands, and the toxicity of the sweat created a rash.

Age thirty-eight, high blood pressure—I had resigned from the large manufacturing plant and was in my second year of the newly formed truck service business. The business desired to insure my life with a large life insurance policy. I busted the physical exam. A series of blood pressure tests averaged 160/95. I was twenty-five pounds overweight. Doctors prescribed a strong diuretic drug. In sixty days, I lost about fifteen pounds, and my blood pressure went back to 120/80. The insurance company issued the policy. High blood pressure should be a wake-up call that the body is ill, but my doctors at that time convinced me that I was healthy and that I inherited the blood pressure problem from my father. "It is necessary to take blood pressure medicine the remainder of your life," they said. Later, after I followed The Four Basic Principles for "Getting Well," I found I no longer needed drugs to control my blood pressure.

Age forty-one, anxiety attacks—at 12:30 A.M., early on a Saturday morning, I was rushed to the hospital emergency with heart attack symptoms. I was diagnosed as having an anxiety attack and was given strong sedative shots that calmed me down. My doctor prescribed a drug package designed to prevent it from happening again. The drugs worked, but they interfered with my ability to think, so I did not take them for job-performance reasons. Over the next year, twice I required treatment at the hospital. It was on-again and off-again with the prescription drug package.

I was sixty-five pounds overweight. Betty insisted I lose weight. I did, and the anxiety attacks began to subside. Later I learned that the increased truck-exhaust toxins that were constantly entering my bloodstream caused the anxiety attacks by disrupting my blood chemistry and interfering with my nutrient-absorption process. My body's cells were screaming for more vitamins and minerals by creating food cravings. I reacted to the cravings by eating more calories. When my blood was overloaded with toxins, my immune system stored the surplus toxins not filtered out by my liver and kidneys in fat cells, out of harm's way. If my immune system detected more toxins than fat cells to store them in, my body was encouraged to produce even more fat cells, so that my immune system had someplace to store the toxins. As a result, a difficult-to-stop weight-gain cycle was created.

Age forty-two, need for glasses—The 20/15 vision I had as a pilot had now weakened. I began to squint when reading the telephone book. Bifocals solve the problem. The doctor said that my eyes looked healthy.

Age forty-seven, major dental problems—Over the years, I had regular checkups with a dentist resulting in about ten silver fillings, two root canals, and five jaw-teeth extractions. The pattern of the extractions reduced my chewing ability. Most teeth were very hot/cold sensitive and infections were common. I selected a former instructor at a dental school to solve my dental problems. He replaced my loose silver fillings with new silver material, performed three more root canals to stop the infection, saved two cracked jaw teeth with gold crowns, and constructed three long gold bridges across the areas of missing teeth. This gave me full chewing power again. However, I was not informed at that time, but learned later, that all silver filling material is made up of fifty percent mercury, twenty percent silver, and approximately ten percent each of tin, zinc, and copper. When I became seriously ill, I learned that galvanic electricity is created among the five metals making up the silver fillings, causing the metals to be dissolved and released into my bloodstream. In addition, each time I would chew food, micro-amounts of mercury vapor were created that also entered my bloodstream. Over time, the highly toxic mercury and very toxic tin built up in my body's organ tissue and contributed enormously to my illness.

Age forty-eight, inability to concentrate—This came on quickly, in less than six months. I lost my ability to organize my next week's work during the last three hours on Friday afternoon. Suddenly, I found myself working all day Saturday trying to get organized. Often, I went to my office on Sundays, struggling to be ready for the Monday morning meeting. Sixteen years later, I discovered the cause of this concentration problem. Large amounts of mercury and tin from my tooth fillings, combined with the lead from the truck exhaust fumes I had inhaled over the years, accumulated in my brain cells. It came on suddenly because of the large volume of mercury vapor absorbed during the major dental work done at age forty-seven, the year before. This disrupted the chemical balance and the normal electrical functions of my brain. At sixty-four, I had all the mercury, tin, and lead removed from my entire body, and my ability to concentrate returned quickly, very close to the level I experienced as an Army Pilot at twenty-four.

Age fifty, birthmark operation—My lower back had a five-inch by seven-inch, very black, skin-deep birthmark. My doctor became concerned because two small bumps began to grow on the surface. Tests showed no cancer, but it was the type of skin pigment that could migrate to cancer. He recommended surgical removal. I was in the hospital for four days. Twenty-two years later, that area of my lower back remains normal, suggesting that certain types of preventive surgery may be wise.

Age fifty-two, gallbladder operation—After two painful attacks, each one-week apart, my doctor insisted I have my gallbladder removed. My surgeon made the big nine-inch diagonal incision on the right abdominal area. Reaching in with both hands and, using a self-retaining retractor (jack), raising my right ribcage, he flopped the liver up under the ribcage, exposing the underside of the liver containing the gallbladder. He removed my gallbladder and then spent about thirty minutes examining the stomach, intestines, and other sections of the abdominal area for disease. He announced that I looked very healthy inside.

Age fifty-three, diabetes arrives—Nine months after my gallbladder operation, I was diagnosed as a type-2 diabetic. The Exchange Diet and a walking program controlled my glucose level for fourteen years. During the fifteenth year, my first drug prescribed was Rezulin®. I needed the maximum-allowed dose to control my glucose. Rezulin® was widely promoted and quickly became the number-one profit maker for Warner Lambert. Three months after I was prescribed the drug, Europe banned Rezulin®, claiming that it was causing deaths by damaging the liver. The Food and Drug Administration (FDA) claimed no deaths in the U.S. and insisted the product was safe.

Twelve months went by, and a few lawsuits for wrongful deaths against Warner Lambert were filed. This concerned me, so, after fourteen months on Rezulin®, I quit taking it. Another twelve months went by, and the FDA ordered the removal of Rezulin® from the market upon finding out that people in the United States had died from using this drug, too. The FDA then fined Warner Lambert for lying and filing false reports about

Rezulin®. Paying the fine was no problem because Warner Lambert had already grossed an estimated 1.8 to 2.1 billion dollars from Rezulin® sales. I learned later that this was not the first time a drug company had been fined for filing false reports to the FDA about the safety and effectiveness of its product.

I was on the FDA watch-list and had my liver tested every month during twelve of the fourteen months I took the drug. Since the time I have been off Rezulin®, I have been unable to take any other drug for diabetes without my liver becoming inflamed within three months. I inject insulin now, along with diet and exercise. Because I was on the FDA's watch-list, I continue to get letters from large law firms asking me to join their class-action lawsuits. Copies of their letters are available on the Web by searching for the word Rezulin®. These lawsuits, based on information I have received, appear to be being settled out of public view. Dr. Guyer recently told me that the type of liver test the FDA monitoring program provided me would not have detected, in time, the type of liver damage Rezulin® causes.

Age fifty-five, energy loss and premature aging—Jim and I had sold our truck-parts business, and I had completed one year of the five-year management contract I signed with the new corporation. My life actually was very easy because I had a large staff of younger managers doing all the day-to-day work. My job was to train them before I retired at age fifty-nine. Fifty-nine was considered early retirement, but most people thought I was retiring late because I looked more like I was sixty-nine. People often mentioned that fact. My energy level continued to decline. I visited my doctor every three months. He could not find the reason for my energy decline, but found it necessary to add more drugs to control my blood pressure. As I approached my last year before retirement, I also was taking medicine for my nerves. My boss, a vice president, often would ask if I was feeling okay and would suggest I take a few days off.

Age fifty-six to fifty-nine—by the time I retired, an assortment of what seemed like minor symptoms began to develop:

- sore tongue: It was so sore that it would sometimes crack and bleed. My doctor would examine the redness and suggest that I was drinking my coffee too hot. He recommended saltwater rinses. I stopped drinking coffee. The rinses helped, but did not cure the problem.
- red streaks: These were on my face, along the side of my nose, and down the cheeks from just below the eyes to the chin. I sometimes looked like I was wearing Indian war paint. The pores on my nose

would often pop open and bleed. The cause stumped my doctor. He prescribed an antibiotic cream. This controlled infections, but the problem continued as an unexplained chronic condition.

- muscle twitch: It first began with an unannounced twitch of the right upper eyelid. It would last for a moment and then go away. Soon muscle twitching began happening at other areas of my body. It would begin while reading the newspaper, at a stoplight in my car, or while resting on the couch. It was not pain, just an uncontrolled twitching of the muscle. If I touched the muscle or moved the muscle, the twitching would stop. My doctor just smiled and said that a lot of people my age had this and that it was nothing to worry about. Today, twelve years later, I know what caused it and no longer have that problem.

- stomach tremors: After eating certain foods, I would sometimes have tremors in my stomach often accompanied with a fast or irregular heartbeat. My doctor had no idea how to address this problem. Later I discovered the tremors were actually coming from my colon.

- food allergies: An allergy is a misjudgment by the immune system. Immediately after a difficult root canal on a jaw tooth, I developed severe allergies to eighteen common foods. My reactions when I ate any of these foods were a nervous shaky feeling, increased heart rate, mild nausea, and tremors in the colon. The eighteen foods were identified by skin sensitivities testing to help me avoid eating them. My allergies were created when mercury, the most toxic metal to the human body, entered my bloodstream. This large dose of mercury came from an infected jaw tooth with a large silver filling covered by a gold crown. A silver filling is fifty percent mercury.

My dentist drilled down through the gold crown, through the large silver filling, and relieved the pressure as a first step in performing a root canal. This tooth was boiling with infection and continued to do so for two months while I remained on antibiotics and the dentist treated it. Finally the infection settled down, and the root canal was completed. It was during the two months when the tooth boiled with infection that the large amount of mercury was carried by the infection into my bloodstream. My immune system, recognizing mercury as the worst possible substance to be in contact with the human body, directed the liver to filter out as much of it as possible and to deposit it in my digestive system. Mercury not filtered out by my liver was removed from my bloodstream by storing it in the fat cells of my organs, namely my brain, heart, and kidneys.

One of the eighteen foods I became allergic to was turkey. (I will use turkey as an example of how my allergies were created.) As the mercury was filtered from my bloodstream by my liver, it was deposited into my digestive system, scheduled for elimination out the colon. When the mercury was transferred from my liver into my digestive system, it mixed with the turkey I had eaten. Detecting the toxic mercury, the immune system became excited and notified my entire body of the danger by pointing to the mercury/turkey mixture. This created a nervous environment causing the heart and stomach to react in an excited manner right away. The immune system continued to follow the mixture of mercury and turkey down the digestive tract. As the mixture entered the colon, the immune system created an immediate tremor in the colon muscle to encourage the mercury/turkey mixture to be discharged from my body faster.

From that moment on, when my immune system detected turkey in my digestive system, it misjudged by believing mercury was with the turkey also. With only turkey present, my digestive tract developed a nervous shaky feeling, my heart rate went up, I became mildly nauseous, and my colon set up a tremor as if it were mercury. When the discharge of turkey was completed, the colon tremor stopped. After I became aware how my allergies were created, I could avoid the allergic foods, or, when I did have an allergic reaction, I could always stop the reaction by flushing the colon. I believe it is the presence of toxins in the colon that causes food allergies. After all toxins and heavy metals were removed from my body, my allergy shots prepared especially for me became effective and all food allergies disappeared, and even my sensitivity to chemicals and common household detergents was gone.

- short-term memory loss—When I was young, I had a great memory. I could easily memorize and recite the long checklists for each type of aircraft I flew. Every Saturday, Betty would read her list of grocery items to me, and I would memorize each item as she read them out loud, then go to the supermarket and buy every item correctly. Fifty items were no problem. By the time I reached age fifty-nine, the amount of items I could remember was down to three. With an assignment to buy just three items, I always took a twenty-five-cent coin with me. Most of the time when I arrived at the store, I could only remember two items and would have to use my quarter to call home for the third item. Sometimes I would forget all three items. I began having problems reading the newspaper. I always understood what the paragraph I was reading said, but would become confused because I had forgotten what the above paragraphs I just read had revealed. I knew what I was reading, but it was not recording in my memory. Watching television was the same. I knew what the people were doing and saying, but often did not understand what was going on because the introduction and early scenes had not recorded in my memory. By following The Four Basic Principles for "Getting Well," my memory returned to normal.

- mental confusion—I sometimes would drive to downtown Indianapolis, park my car, and then just stand motionless trying to figure out why I was there. I would search my car trying to find a note or clue to explain why I was there. Confused, I would return home and try to determine the important things I should be doing. I had a lot of days that passed with me not remembering anything that happened by the next day. One Sunday, I got lost driving to church. I would sometimes forget the names of my two grandsons. I would strain for hours trying to remember. Often I would have to give up and go to my private journal where I had things important to me written down. My family became very concerned and began talking behind my back when I started telling the same story in great detail three or four times within the same hour of conversation. Today after treatment that problem has been completely cured.

- fifty-cent pain—For no reason at all, a spot of sudden pain, about the size of a fifty-cent coin, would discharge from my skin. The pain was so intense I would wince. The pain lasted only one or two seconds. By the time I was in a full wince, the pain would completely vanish. The sudden spurts of pain moved around to various parts of my body, seldom repeated in the same spot. About ten or twelve spurts of pain would invade as a group and would play out over a one- to two-hour period. The groups of pain would reappear about once or twice each week. My doctor and I suspected that it was a nerve spasm but could not determine the cause. My doctor didn't have a name for this symptom, so I named it "fifty-cent pain." Later after the toxic heavy metal tin, which attacks nerves, was removed from my body, this type of pain became history.

- big toe pain—Sometimes it would be my right big toe, sometimes my left; I would be awakened from my sleep with great pain coming from my big toe. It felt like a burly wrestler was bending my big toe up and back as hard as he could. To stop the pain, I would force the toe back to a straight position, hold it there, and feel for a small knot on the bottom of the foot. By holding pressure on the knot, then gently kneading the knot for about ten minutes, the toe would relax and the pain would stop. My doctor listened to my story and wrote a prescription for gout, but the medicine didn't solve the problem. Later after all the toxic heavy metals were removed from my body, the problem did not return.

By the time I reached the age of fifty-nine, the above symptoms had fully developed. I felt that I was getting very ill, but my doctor still could not find much wrong with me except high blood pressure and being overweight. My long list of symptoms was being addressed with drugs or just ignored. However, my body began to grow weak. I no longer felt like taking a one-mile walk, and I would sometimes get out of breath climbing stairs. My doctor reminded me that I was getting old. He said, "Unexplained symptoms happen to almost everybody as they age." But little did my doctor or I know that catastrophic illness was just around the corner. As I passed my sixtieth birthday, things began to happen fast.

Doctor's Commentary

Contrary to popular belief, chronic illness does not occur suddenly—it does not fall out of the trees. A person cannot "immediately" acquire asthma, heart disease, cancer, chronic allergies, or chronic sinusitis. It is certainly rare that the etiology (underlying causes) was an acute and immediate process. In general, for most individuals we tend to associate our label at the juncture when we are given that diagnosis, but often, as in Wayne's case, many of the health problems and root causes obviously started and were acquired over many years.

I am reminded of a conversation I overheard in an airport while waiting for a connecting flight on my return from a medical meeting some years ago. Another family seated close by in the airport terminal was discussing an uncle who had just passed away. Apparently, this gentleman had smoked for about 40 years, overused alcohol, and was sedentary and quite overweight. His doctor had encouraged him to quit smoking and take better care of himself for many years. He finally acquiesced about two years previous. Soon after, however, he developed a diagnosis of lung cancer, and, as would be expected with that unfortunate diagnosis, he soon passed away. The interesting observation was that most family members attributed his terminal plight to the fact that his doctor "forced" him to quit smoking. They believed he would be alive today if he had not quit smoking and drinking. The evidence of that conclusion rested in the observation, for his family at least, that he seemed to be healthy, i.e., functional, until he gave up his bad habits and then rather abruptly succumbed to a terminal illness. Obviously, one would logically construe that this gentleman's problems began many years ago with a chronic exposure to the toxins laden in tobacco smoke, the use of alcohol, a rather sub-optimal diet, and no exercise.

The important focus, of course, is to pay attention, as Wayne discusses, to what is going on in your body and to the choices you make on a daily basis about how you treat it. I have often joked that men are generally insensitive creatures in this respect.

In any event, if you follow the course of Wayne's evolving *un-wellness* (as outlined in Chapter 3), you can see consistent patterns developing, and the usual medical approaches as previously noted are woefully inadequate except for symptom control. In fact, I have heard the statement that one of the most unfortunate inventions in modern medicine was the prescription pad, in that it gave the doctor an immediate excuse to scribble on a piece of paper and exit the exam room to move on to the next of his or her 50 or 60 patients he was scheduled to see that day. In reality, rarely can the prescription medicine address the cause of illness. Medicines as a rule are generally "anti-" something. There are anti-inflammatories to treat headaches or pain, anti-insomnia drugs for people with sleep problems, and anti-depressants for people plagued with poor moods. Rarely is the office visit devoted to uncovering root causes of medical plights. Obviously, sleep disturbance, headache, chronic pain, and mood disturbance, such as depression, all have basic biological reasons. However, the more productive path of casting a broader net to diagnose the underlying cause is infrequently embraced.

As one looks at Wayne's course starting at 29 with the sinus infections, one would presume that, even then, because of the toxin exposures and most likely numerous other features, his immune system was declining, and those sinus infections and allergies representative of immune imbalance were setting in. Shortly after, he gained weight and developed skin rashes—all consistent with toxin overload—but also suggesting some hormonal anomalies created by toxins and chronic illnesses, such as low thyroid function that can be associated with weight gain. Next, Wayne experienced high blood pressure, followed by anxiety or panic attacks, as his circulatory system, heart conduction system, and capacity to manufacture and maintain normal balance of neurotransmitters continued already on a downward spiral. At that time, nutritional supplements to preserve that balance and efforts to get rid of accumulative biological toxins would have likely been a significant benefit to Wayne, but he never had the opportunity to work with physicians who were focused on root causes.

Shortly after, dental problems arose. This tends to be a major area of medical challenge, and the respective fields of medicine and dentistry have long since gone their separate ways. Historically, the practice of human healing encompassed both dentistry and medicine. Now, however, most physicians look at the oral cavity as functioning no more than for necessary mastication of food. Most dentists are unaware that the health of the oral cavity is profoundly important to overall health. Anomalies in the mouth, such as dental fillings that can release mercury vapor into biological systems, chronic infections that can derail almost every facet of normal biological function, and electrical alterations from dissimilar metals and conductive anomalies can all co-create many variations of medical problems. Wayne experienced this in a rather classic setting that is often discussed by his endodontist. Wayne developed what is known as a cavitational infection or a chronic infection in the jaw. This was diagnosed with regulation thermography, which was then followed up with a dental bone scan. At the time, Wayne had chronic atrial fibrillation, and he was scheduled to have surgery of the chronic infection so it could be appropriately drained. This was done under general anesthesia, and the interesting finding was that the heart monitor was reading chronic atrial fibrillation while Wayne was asleep, but, as the endodontist opened up the infected area with a scalpel and drained out the pus, his atrial fibrillation returned to a normal sinus rhythm. This was felt to be an exceptional finding in that clinical setting, but I must say that I have seen many, many cases of chronic dental infections, when treated, that improved all sorts of biological abnormalities.

Another interesting experience relates to the function of the autonomic nervous system. In Wayne's case, he had a birthmark operation at age 50, but it was not long after at 53 that he was diagnosed with non-insulin dependent diabetes. A technique called neural therapy uses the injection of an anesthetic such as Procaine® into areas of body trauma like surgical scars. An important observation in Wayne's case is that when we injected his gallbladder scar with Procaine®, his type-2 diabetes went into acute remission to the degree that he was able to discontinue three anti-diabetic drugs that his primary care doctor had placed him on. This is an example of the significance of how trauma to the body can disregulate the function of the autonomic nervous system, which helps maintain normal homeostasis or balance body functions. We will be discussing more about this very effective therapy in later chapters.

The take-home message, however, is that one must pay attention to even the vague nuances of physical changes in our bodies. Wayne mentions many symptoms in terms of the chest pain, toe pain, allergy symptoms, sinus congestion, muscle twitches, skin rashes, red streaks, and so on, all of which sound relatively vague when physicians are looking at a textbook diagnosis, but, when viewed holistically in a paradigm where all things are related to each other, one can gradually unravel meaningful information of how the body may be operating in a dysfunctional pattern.

—Dale Guyer, M.D.

Chapter Four
A Rude Awakening

As I passed my sixtieth birthday in October 1992, I continued to have real concerns about my health. My thirty-eight-year-old primary care physician was addressing some of my symptoms with prescription drugs, and he believed that natural aging caused the other symptoms. In December and January, I continued to have electrical and hot/cold sensations in and around the fourteen silver fillings in my teeth. These symptoms were accompanied, frequently, by mild jawbone pain. X-rays failed to show infections, defects in the teeth or gums, or root canal problems. Two months of antibiotics quieted the pain a little.

I attempted to discuss my teeth and jaw pain problems with my medical doctor, but he always advised me to talk to my dentist. When I talked to my dentist, he always replied, "I cannot find anything wrong with your dental work." By March, the jaw pain had spread to my right ear. My ear was not infected, but my doctor prescribed two more months of antibiotics anyway. In May, I began developing pain in the rectum. A specialist doctor diagnosed a severe infection of the entire rectum and said that it had also spread out into the right hip. Fearing infection spreading to the hipbone, the specialist M.D. ordered me to bed twenty-four hours a day, back on more antibiotics and taking five sitz baths daily hoping to collect the infection and prevent its spread. After I spent five weeks in bed, the infection collected to a golf ball-size cyst that a surgeon removed. Six more weeks of antibiotics and I was declared good as new. I asked my doctor, the specialist, and the surgeon what caused this big infection, and all three said, "I don't know."

I began losing weight, was not feeling well, and was determined to get to the bottom of my health problems, so I asked my primary care physician to conduct a complete physical exam. He called for an electrocardiogram, chest x-ray, complete digestive tract exam, a colonoscopy, a complete blood profile, and a hands-on exam. He found nothing wrong that he did not already know. He felt that my lack of energy might be caused by the 50mg of a beta-blocker drug for high blood pressure, so he converted me, over thirty days, to an ACE-inhibitor drug. Five days after full conversion to the ACE inhibitor, in the middle of the night I was rushed to a hospital emergency room. A nightmare of the worst kind was in process.

The Rude Awakening Had Arrived

The date was September 10, 1993. At 3:00 A.M., I suddenly awoke with great stress in my chest. I felt very strange. I walked over to our bedroom desk and attempted to take my blood pressure. What I heard in the stethoscope startled me...no, it *terrified* me. It sounded like a bass drummer and a snare drummer playing as fast as they could, both at the same time, each with a different beat, resulting in a sound of pure chaos. I placed my hand on my heart, and it was shaking. I woke up Betty. I said, "No, don't call 911; I want you to drive me to the hospital." In less than three minutes, we were on the way. I did not feel weak or disorganized, just stressed out.

Without traffic, we arrived at the hospital in twenty minutes. I sat down in a wheelchair and told the attending nurse that my heart had a funny beat. She listened to the beat for about three seconds and without even knowing my name wheeled me directly into the big emergency room.

When the doublewide automatic doors to the emergency room swished opened, about twenty medical people turned and looked at me. My wheelchair nurse whispered something to one of the nurses. Immediately, six of the medical people treating other patients at the ten beds left their patients and headed straight to me. As a team they removed my shirt, lifted me into the bed with my pants and dirty shoes still on, ganged around me, connected me to a big monitor, and at the same time began injecting drugs in my upper arms and drawing blood from both lower arms.

The entire process took about forty-five seconds. At the one-minute mark, three of the medical people returned to other duties, leaving the emergency room doctor and two nurses at my bedside. The doctor explained that the shots were an attempt to calm me down and to thin out my blood. The blood draws were to check my overall blood chemistry and specifically to check to see if I was having a heart attack. The doctor began asking me a series of questions, and one nurse began to write. The other nurse continued to hold my left hand and massage my neck, shoulder, and arm.

At the three-minute mark, two technicians arrived pushing a large portable x-ray machine. They parked it at the foot of my bed, slipped a big frame of film behind my back, set up portable shields around my bed, asked the doctor and two nurses to step behind the shields, and then began shooting a series of chest images. The process lasted about two minutes, but the doctor continued to ask questions by yelling over and around the shields. By the time the shields were down, a female M.D. was standing beside him. The doctor introduced her as the cardiologist on duty and explained that she was taking over my emergency treatment.

The cardiologist said that my heart's rhythm was atrial fibrillation. The lower two chambers were keeping me alive by beating in an irregular pattern at 160 beats per minute (bpm). My upper chambers were not pumping blood at all, but instead were quivering at a 320-bpm rate. She said that my condition was serious because this was my first indication of heart problems, and there was no heart history for reference, except the perfect EKG that had been made about two months before, during my physical exam. She said she would be making decisions as to how to treat me on the run as we gathered test data. About that time, a nurse handed the doctor some paperwork. She glanced at the first page, looked up at me, and said, "Good news. There are no indications that you have had a heart attack."

She excused herself and went over to a small desk in the corner of emergency room, looked at the paperwork, and began to write. In about three minutes, the cardiologist was back at my bedside and announcing her plan to get my heart back into normal rhythm. She had decided to use an assortment of drugs to slowly return my heart to normal rhythm. She wanted to do it slowly because she did not know the condition of my heart and did not want to risk damaging it. Beginning with my heart beating 160 bpm, she would inject enough drugs to reduce my heart rate, hopefully, to 140 in one hour. Sure enough, in about one hour the alarm on the monitor sounded, and my heart rate was 140. She gave me another round of shots, and again in one hour the alarm went off, and my heart rate, although still irregular, was reduced to 120 bpm. She repeated drugs for a third round.

About thirty minutes later, the alarm on my big overhead monitor sounded because my heart rate broke through 100 bpm. The irregular rate stabilized at 90. As the cardiologist and my two nurses watched the monitor, I could feel my heart shaking, then stopping, hesitating, then starting again and really straining, trying to change. Then all at once all the stress left my chest. I felt completely normal, and I knew something good had happened. Again the monitor's alarm sounded. I looked around the emergency room, and all twenty medical people were staring at my monitor. A male nurse rushed to a printer where a red light was flashing and tore off about a three-foot-long piece of tape; slipping the tape through his fingers, he began to read and yell, "Mr. Cox has converted, Mr. Cox has converted! He has a perfect rhythm at 72 beats!!!" Without hesitation, all twenty medical people in the emergency room raised a closed fist in the air and sounded a cheer, a cheer much like a touchdown had just been scored.

Puzzled, I turned to the cardiologist and asked, "Why did everyone cheer?"

She said, "Oh, I forgot to tell you, when someone comes to emergency with a heart beating like yours and we don't have any past history on their heart, anything can happen, and usually does. About sixty-five percent of cases like yours go 'straight-line' on us and, even with our best efforts, die. You are what we call a thirty-five-percent-er, and that is why we cheered. Congratulations!"

About halfway through this five-hour experience in the ER, I became very confident that this emergency team knew exactly what my outcome would be. In fact, I had thanked God several times for providing me with this very professional group of medical doctors and nurses. Now because of the cheer, I found out that they really didn't know. This shook me because I suddenly realized they were aware that I was "knocking on death's door" and that the outcome could have been beyond their abilities. A lump immediately formed in my throat, and I began to cry. I realized that God Himself was in control and had guided this talented medical team on my behalf. I immediately prayed and sincerely thanked God. I was overwhelmed, but could not get out of my mind "Why did God do this for me? He must have a reason, but I can't think of one. I am almost sixty-one years old and too sick to work. What does he want me to do? He knows I can't do things like I used too. How can I ever pay Him back for this?" Worn out, I asked God to erase these types of thoughts from my mind so I could get some rest, and He did.

The Next Two Days

Although my heart was beating normally, my emergency room cardiologist moved me from the big, busy emergency room to a monitoring room next door. Before going off duty, she also informed me, she had telephoned my family doctor, and he in turn had selected a new doctor to be my new personal cardiologist. "Your new cardiologist will be coming to the monitoring room to meet you shortly" were her departing words.

The monitoring room was dimly lit with six monitored beds. The male nurse on duty sat at a station positioned so he could see each of us and at the same time watch our heart-performance data on his big monitoring screen.

After I had been in the monitoring room for about an hour, in walked my new cardiologist. He reviewed everything that happened since I entered emergency and advised that I needed several additional tests right away to determine the extent of my heart problem and what caused the atrial fibrillation. When I told him that in the previous hour I had developed a new kind of pressure in the center of my chest, he began to examine me. He said that I had the symptoms of a heart attack developing. He ordered additional medicine administered, and in a few minutes the pressure left. This chest pressure repeated three more times, and each time the medicine relieved it. My cardiologist continued to check on me during the next two days. By noon the second day, I was pronounced stable, and the chest pressure did not return.

On the third day, he scheduled me for a Cardiolite Stress Test, an echocardiogram, and other tests. At the end of the day, my cardiologist reviewed the test results that reported no indication I had had a heart attack. My cholesterol was 160. The echocardiogram showed my heart muscles and valves to be working properly. My cardiologist said that they had run about twelve tests trying to determine what caused the atrial fibrillation; not all tests were completed, but as of then he didn't know the cause. He showed me my Cardiolite Test, which indicated that my left-descending coronary artery was about seventy-percent blocked, restricting blood flow to the left-front and bottom of my heart. He informed me that this lower-left area usually ends up damaged from a heart attack. He recommended I stay in the hospital and have a catheterization the next day to determine if bypass surgery was needed on that left artery. I agreed.

The Big Move Upstairs

At 7:00 P.M. that same (third) day, they reclassified me from an outpatient in emergency to an inpatient and moved me to the seventh floor. When I arrived, my wife Betty, my daughter-in-law Diane, and my three-year-old grandson Caleb were waiting for me. While we were visiting, a nurse came into my room to ask some questions. In turn, I asked her what they did on this seventh floor. She said, "We prepare you for major surgery and care for you after surgery."

"But, I am only getting a catheterization at one o'clock tomorrow afternoon and will then go home." I asked, "If I need surgery, we can plan it later. Okay?"

She didn't answer me, but instead gave me one of those "I know something that you don't know" smiles.

My family left at 8:30 P.M., thinking that my catheterization would be in the early afternoon the next day. A few minutes after they were gone, I requested something to eat. Because of tests that day, I had not eaten and was hungry. I was refused food because the hospital schedule indicated I was scheduled for surgery at 9:00 the next morning.

"No, I am not," I insisted. "My cardiologist told me that I am scheduled for a catheterization at 1:00 P.M. tomorrow and that then we would talk about surgery if I needed it." Again, she gave me that "I know something that you don't know" grin.

Preparing for the Next Day

At the foot of my hospital bed was a big clock. As I pulled the blanket up around my very tired body, the clock on the wall read exactly 9:00 P.M. I fell instantly to sleep. At 1:00 A.M., I woke up thirsty, reaching for my pitcher of ice water, and it was gone. I then realized they were serious about 9:00 A.M. surgery. Still very tired, I fell back to sleep.

Then all at once, I woke up in a rage. I glanced at the big clock on the wall. It was 3:00 A.M. I had been in bed six hours. My heart was beating really fast, well above 100 bpm. I had a headache that was about to burst, my chest and shoulders were throbbing with pain, and I was angry with my cardiologist for scheduling me for bypass surgery without fully discussing it. I was frightened, and disgusted with myself for losing control of what was happening. Other people were deciding what was best for me. They were deciding without even asking me. I was in such a rage that I got out of bed and started walking around the room, trying to settle down. I kept saying to myself, "If you don't calm down, you are going to have a heart attack and die right here in your hospital room." I kept thinking that this was the first time in my life I had been out of control. The Air Force had beat into my head always to stay in control of the aircraft I was flying. My employer had insisted I maintain control of the 100 men I supervised. The survival of my own business depended on tight-fisted control of everything. Maintaining control was what I was all about. Now when I needed to reach out and take control of what was happening to me, I didn't know what to do.

I was frightened, and I began to cower like a weak man who cannot act.

All at once, I got this idea.

I will get back in bed and pray. I go to church every Sunday. God knows who I am. He guided my treatment in emergency just three days ago, so I am sure that He will guide me back to normal now.

I began my prayer with "God if I ever needed you it is NOW! Please have mercy on me and please return my life to what it used to be." For about twenty minutes, I prayed and pleaded for help. God was silent—He didn't say a word. I asked time and time again for his mercy. God did not respond. When He did not respond, I became really frightened, weak, and hopeless. I didn't know what to do. I just lay there, my body shaking from crying hard. My life was passing in rapid dark swirls through my mind.

All at once in a swirl of red, the name JESUS flashed by. I reached out my hand at 3:20 A.M. on September the 14th, 1993, in a hospital room in Indianapolis, and said aloud, "Lord Jesus, please come into my life and take charge." Instantly the rage left my body. My heart rate dropped from above 100 bpm to about 70. The pain in my head stopped. My chest, my shoulders, my neck, and my whole body relaxed. A new warm feeling was throughout me and around me. I realized I had forgiven my cardiologist, my family, and all people I knew and that I had accepted my illness as a teacher and a challenge. I knew all of this instantly. I didn't have to think about it. All fear was gone. My mind was reprogrammed at the speed of light. All my old negative thoughts were gone and forgotten. My thinking was new. I was truly a new person. Instead of being a boss, I would now have to learn to be a servant. I knew all this, instantly.

This event was so dramatic that my first conscious thought was "This must be death." It was such a good warm feeling, and, if it was death, I was puzzled because I seemed eager to continue. But, I could still see that I was in my hospital room, and it remained 3:20 A.M. Confused, I raised myself up in my bed and stared down at the hospital parking lot. I saw a nurse dressed in white lock her car just as a security vehicle picked her up and drove her to the front entrance where another security guard stood.

Seeing the nurse, I knew I was still alive but could not understand why I felt so warm and secure. Through conscious logical thinking, I figured out that I was being held in the arms of Jesus himself. He is the Good Shepard, just like the Bible says, and I am the Lamb that he values so much. That is why I felt so warm and secure.

For the next forty minutes, I just lay back in the bed, thinking about how great it was to be alive, how warm and secure I felt. How wonderful was God's love. I continued to cry as I talked to the Lord and thanked him for my conversion. I even sang a hymn aloud, "Oh How I Love Jesus"—"Oh How I Love Jesus"—"Oh How I Love Jesus"—"Because He First Loved Me." Over and over, I sang while shedding tears of joy. The last time I looked at the big clock on the wall, it was 4:00 A.M. My conversion had taken one hour. Completely calm and relaxed, I fell sound asleep.

Doctor's Commentary

Again, Wayne draws attention to the impact of dental amalgams and other oral problems on health. In my clinical experience, many people suffer health complications as a result of exposure to chronic mercury from dental fillings, chronic infections, and electrical dysfunction that can have a negative effect on the immune system and overall health. As immune system defenses weaken, we become predisposed to many infections, as was the case with Wayne.

Surgery and antibiotics appropriately treated his rectal infection. However, when his physicians were posed with the question of cause, the overwhelming response was "We just do not know." This is a typical experience that many frustrated patients will encounter. The reason is that very little effort is devoted to looking at root causes of overall body dysfunction. Many chronic ongoing issues, particularly relating to toxin exposure and chronic infection, can lead to chronic and potentially serious conditions, ranging from cancer to heart disease to neurodegenerative disorders among many others.

Heart disease remains an elusive and little-understood disease process. While we like to put all the blame on known risk factors, such as cholesterol, triglycerides, gender, smoking, hypertension, diabetes, and so on, very often—especially for many men—the first symptom of heart disease is sudden death. It remains unclear why individuals develop heart disease in the first place, as they may not have had any of the typical risk factors. Even diagnoses can be difficult, as often examinations and diagnostic approaches, such as EKGs and stress tests, will show definite problems only if significant arterial narrowing creates an electrical aberration that is measurable on these tests. Otherwise, many patients can have ongoing extreme narrowing of the coronary or other arteries in the body, but experience relatively few symptoms. However, the proverbial house of cards can come immediately crashing down when the body produces a clot that will lodge in these otherwise normally functioning but narrowed arteries. Other risk factors go significantly beyond typical parameters of cholesterol and biochemical anomalies, such as elevated C-reactive protein (CRP) or fibrinogen or alterations from viral and chronic bacterial infections, such as nanobacteria and atypical bacteria like *mycoplasma* or *Chlamydia*, probably playing distinctive pro-inflammatory roles and accelerating atherogenesis.

My personal experience confirms this observation. Prior to entering medical school while in college, I accompanied my grandfather who had retired from the tool-and-die profession to his yearly physical at a local hospital in Indianapolis. After a two-hour wait and a 15-minute evaluation, I walked down the marble halls of this hallowed institution and asked my grandfather how the examination went and about his health. He confidently boasted that the doctor pronounced him "fit-as-a-fiddle." Everything was fine. I asked my grandfather what was done. I wondered how his attending physician could have ascertained such a confident conclusion from cursory lab testing and the ritual passing of a stethoscope over the chest. At that time, I knew little about medicine, but it did not make intuitive sense that such a proclamation could be so confidently pontificated by his physician. A few months later, my grandfather passed away from heart disease. The event set me on a path to look more deeply in a comprehensive fashion at individual health and medical challenges.

Another health factor often neglected in the conventional scientific mindset is the role of spirituality. The whole concept of mind-body-spirit is an important interwoven phenomenon that cannot be separated from physical health alone, although some medical consumers and medical professionals try. I have seen patients who spend hours in deep meditation daily, but participate very little in their overall health. At the other extreme are individuals who lavishly attend to overall health but spend very little time attending to spiritual and emotional needs. Both extremes create imbalances. Often an invitation to restore balance is catalyzed by a dramatic, often life-threatening, event.

It is through these channels, however, that doctors are often asked to take a back seat to God. The role of spirituality can supercede in a most dramatic sense the biochemical nostrums and incantations of the most well-informed physician. However, there is often reluctance on the part of many physicians to acknowledge this important contribution. Only recently have studies on the impact of prayer been conducted and evaluated. The concept of prayer is often not directly discussed, as clinical studies will give the concept a new name. Prayer, therefore, becomes "non-local healing." Megavitamin therapy becomes "enzyme activation therapy." While the same approach, the nomenclature lends greater comfort to the academic mindset. In any event, both boast numerous studies supporting their efficacy, and will continue to acquire greater confirmation as medicine evolves. Slowly, doctors are being forced to relinquish the self-adopted attitude that the abbreviation M.D. following their name stands for "Minor Deity" as the acronym was jokingly referred to during my medical school training.

Always remember that you, the patient, know your body better than any physician or even well-meaning family or friends. Therefore, you have to pay attention and trust your intuition, as not all advice you receive will be ideally suited for you. Do not hesitate to ask questions. Get second, third, and fourth opinions if required, and never relinquish your power over your own body.

—Dale Guyer, M.D.

Chapter Five
One Hour Later, the Same Day

I was still in my hospital room, sound asleep. I felt a nurse gently shaking my left arm. Don't wake up, she whispered. I remembered her saying, "I am going to pass a stethoscope around over your body and check your vital signs. Please just stay relaxed and try to go back to sleep." There were no lights in the room, but I could see the big clock on the wall. It was 5:00 A.M., only one hour since the Lord quieted me down from that 3:00 A.M. rage. I felt very relaxed, like I just slept eight full hours.

She spent several minutes quietly listening to the front and back of my chest. She worked her way down and across my abdominal area. As the stethoscope slid past my groin area and proceeded down my right leg, I fell back to sleep.

All at once, a bright light turned on directly above my face. This same nurse, now in a louder voice, said, "Wake up, wake up!" I blinked several times and focused on the face of an African-American nurse. As I looked her over, I said to myself, "She is the senior nurse. Look at all those award pins on her big white cap." She looked down at me like I was one of her little boys.

She began with, "Mr. Cox, are you sure you need the procedure you are scheduled for? You are supposed to have severe blockage in your arteries. I have checked your entire body, and I cannot hear blood flowing through restricted areas anywhere."

I responded, "I don't even know what kind of procedure you are talking about. The last I heard, I was to receive a catheterization this afternoon at one o'clock."

She looked at her paperwork and then said, "According to this, you are our first patient today for the Cath Lab, and you are then scheduled for surgery at 9:00 A.M."

Without further discussion, she raised her voice a little, handed me a bar of soap, and ordered me to take a hot shower. Her instructions were to "scrub every inch of your body, every inch, you hear, even the bottoms of your feet. Then put on these little booties. While you are in the shower, I will put a new sterile sheet and blanket on your bed. After you make your body sterile in the shower, get back in bed without any clothes on. Pull up the sterile blanket, stay warm, and wait for surgery to come for you. Understand?"

"Yes," I replied.

Later, she stopped by my room to see if I was okay. She whispered in my ear, "May God bless you, Mr. Cox."

By the time I got back in bed it was about 6:15 A.M. On the nightstand were a telephone and a Gideon Bible. I dialed home to let Betty know I was headed for my catheterization in a few minutes. There was no answer. Betty is an early riser so she was probably at a restaurant having breakfast, I thought. I laid the telephone down, picked up the Gideon Bible, and turned to the index. The first word I saw was "anxiety." I remember thinking, "That's me, alright." Recommended reading for anxiety was the fourteenth chapter of John. I began to read.

In this chapter, Jesus is speaking to His disciples. "Do not let your hearts be troubled. Trust in God; trust also in me."—"In my Father's house are many rooms..."—"I am going there to prepare a place for you..."—"You know the place where I am going...."—"Thomas, a Disciple, interrupts and says, 'Lord, we don't know where you are going, so how can we know the way?' Jesus answered, 'I am the way and the truth and the life. No one comes to the Father except through me.'"—"If you love me, you will obey what I command. And I will ask the Father, and He will give you another Counselor to be with you forever."

As I lay there meditating on these words of Jesus, I began to realize I was in a no-lose situation. I had asked Jesus to take charge of my life. Through Him, I was in touch with God, the Father Himself. If I was to get well, I would need to make many difficult medical decisions. The Father, because Jesus asked Him to, had placed a great Counselor, the Holy Spirit, within me to help make intelligent decisions. With this kind of help, I had a good chance of "Getting Well." But, if I were going to die, Jesus had prepared a place for me at His Father's house, where life continues forever. Thinking about life and death, in the light of John 14, on that day brought a calmness and strength to me, remaining today.

I Am Ready

I was reading John 14 for the third time when in through the open door came a nurse dressed in surgical green. Right behind her was a good-size male dressed in dark blue, pushing a gurney. I looked at the wall; it was 6:45 A.M. As they approached me, I motioned for them to stop. I asked, "Can I make a phone call first?" The nurse smiled and said, "Fine."

Suddenly, I realized that none of my family or friends knew I was on my way for catheterization. Nobody would be praying for me. I grabbed the telephone and dialed the only number I could think of, the telephone receptionist at the truck parts company from which I retired. I asked for the President, Bill Mutz. Bill, young enough to be my son, was my last boss before I retired. God guided his life. He always prayed at our staff meetings.

Bill had not yet arrived at his office. I explained my situation and why I needed Bill to pray for me as soon as he arrived. She assured me she understood and would give Mr. Mutz my message. As I hung up the telephone, the thought occurred to me, "What if Bill has a breakfast appointment and comes in late? No one would be praying, so I better make sure and pray for myself." While still in the bed, I clasped my hands and bowed my head and said aloud, "Father, in the name of Jesus, I request that the procedure I am about to receive will not result in needing surgery, and I can go home today and continue to serve You, Amen." I looked up and said, "I am ready," only to find that the nurse and the aide had also bowed their heads.

Where Have You Been?

They wheeled me out of my room onto the elevator, down to the surgical floor. As we traveled, I kept thinking, "What a wonderful day." I must have smiled and said hello to a dozen or so people along the way.

When we arrived at the surgical receiving area, a sharp-looking young nurse looked down at me and said, "Where have you been? We have been waiting for you. You're our first patient for the day." She pushed my bed into a stall and drew the curtains. She then introduced herself by saying, "I am known around here as 'the mouthy nurse.' I talk all the time. If there is anything you want to know, just ask." She said that it was her job to keep me calm and to answer all my questions.

"My first question is," I said, "why I am scheduled for surgery when they haven't done a catheterization yet."

"First," she said, "your tests that they ran yesterday indicate that you have blockage severe enough to warrant bypass surgery. The angiogram we are about to do in the Cath Lab is considered the 'gold standard test.' This will provide the very best information needed for you and your cardiologist to make the best decision for you concerning surgery."

"But, that still does not explain why I am scheduled for surgery at 9: 00 this morning. It sounds to me like the decision to do bypass surgery has already been made by somebody, and I don't know who that somebody is."

"The second reason you are scheduled for surgery is that we had two bypass operations cancelled during the night, which means that two surgical teams will report to work this morning with nothing to do. A review of all the heart patients in the hospital was made, and you were selected as the most likely patient needing surgery. But, don't worry about it. You will not have open-heart surgery unless both you and your cardiologist agree you need it."

"Why did the two patients cancel surgery last night?" I asked. She replied, "One died, and the other just plain chickened out. You're not going to chicken out on me are you?"

"I'm not promising anything," I replied.

She then explained in great detail everything that would happen during the catheterization. I was beginning to understand why they called her the "mouthy nurse." She was truly a talking machine. By the time she stopped talking, I knew all about her husband, her two boys, and her neighbors. She answered every question I could think of. She stayed by my side all the time. She helped another nurse shave my groin and change out with new sheets and blankets for final catheterization preparation.

Mr. Cox Has Arrived

My nurse called out, "Mr. Cox has arrived," as she pushed my gurney into the Cath Room. She and three other nurses slid my body over onto the procedure table under a maze of overhead equipment. I looked at the clock on the wall; it was 7:55 A.M. The catheterization was scheduled to last thirty minutes.

A few feet away was a cardiologist getting dressed with what looked like heavy firemen's bib coveralls with no back, a coat with no back, and a funny looking hat with a clear plastic face-shield. He explained his clothing protected him from the radiation.

I asked, "How many of these catheterizations have you done, doctor?"

He replied, "Catheterizations are all I do. I have performed well above 1,000 of them."

"Good," I replied. "Sounds like you are my type of doctor."

My mouthy nurse was at my left arm giving me a big shot of Valium® to keep me settled down during the procedure. I was told if I needed additional shots to just hold up my hand.

"How will I know if I need another shot of Valium?" I asked.

She said, "If you feel like jumping off the table, hold up your hand fast because you need more shots."

"Okay. I understand."

The doctor inserted the metal sheath into the artery at my right groin, and the procedure began. The three nurses stood behind small radiation protector areas around the room as the doctor inserted the catheter and kept shooting dye ahead of the catheter as he recorded what he was seeing on both audiotape and still-film shots. Three or four times, the cardiologist stopped, and the three nurses stepped out from their protective post. Two nurses opened up the equipment above me and changed film and dye containers while the mouthy nurse came to my left side, patted my arm, and asked if I was okay.

The clock on the wall said 8:25 A.M. when the procedure stopped and the three nurses and the doctor huddled at the far side of the room. The doctor was talking, but I couldn't hear him. He then came to me and said he needed to take more pictures. I wanted to ask why, but he walked away. I could feel myself starting to get upset. Instead, I just closed my eyes and prayed, "Holy Counselor, please remind Jesus that He is in charge, Amen." With that, I relaxed and became less concerned about what was going on around me.

This time, the two nurses changed the entire set of cameras. The mouthy nurse gave me an additional shot of Valium®, the nurses returned quickly to their protective post, and the doctor instructed me to lie very still, hold my breath, and not to move. I felt a big rush of hot dye being released into my heart, and at the same time I could hear two high-speed movie cameras making a Z-Z-Z-Z-Z sound for about twenty to fifty seconds. Cameras were reloaded and activated two more times and then the doctor announced he was finished!

The nurses left the Cath Room, leaving only the doctor and me. I lay quietly on the procedure table, and the doctor with his backless jacket and backless pants wrote his report at a stand-up desk. After about a minute, I couldn't stand it any longer and asked, "Do I have blockage?"

He replied, "Yes."

"Can you fix it with a balloon?"

"No, you are not a candidate for angioplasty."

"Does that mean bypass surgery?" I quickly followed up.

"Not necessarily," he mumbled as he continued to write. Then all at once he stopped writing, turned to face me, and said he was talking when he shouldn't be. He then explained that about thirty minutes after I would be returned to my room, my cardiologist would give me a full report and a recommendation as to what should be done next. He explained that he was preparing for a meeting that was being organized at that moment, consisting of my cardiologist, one more cardiologist, three heart surgeons, and him. At the meeting, he would present what he found concerning my heart blockage, my cardiologist would present the history of my heart problems, and together the six-person group would discuss it all. "We as a group will then make a recommendation to your cardiologist."

"Thank you," I replied. "I understand." This discussion made me feel good, because it indicated I had just a small amount of blockage and that surgery was not needed immediately. A big smile came on my face. I closed my eyes and whispered aloud, "Oh, thank you, Lord. Oh, thank you from the bottom of my heart, dear God."

The four nurses came back in the Cath Room, lifted me gently onto a gurney, and wheeled me behind the curtain in the holding area. Two nurses stayed with me. Together they coordinated a maneuver to remove the large metal sheath from the artery in my right groin. Something went wrong. Blood spurted everywhere—on the wall, on my bed covers, and on the front of one nurse, and a bunch ran down between my legs. None of my bedclothes got soiled because I wasn't wearing any. The mouthy nurse finally got a pad over this little gusher and shut it off with hand pressure. They called another nurse who went "yuck" when she took a look at me. They all began to chuckle quietly as they exchanged glances with each other while looking at the big mess. My mouthy nurse stayed directly above me holding the pressure, while the other two nurses cleaned me up, first with wads of gauze and then with washcloths, warm water, and soft towels.

While they were cleaning me up, one of the nurses said, "Don't worry about it Mr. Cox; this is what we nurses do every day for a living." Everybody sort of chuckled again. After my bed sheets were changed and the two clean-up nurses left, my mouthy nurse, still holding the hand pressure on my groin artery, said, "I am sorry, Mr. Cox. This was not supposed to happen."

"No harm done," I said.

She then explained that she would be holding pressure for a few more minutes until a seal was formed over the hole the doctor made in my artery. She would then cover it with a big Band-Aid and would move two fingers of my right hand to the artery, and it would be necessary for me to keep my leg straight and to hold the pressure for the next five hours, before I could get up and walk. I said, "I understand," and we began to do small talk.

She loved to talk, so, while I lay there very relaxed, she told stories about her two boys and the dumb things one of her neighbors does. All at once she stopped talking, and then said, "I saw your pictures."

"What did they look like?" I asked.

"Boy, do you have big-time blockage," she replied. Her comment froze my thinking instantly. I started to get upset. I found out later that she was told to make that comment to check my reaction. The six-man doctor team was still discussing what to do with me and wanted to check my reaction to bad news. When I froze, I just lay there for a few seconds and then closed my eyes and whispered, "Holy Spirit, did you remind Jesus that He is in charge?" "Yes, I did," he replied, "and He already knew it." After that brief prayer, I became fully relaxed and continued the small talk with my mouthy nurse.

Back in My Hospital Room

Just before my mouthy nurse sent me back to my room, she said to expect a nurse to take my blood pressure every fifteen minutes because my catheterization had been extra long and stressful. "It will take a while for your body to settle down." Sure enough, as soon as I was comfortable in bed, a young nurse took my temperature, pulse, and blood pressure. She walked to the foot of my bed, picked up my chart, wrote something on it, and then came back and took my blood pressure again.

I said, "What was it?" She said, "115 over 70." Fifteen minutes later she was back and took my blood pressure again. I said, "What was it?" She said, "110 over 70." That was the last time I saw that nurse. What she did not know was that Jesus was in charge and that included blood pressure.

The day before, the last words from my cardiologist were "Within thirty minutes after you are back in your room tomorrow, I will come in, and we can talk about the results of the catheterization and decide what to do next." I had been back in my room for an hour then, so where was he, I wondered. All at once into the room rushed my cardiologist's nurse, Nina, with her arms loaded with records. She asked if I had seen my cardiologist.

"No," I replied.

"If you see him, tell him I am looking for him."

"Okay," I said. In a hurry, she ran out of the room. Less than five minutes went by and, almost at a run, in rushed my cardiologist. He asked, "Have you seen Nina?"

"Yes, she was here two minutes ago looking for you."

"Did she tell you the results of your tests?"

"No," I replied, "she just had an arm-full of records." With that he turned and started to run out of my room. I yelled, "Hey doctor, what are the results of my tests?"

He turned and yelled back, "We don't know yet. We need to compare all the tests we made yesterday with what we did today before we can decide. Nina has your records that we need in the meeting."

"How long will that take?" I asked.

"At least three to four hours," he answered, and rushed out of the room. Betty and I looked at each other as if to say, "What is going on here?"

God Answers Prayer

Five hours passed, my artery sealed, and I no longer needed to hold pressure, but I was still in bed. It was 3:30 P.M. Betty had been in a chair next to me all this time. In walked my cardiologist, relaxed, with a smile on his face. He began, "I want you to know that in the past four days during your stay at the hospital you have not had a heart attack, and we can find no indication that you have ever had a heart attack. However, I have some bad news, but I also have some more good news. First," he said, "let's cover the bad news. You know that left coronary we thought was seventy-percent blocked and might need bypass surgery? We were wrong. It is blocked 100 percent, solid as a rock. There is no blood at all flowing down that artery."

I interrupted him, "So, that means bypass surgery?"

"No," he responded, "the good news is that the bypass has already been formed."

Puzzled I said, "What are you talking about?" With that, my cardiologist held up in front of me a diagram of my heart showing the details of my three coronary arteries. He pointed to the blackened-out area up high above the first branch on the left artery with 100 percent written beside it. He then pointed to the area next to the blockage and said, "This area has a new artery flowing a small stream of blood around the blockage. Also [as he began to draw several arrows on the diagram from the right coronary artery to the left artery], there are several small new collateral arteries growing from your right artery, and they have connected to the area below the blockage in the left artery. The best that we can tell, all areas of your heart are getting sufficient blood right now, so we have called off the surgery."

"What caused these new arteries to grow?" I quickly asked.

"We don't know," he replied calmly.

"When did this happen?" I asked.

Shaking his head, he said, "We don't know that either." I remained silent for a moment, pondering that six of the best heart doctors in Indianapolis did not know how or when this happened, but I, with no medical training at all, knew!

Instantly my thoughts returned to the prayer from earlier that morning, "Father, in the name of Jesus, I request that the procedure I am about to receive will not require surgery, and that I can go home today and continue to serve you. Amen." Big tears started forming, and I began to cry. My cardiologist excused himself and stepped out into the hallway.

After I gained my composure, my cardiologist returned. He began by saying, "I have signed your release, and my treatment plan is to enter you into a good heart rehab program and see if we can expand the size of those new little collateral arteries and increase your blood flow. This will also give us a chance to study the locations of those new arteries in case we need to do surgery later. We will then better understand how to plan the surgery. Nina has the prescriptions for your new drug plan, and she will explain what each drug does. After you are comfortably on the new drugs package, call me; I will get you enrolled into rehab." With that, we shook hands, and he departed.

A few minutes went by, and into my room a doctor arrived in surgical clothes with a mask dangling around his neck. He introduced himself and said, "I just wanted to meet the guy who threw a monkey wrench into my schedule this morning." We both laughed, and he offered his congratulations, and we shook hands.

No sooner had that doctor departed than another surgeon landed into my room. He said, "I want you to know that, because of you, we in surgery this morning didn't know whether we were pitching or catching." He stuck out his hand and uttered, "Congratulations."

Nina, my cardiologist's nurse, entered my room next. Her opening statement was, "I saw your movies this morning. Watching the blood in your heart flow sideways from the right artery to your left artery was very exciting. I have never seen that before." She then gave the four new drug prescriptions to Betty as she explained what each did and how to take them.

Finally a nurse whom I had not met was suddenly at my bedside, introducing herself as the "Head Nurse" of the seventh floor. She said, "I have your release. Please get dressed. You are free to go home and, by the way, congratulations."

"Congratulations for what?" I asked.

"Not often does a patient check in on my floor one day and then check out the next day like you are doing," she replied. They wheeled me to the parking garage, from which Betty and I happily departed for home.

Doctor's Commentary

Unfortunately for Wayne, he was swept up into the medical "gauntlet" experience. Many patients experience being ushered into a system of elaborate tests, opinions, diagnostic decisions, and therapeutic interventions for which they feel little sense of understanding, control, or active participation, especially patients with potentially life-threatening problems. Heart disease is certainly a common label for patients thrust into this dysfunctional ritual. The average consumer is not remotely aware of much of what goes on behind the scenes. I have observed that the typical patient enters this system with blind faith that the scientific rigor of the medical establishment will not lead him or her astray, that doctors always know best, and that they will be expected to blindly succumb to whatever treatment, therapy, strategies, or interventions the doctors deem necessary. However, it is unfortunate that more appropriate, perhaps less invasive or risky, therapeutic strategies are not even presented as reasonable options for a patient.

How could this be the case? Primarily, most patients do not realize that the bulk of medical practice is tightly tied to maintaining a status quo, favorable to the prevailing politics and economic goals of the times. Heart disease is very profitable for a medical institution, and almost anyone reading this book in any large city in the United States can look around the local architecture and note that the most magnificently engineered and architecturally stunning buildings are the heart centers at local hospitals. That is because heart surgery and heart procedures are billed to insurance companies for many thousands of dollars that enables one to build lavish buildings with marble throughout. The entire process is underwritten financially by the insurance companies' medical status quo and the pharmaceutical industry—all primarily supported by ever-increasing monthly insurance premiums.

More often than not, other supportive therapeutic avenues, such as nutritional intervention, which Wayne will discuss in the next chapter, are rarely discussed. As a matter of fact, that option is often scorned in prevailing medical circles. Wayne was perhaps the lucky recipient of divine intervention that allowed him to avoid a potentially invasive surgical procedure that could indeed have proven fatal. Intense desire, belief, and prayer can impel action. The main distinction is the intensity. A quotation attributed to Norman Vincent Peale that I have seen played out on many occasions is *"If we are really willing to take responsibility for our own health and engage it intensely, then seemingly magical changes can occur, but for so many complacency is the normal life experience."* That is one reason why I feel that Wayne's message is so germane to enhancing the reader's motivation to embrace his or her health potential.

—Dale Guyer, M.D.

Chapter Six
Following Doctor's Orders

Betty and I arrived home in Brownsburg at about 6:00 P.M. We were both worn-out from our day at the hospital, so we lay down in street clothes on our king-size bed. Soon, I began talking about what happened to me during the past four days that she didn't know. I told her about my inviting Jesus into my life to take charge. I told her about my call to Bill Mutz asking for prayer and my own prayer just before they took me from my room for catheterization. I described the catheterization and my short prayers that got me through it. I told her about the mouthy nurse and about the mess made when blood spurted everywhere. I ended up by asking, "Honey, are you surprised I have committed my life to Jesus?" She replied, "No, I am not surprised. I could tell something wonderful had happened to you."

The next day was Wednesday, September 15, 1993. I drove to Indianapolis to see if Bill Mutz had received the prayer request I made the previous morning. Bill showed me an email he had sent to his twelve truck-parts stores located in Indiana, Ohio, Kentucky, Tennessee, and Florida. It read, "Attention all Christians. Stop what you are doing and immediately conduct prayer for Wayne Cox. Wayne is in a local hospital and is undergoing heart procedures at this very moment." I glanced at the time the email was sent, 7:55 A.M., the exact time that the four nurses placed me on the procedure table in the Cath Lab. I thought, "With twelve employee groups praying for me, no wonder my catheterization resulted in good news!" Before I left Bill's office, he laid hands on me and prayed, "Giving praise and thanks to the Lord," for the good news.

The next day, I visited my pastor and told him about my four-day experience in the hospital. He reminded me that God had not done this because I was special. "God did this," my pastor said, "because He expects you to be grateful and expects you to spread the good news about Jesus to others." On the next Sunday, September 19, 1993, my pastor, at the beginning of the 8:30 A.M. service, called me before a seated congregation of 1,200 people and announced that I had come forward to re-commit my life to Christ. He said, "Wayne has previously been baptized at age thirteen in White River." He then placed his right arm around me and asked that I raise my right hand and repeat after him. "I believe that Jesus is the Christ, the Son of the living God, and I accept Him as my personal Lord and Savior, Amen." When I finished, 1,200 people clapped and called out praises to God. Betty sat on the front row seat and wept, because, as she said later, "I am so proud of you."

The New Medicine Package

It took three weeks for my heart to settle down taking the four new drugs. My body disliked and fought a drug called ISMO. It is a very powerful nitrate drug designed to expand my arteries. One coated tablet reacted in my body for exactly seven hours. I took one at 6:00 A.M., which would start a throbbing headache and a throbbing pulse. The throbbing pulse would usually start in my neck and then move to the stomach, then move to a leg or arm, even on to an elbow or knee. I could not tell where the pulse would show up next. That really unnerved me. The 6:00 A.M. pill would wear off after lunch at 1:00. I was required to take an additional pill then, and it would wear off at 8:00 that evening, just in time to relax a little and catch a good night's sleep. This nerve-racking situation continued for three weeks, and then all at once, as if I had flipped a light switch, my body gave up and accepted the ISMO drug. From that moment on, I looked forward to being on ISMO for fourteen hours each day. It gave my body a pleasant buzz, sort of a little high, a simulation of extra energy.

Heart Rehab, the Long Road Back

I informed my cardiologist that I was on the drug package successfully. He advised me to report to the heart rehab center for an acceptance interview. The next morning, an R.N. specializing in heart rehab interviewed me. She had my records and had been briefed by my cardiologist. She informed me that my insurance company had agreed to pay for three months at the center. Her opening question was "What do you expect to accomplish here at rehab? What is your goal?"

"My goal," I said, "is to reverse the blockage I have accumulated in two of my coronary arteries."

"That is not a realistic goal," she responded quickly.

"I just finished reading *Reversing Heart Disease*," I said. "Doctor Dean Ornish says it can be done, and he has reversed five patients, and I want to be the sixth."

"We don't accept Dr. Ornish's work as valid; have you seen the results of your angiogram?" she asked, as she held up a copy of the diagram of my heart that my cardiologist showed me in the hospital. She pointed to the diagram, saying, "Look here, your left-descending coronary artery is blocked 100 percent. That blockage will always be there, with no way to remove it except surgery. So, why don't you pick another goal?"

Disappointed, I remained quiet for a moment and said, "I can't think of a goal."

The R.N. said, "If you don't have a stated goal, I can't enroll you into the center's heart rehab program."

Again, I hesitated and said, "Why don't you pick one for me?"

"Fine," she replied, "how about, your goal is to increase both the blood flow at your heart and your overall physical conditioning by twenty-five percent by the end of the three-month rehab program?"

"That sounds good to me," I replied. With that commitment, I was officially enrolled on that mid-October 1993 day.

Rehab Procedure

Up at 5:00 A.M. each Monday, Wednesday, and Friday, I would arrive at the rehab facility at 6:30 A.M. Standing looking at a mirror, I would attach four sticky snap-button patches to my chest in a pattern diagrammed on a chart taped to the mirror, and also strap a battery-powered transmitter around my waist and attach the four color-coded wire leads to the four snap-button patches on my chest. I would turn on the transmitter, walk up to the nurse with the monitoring screen, and give her my name and the transmitter number I was wearing. She would identify my heart pattern on her screen and label it with my name. Next, I would line up for a blood-pressure reading. Then, I would hold one of the paddles to a heart defibrillator machine slightly above my heart, and the nurse would place the other paddle to the left side of my heart, press a button, and make a six-inch-long printed EKG for my daily rehab record. This cleared me to begin walking around the indoor carpeted warm-up track, followed by twenty minutes on the treadmill, twenty minutes on an Airdyne bicycle, and twenty minutes of supervised floor exercises with light hand weights. My blood pressure was checked again twice during exercise and after cool down.

My First Three Months in Rehab

At the beginning, my twenty-minute scheduled periods of exercise on the treadmill were only five to ten minutes long. My exercise specialist would stand right beside me as I took small, slow steps. She would increase speed while watching hand signals from the nurse monitoring my heart pattern. At first, I experienced very sharp knifing pains in the area directly over the 100 percent blocked artery. She would then speed up the treadmill until I experienced pain in my chest and would then slow it down, a little faster each day and a little longer as she coached my heart muscles to be

51

stronger. After two weeks of her teaching me how to exercise my heart, I took over the controls. By the end of the three-month program, I had worked up to the full one hour of daily exercise. I purchased an Airdyne exercise bike for home use and increased my exercise periods to six days a week.

At the end of my three-month rehab period, my overall physical strength was tested at thirty percent improved, and my chest pain while exercising was greatly reduced. There was only one problem, and it was a serious one. The fibrillated, irregular heartbeat problem returned. Almost every day, usually around midnight while in a deep sleep, I would be awakened with an irregular heartbeat. It would last for one to six hours. Increasing my medicines to larger doses did not help. The more I exercised, the more frequent and more intense the atrial fibrillation. Occasionally, I would suddenly go into atrial fibrillation while exercising at rehab. I would immediately lie down, cross my arms across my chest, and just hang on until it stopped. When this happened, the monitoring nurse would place my transmitter on full record and provide a long EKG tape for my cardiologist's review. One time, my heart rhythm, while exercising, slipped into "atrial flutter" at a very stressful, staccato 130 beats. The rehab nurses became very excited, rushed me to the hospital emergency room down the hall, connected me to a full-scale monitor, and called my cardiologist. By the time he arrived at emergency, I had already converted back to normal rhythm. He did a quick exam and released me back to rehab. I asked the nurses why they were so excited, and they replied, "Atrial flutter is what we nurses often see just before straight line, that's why!" In the future when I experienced atrial flutter, I always thought about what they said.

I Didn't Give Up—Rehab Continues

At the end of my three-month rehab program, my heart and my body overall had gained strength. I was very skinny at 155 pounds, on a vegetarian diet with a cholesterol level of 130. Because of the atrial fibrillation problem, my cardiologist asked that I remain in the rehab program so they could continue to study my irregular heartbeat. Without success, my cardiologist ran twelve different tests trying to determine the cause. I was asked to wear a heart-rate monitor twenty-four hours a day, set to alarm at 120 bpm on the high side and fifty-five bpm on the low. In a deep sleep, my heart rate would often drop to forty bpm, and, if I slipped into atrial fibrillation, the heart rate would be around 180 bpm. In either case, they wanted me awake while the heart was beating either fast or slow. There were so many alarms going off some nights that Betty had to move to our guest bedroom. I experienced heart rate alarms for over a year, but I didn't give up and remained in the rehab/research program at the heart rehab center for three years trying to find a cure.

A Progress Meeting with My Cardiologist

After nine months in the rehab program, I was fitted with a forty-eight-hour Holter computerized heart monitor. I met with my cardiologist in mid-July 1994 to review the results. It was not a good report. My heart was going in and out of a-fib several times a day. The beats per minute were up around 190. My drug package was not working. I had developed several types of additional arrhythmias to include the unusual atrial flutter. The various irregular heartbeats were jumping back and fourth and mixing together. My cardiologist said that a six-doctor advisory committee had reviewed my case and considered a pacemaker and a defibrillator, but the committee had decided that my heart was way-too erratic for either to work well. He said that they didn't know what they were going to do with me if my heart didn't settle down. I could detect the frustration on my doctor's face. It was beginning to sound like the irregular way my heart was beating was my fault.

I made a suggestion. I told my cardiologist about a doctor whom I recently read about in *Reader's Digest* who developed a new way to locate the exact nerve in the heart causing the fibrillation. After locating the bad nerve, he would then destroy it with a radio frequency probe. My cardiologist responded immediately, "That procedure works for ventricular fibrillation only; it won't work for you. And, another thing, that doctor used to work with us. We taught him most of what he knows. The three best heart electricians in the Midwest are right here in our group. One of them has been studying your case for the past month or so."

"What is his recommendation for me?" I asked.

"We are not yet finished with your study, but I believe we will all agree that stronger drugs will be the best treatment for you. Here is a list of fifteen anti-arrhythmia drugs we will consider using. Look them over, and I want you back in a month, and I will have the committee's final recommendation. We can discuss it when you return." I left this appointment wondering if my doctors knew what they were doing.

Taking the Practice of Medicine into My Own Hands

I arrived at home to find that my sister Pat Blackwell from Cleveland had sent me a newsletter written by Donald J. Carrow, M.D., *Be Still My Heart*. Dr. Carrow was an anesthesiologist who spent his career with a surgical team that had been personally trained by the inventor of bypass surgery, Dr. DeBakey himself. Dr. Carrow had participated in over 2,000 bypass surgeries. Being faced with an irregular heartbeat was a daily occurrence for him. He had converted back to a normal rhythm hundreds of patients who developed various types of arrhythmias during surgery.

Be Still My Heart began with Dr. Carrow describing the various types of arrhythmias and the seriousness of each. On his list were my problems, with atrial fibrillation described at low heart rates as not very serious, but as the heart rate rises around or above 200 bpm, it can become very serious due to the risk of damaging the heart valves or creating a stroke. Atrial flutter was described as unusual and often dangerous and difficult to treat.

He then listed the fifteen drugs normally used for treatment. I compared his list with the one my cardiologist gave me, and they were identical. Dr. Carrow went on to explain that he always had to experiment to find the drug that would work. "Experimenting with anti-arrhythmia drugs is a very dangerous process and must be done in a hospital. Any anti-arrhythmia drug that will stop a given type of irregular heart beat," Dr. Carrow wrote, "can also create a new different type of irregular heart beat, sometimes worse than the one the drug just stopped." This sounded a little scary to me because I had a mixture of irregular heartbeats that would stop and go and even mix into a combination of beats.

Dr. Carrow said that all of these anti-arrhythmia drugs had some undesirable side effects and suggested my consulting with a good pharmacist to understand the possible side effects before taking any of them.

Dr. Carrow then listed ten vitamins and minerals to experiment with to see if I might get control myself. He suggested starting slow with just one or two on the list and then rating the results before moving on to others. I selected CoEnzymeQ-10 (CoQ-10) that improves cell communication, magnesium citrate as a quick source of magnesium, and Tums® as a quick source of calcium.

That very night, my monitor's alarm woke me up at 1:30 A.M. I was in atrial fibrillation at an average heart rate of 172 bpm. I had a dry mouth, so I headed for the lavatory and began rinsing my mouth with salt water. When salt water entered into my mouth, I could feel electrical currents jumping around between my teeth fillings and gold crowns. Twice while salt water was in my mouth, my heart jumped back into normal rhythm at 72 bpm. "Interesting," I thought. "I haven't noticed that before." Then, when I would spit out the salt water, my heart rhythm would go back to a 172-bpm irregular beat. I then downed 200mg of CoQ-10 and two ounces of magnesium citrate (which is 3,500mg of magnesium) and chewed up six Tums® (which is a big dose of fast-acting calcium). Tums® is not normally used as a mineral supplement, but works quickly.

I moved gently back into bed with my heart rate alarm still sounding. Twenty minutes went by, and all at once my heart stopped, waited until the count of ten, and then came back to life with one big thump, followed by five seconds of quivering. Then, it slipped back into atrial fibrillation. Over the next five minutes, my heart stopped and repeated this process about four more times and then converted to a normal rhythm at a 70-bpm rate. The alarm went quiet. This was pure excitement for me—now I had some control! I had experienced over fifty attacks of atrial fibrillation during the past nine months, and all I could do was curl up into a fetal position and hang on until my heart converted back to normal rhythm, which took anywhere from one hour to six hours. Over the next month, this treatment that I learned from Dr. Carrow's newsletter worked every time. A few times, I had to double-dose and wait ten to thirty minutes longer, but it always worked for both atrial fibrillation and atrial flutter. I could hardly wait to tell my cardiologist about this, hoping that my experiment would spur an idea of his own, and he could then fix my problem.

A Meeting with the Boss

About five days before my August 1994 appointment with my cardiologist, I was notified that he would be out of town, and that I would have to reschedule. I asked to keep the August appointment and to see his boss instead. Scheduling called back and said okay. I met with this senior cardiologist who immediately spoke up and reviewed my past nine-month heart history. He said that he was a member of the committee that was following my case. When he finished, I told him about the Dr. Carrow newsletter and the encouraging results I was getting by experimenting with CoQ-10, magnesium, and calcium. I followed up by asking him to refer me to a medical doctor who was also knowledgeable about vitamins and minerals. I told him that I thought I was on to something and that if I had an M.D. who knew how to treat with vitamins and minerals, I believed we could make some real progress controlling my irregular heartbeat.

This senior cardiologist ignored my request, but responded, "The best thing, I believe, you should do is check in to the hospital for a week. You forget about experimenting and let us do the experimenting with drugs that have already gone through performance testing by the FDA."

I didn't respond. Instead, I said, "When I first checked into rehab nine months ago, my attacks of irregular heartbeats were mild and infrequent.

As my heart grew stronger from exercise, the attacks became more frequent and more intense. There must be a reason for that. Why don't you place a big piece of graph paper on the wall and plot the dozens of my EKG recordings you have on the graph paper? Then, analyze it, and maybe that will lead you back to the source of the problem, and then we can work on fixing it instead of covering up the problem with drugs." He didn't answer me immediately, but instead began thumbing through my large file of records and unfolded a three-foot-long EKG tape that had been recorded by the big monitor in rehab when my heart went irregular while exercising.

Raising his voice a little he said, "You ask me to analyze. First, let me say that you can't analyze chaos! Look at this tracing. See, in this area your heart is clearly in atrial fibrillation at 145 bpm. Then, all at once it appears that other arrhythmias join the a-fib and look what you get." I looked at where he was pointing. An area about two-inches long looked like a kid had taken a lead pencil and then scribbled up and down as fast as they could.

I said, "I see what you mean about chaos, doctor."

At that moment, I realized that none of the six cardiologists involved with my case had the faintest idea what was causing my heart rhythm problems and that I was going to either become a drug zombie for the remainder of my life or die during one of the attacks.

My October Appointment

During the first week of October 1994, I again met with my regular cardiologist. He confirmed what I had learned during my last meeting with his boss. The committee had recommended that I become a patient in the hospital for a week while they experimented with stronger anti-arrhythmia drugs. Immediately, I told him that I felt I was addicted to ISMO and should be taken off of it.

"What makes you think you are addicted?" he asked.

"Because during the ten hours each night when ISMO is not in my bloodstream, I crave it," I replied. Then, after about three to four hours of craving, my heartbeat often becomes unstable and sometimes throws a temper tantrum. This is followed by atrial fibrillation at a high rate up around 200 bpm."

He replied, "Since this happens when ISMO is not active, it suggests that you need a nitrate drug twenty-four hours a day, not fourteen hours like ISMO. I can take you off of ISMO, but I must put you on another nitrate drug designed to work twenty-four hours a day."

"What would happen if I stopped ISMO and no longer took any nitrite drugs?" I asked.

"You would have chest pain again, and would get into serious trouble," he said.

I thought about it for a few moments and then commented, "I think I am taking so many drugs now that my heart is very confused as to how it's supposed to act." My cardiologist did not reply. I then told him that I felt we should run some more tests and try to determine the cause of the irregular heartbeats before we caved-in to more powerful drugs. I asked him to refer me to a nutritional doctor because "I have been experimenting with vitamins and minerals and getting some improvement controlling my irregular heartbeat, but I don't know what I am doing. I need a doctor to guide me. Also, I have been reading about people controlling their heart rate and blood pressure with biofeedback, and I would like to try it."

He said, "Let me think about all this, but for right now I want to fit you up today with a forty-eight-hour Holter Monitor, and let's gather more information about your heart rhythms before we make any final decisions."

I said, "That sounds good to me." I departed with eight sticky snap-buttons attached to my upper body with a maze of color-coded wires connected to a high-tech digital recorder attached to the right side of my waist. I could not remove it even for showering or sleeping for the next two days, and in a special logbook provided, I was directed to write each hour, for the next forty-eight hours, details of my activity.

The Next Chapter

Chapter 7 that follows was not written for this book. Instead, I made detailed personal notes on October 21, 1994, the day following a meeting with my cardiologist and primary-care physician on the twentieth. Chapter 7 is from my personal journal. I do not recommend that you follow in my footsteps and reject your doctor's advice. However, after much debate, I included Chapter 7, "Moment of Truth," simply because this is what happened, and it became a major turning point in my "Getting Well."

Doctor's Commentary

Wayne is arriving at a new vision. A life-changing event through various avenues of intervention is leading to a new life experience, a greater sense of connection to wholeness outside of one's individual ego. For many, the process enables letting go of the enormous weight of negativity, desperation, fear, and uncertainty.

Unfortunately, Wayne was facing the next medical gauntlet—pharmaceutical interventions. While drug therapy is often necessary for life-threatening problems, in many cases pharmaceutical intervention has so many side effects and long-term complications that the problems created outweigh whatever potential benefits might be derived. Note that the constant litany of new anti-arrhythmia drugs Wayne was prescribed to prompt his heart to maintain an acceptable normal rhythm actually worsened his medical condition—another common scenario in medicine. The drugs may not work, but it boils down to the hammer and nail attitude. If the only tool you have is a hammer, everything else must be a nail. In medicine, if the only tools are pharmaceuticals, that will be the only approach administered. It took Wayne's own research for him to learn that nutrients, such as CoQ-10 and magnesium, and medical treatments, such as chelation therapy, can often improve one's condition without pharmaceutical intervention.

Several years ago, a patient shared a personal struggle. He was experiencing poor circulation, a sluggish heartbeat, and ongoing fatigue. Local doctors referred him to a well-respected specialty care facility. Extensive evaluations determined that he did indeed have mild heart disease and circulatory sluggishness. The staff cardiologist who met my patient disclosed to him in confidence that his own father was undergoing chelation therapy at a local clinic, with wonderful results. He suggested that he may want to consider the same therapeutic option himself. He stated very clearly that he would not make this part of his official medical record, and, if anyone ever asked him about this in the future, he would deny ever having had the conversation. Such is the unfortunate reality of "peer fear" within the medical community.

More recently, an acquaintance of mine, another family doctor, who happens to be very knowledgeable in nutritional interventions in medicine but also practices in a group setting, was asked by his partners to no longer give nutritional advice to patients, as they did not want the image of their clinic to be tarnished with this so-called unscientific approach. Unfortunately, he was required to acquiesce as he had already had significant investment in the clinic, an established practice, bills to pay, and a family to provide for. That is the model of how medical complacency sets in among physicians. Even those who know better are not often allowed to practice better. It is much more comfortable to remain in an arena of ignorance.

—Dale Guyer, M.D.

Chapter Seven
Moment of Truth

October 20, 1994. Brownsburg, Indiana. I am upset and need support. Without an appointment, I have walked into the office of my family doctor and requested to see him. It is 1:30 P.M. His receptionist replies, "Please take a seat, Mr. Cox, and I will see what Dr. Branden says."

Forty minutes go by, and I find myself face to face with Dr. Branden. Both of us remain standing. I begin talking. "This morning, a nurse called, advising me to go to my cardiologist's office right away and to come prepared to spend up to a week in the hospital. When I arrived, my cardiologist saw me immediately. He reviewed the EKG recordings of the forty-eight-hour heart monitor I wore last week. He said that my heart rhythm patterns are now worse than a year ago when he began treating me. My heart is going in and out of atrial fibrillation several times a day with the lower chambers beating irregularly at rates up around 180 to 200 beats per minute, and the upper chambers are fibrillating around 360 beats per minute. He also said I was starting to develop periods of atrial flutter at a staccato beat around 130 beats per minute. Yesterday, he said, a panel of six cardiologists had reviewed my case. All had agreed my life was in danger, my present drug package was not getting the job done, and I should be placed in the hospital while they try an assortment of more powerful drugs. They had considered a pacemaker and a defibrillator, but decided that my heart rhythms were way-too erratic for them to work."

All at once, Dr. Branden, my family doctor, interrupts me. "Why aren't you in the hospital right now?" he asks.

"Because, like I told my cardiologist, I think there are some other things to try before it is necessary to start taking those last-resort-type anti-arrhythmic drugs that produce such terrible side effects."

"I know," Dr. Branden replies, "the side effects of these drugs are unpleasant, but isn't it better to put up with a little *brain fog* or *bladder incontinence* than have a bad stroke or heart failure?" I don't answer.

Looking puzzled, Dr. Branden asks, "What did your cardiologist say when you refused to be admitted to the hospital?"

"He said, 'If you are not going to follow my professional advice, what do you want me to do?'

"'First,' I told him, 'I want you to conduct more tests and compare the new test with the test you did last year. Analyze the change, and this should tell you what caused my heart rhythm problem to get worse. Then, fix the cause.'"

I tell Dr. Branden that my cardiologist bristled a little and then said, "There are twelve different tests to determine the cause of atrial fibrillation. We have conducted all of them at least once, some several times, and none has revealed the cause of your problem. Additional tests will not help.

I provide Dr. Branden with my response to my cardiologist. "'Next,' I told him, 'I want you to take me off of the nitrate drug ISMO. I feel I am addicted to it. My heart craves it. I think one of the reasons my heart rate is so high during a-fib is that my heart is throwing a *temper tantrum* asking for more ISMO.'

"He resisted. 'We can't take you off of ISMO. Without a strong nitrate medicine, you will experience severe chest pain and get into serious trouble.'"

I continue to recount my morning visit with my cardiologist as Dr. Branden, my family doctor, sits down on a stool, crosses his legs, and starts thumbing through my medical records. I remain standing.

"'If you can't take me off ISMO,' I said to him, 'then why not refer me to a medical doctor who is also a nutritionist? I have been experimenting with vitamins and minerals, especially vitamin E, CoQ-10, and the minerals magnesium and calcium, which have been helping me get back in rhythm. I think a nutritional doctor could do me a lot of good.'

"'Your nutrition is okay,' he snapped as he read from my medical file. 'It has been checked twice during the past year by our staff nutritionist. She gave you high marks. Your weight is just right at 155, your cholesterol is at 130, and all your minerals check within the brackets, including your magnesium and calcium.'

"'I have read,' I told the doctor, 'about people who have learned to control their blood pressure and heart rate using biofeedback. Do you know of anyone who could teach me biofeedback? I would like to try it.'

"'Biofeedback is not a medical procedure,' he insisted, 'and as far as I am concerned it is primarily trickery.'

"Realizing I was up against a brick wall," I tell Dr. Branden, "I slid down off of his paper-covered examining table and begin buttoning up my shirt, preparing to leave when he broke the silence by saying, 'Can I make a phone call right now and have you admitted to the hospital?'

"'Not now. Maybe someday, doctor,' I answered and reached for the doorknob.

"He stopped me by saying, 'What do you want me to do?'

"'I want you to continue to be my cardiologist, and if I ever end up in emergency, please do the best you can.'

"We shook hands, and as I walked out the door he said, 'Here is a prescription for a different type of nitrate drug. Please have it filled before you decide to discontinue ISMO; believe me you will need it.' I could see by the look on his face his genuine concern for me."

Dr. Branden stands up and says, "Yes, I understand everything you and your cardiologist talked about this morning, but why are you telling this to me? What do you want from me?"

"I drove directly to your office, Dr. Branden, because you are my primary-care physician. I need your support. I need you to help me get off ISMO, find a nutritional doctor, and direct me to biofeedback training. Will you work with me to help find the cause of my atrial fibrillation? I don't have anyone else to turn to right now."

"First of all," Dr. Branden begins, "it is my understanding that you still have a cardiologist, so I am not willing to change any of his decisions or recommendations. But, while you were talking, I began reviewing your medical file. You sure have had a lot of medical problems cropping up during the past two or three years—infected lower left jaw from a root-canal tooth; it took over two months and a bunch of antibiotics to clear it up—followed by an infected right ear and more antibiotics—then five weeks confined in bed while an infection in the right hip collected, so a surgeon could remove a big abscess. Last year you found yourself in emergency for three days on the verge of having a heart attack. I don't understand how you avoided it because you have more calcified plaque in your coronary arteries than any patient I have. You probably should have bypass surgery right now, but all you want to talk about is somehow reversing the blockage."

Dr. Branden's voice rises a little as he continues. "There is no way to reverse hard calcified plaque like this." Then, emphasizing his words by pointing to a sketch of my heart, he says, "Look, your left coronary artery is 100-percent blocked, solid as a rock; zero blood is flowing down it, and your right artery has some additional blockage. Removing this blockage safely is not possible. It is only because of those new collateral arteries developed in your heart at rehab last year that you are still alive today. I hope you understand that!

"Your problem is," he says, as he points his index finger at me, "that you are unwilling to accept the seriousness of your illness. You are in what we call denial, and it is my job to get through your thick head that you have a degenerating disease called *heart disease*, and you are as well right now as you are ever going to be. The best your cardiologist and I can offer is to try to keep the disease under control and from getting worse. We need your cooperation to do this. Based on my experience, your type of heart disease will always get a little worse each year. You will be lucky to live your full, expected lifespan. I am sorry I have to tell you this, but I believe these to be the facts of your illness."

I just stand there for a moment, not knowing what to say. I know Dr. Branden's intentions are good; he is trying to help me make the decision to be admitted to the hospital like my cardiologist recommended. Finally I look at Dr. Branden and smile. He smiles back, we shake hands, and, without another spoken word, I step out into the hallway to the checkout nurse. She says, "There will not be a charge today." I say, "Thank you," and walk out to my car.

I start to insert the key to unlock my car but notice that my hand is shaking. I walk across the street to a McDonalds and buy a large decaf coffee. I sit there for about thirty minutes sipping coffee and thinking about the happenings of the day. After my hand stops shaking, I drive home. Betty is not there. She had been with me that morning at my cardiologist's office, but asked me to drop her off at home before my seeing Dr. Branden.

I loosen my belt, take off my shoes, and lie down on our bed. Immediately, I begin to cry. I cry hard for ten minutes or so. I feel a lot better. I decide to slip down off the side of the bed to my knees and talk to God. I remain on my knees, with my elbows on the bed and my head resting in my hands, quietly for about a minute or two. I can't think of anything to say. Then all at once I blurt out, "Father, I don't like my doctor's attitude!" Immediately, God blurts back, "Neither do I. Go find yourself a new doctor." (That is my shortest prayer I can remember, however it is not God's shortest answer to me. He has sometimes answered No.)

Without further discussion with God, I drive directly to a CVS drugstore and purchase six ten-ounce bottles of magnesium citrate and two big bottles of Tums®. I place them on the kitchen countertop and lie down on the bed again.

Betty comes home and asks, "What's all that stuff in the kitchen?"

"That's the stuff I have been using to help me get out of atrial fibrillation, remember?"

"Yes, I know," Betty replies, "but why did you buy so much?"

"Because I am going to take myself off of ISMO, and I want to be prepared in case I need it."

"Who told you to do this?"

"Nobody. I decided on my own to try it."

"When are you going to do it?"

"I don't know yet, but soon."

"I sure hope you know what you are doing."

Of course, I really don't know what is going to happen. But, I have gained a lot of experience over the previous three months conducting my own experiments trying to control my irregular heartbeat attacks guided by Dr. Carrow's medical newsletter *Be Still My Heart*.

Day of Decision

The next day is Friday, October 21, 1994. I am up at 5:00 A.M., I shower, I take my ISMO and morning drug package, and then I am off to heart rehab for exercise. I am back home by 8:30 A.M., in time for breakfast.

After breakfast, I settle into my downstairs office, read the newspaper, check my calendar, and begin to plan my day. My thoughts immediately turn to ISMO. Should I stop taking this powerful drug? I open my NIV *Life Application Study Bible* and read several passages related to wisdom and decision-making. Stimulated by what I read, I pray and ask God for guidance. Shortly after prayer, I make the decision to stop taking ISMO in two days, on Sunday, October 23, 1994, my sixty-second birthday.

Next, I begin to make a list of things to do in preparation for Sunday. First is to call my pastor, explain why I need prayer, and ask that I be placed on the church's official prayer list. Feeling that I need a more personal-type prayer support, I begin to write down names of people who know God, but who also know me. I end up with five names whom I telephone, explaining to them my ISMO story and requesting their prayer support through Sunday.

#1 Bill Mutz: He had arranged prayer for my catheterization in Chapter 5. Bill presently owns and manages the Lakeland Ford dealership in Lakeland, Florida.

#2 Jim Jack: A Racers For Christ chaplain from Gilbert, Arizona. Jim always stayed at our home when conducting Sunday morning church services at Indianapolis Raceway Park.

#3 Larry LePage: Larry and I have a close personal relationship that began when I hired him as an accountant and credit manager in the truck parts business. Other employees always recognized Larry, an Elder in his church, as a strong Christian. Larry and his family presently live in Bluffton, Indiana.

#4 Greg Baugh: An Elder in his church. When I became seriously ill, Greg invited me to join him along with 400 other men to study the Bible non-denominationally each Monday evening. Five years with this Bible Study Fellowship group is how I learned to place all my trust in God.

#5 my uncle, Lloyd Powell: He is an eighty-two-year-old retired Texas Instruments employee who maintains a strong personal relationship with God. That relationship has grown stronger over the years because he studies the Bible and prays faithfully every day.

Each of my prayer warriors understands my challenge and agrees to provide prayer support for my drug withdrawal decision scheduled for Sunday. I feel very comfortable exchanging my trust in my *cardiologist team* for my trust in my new *Prayer Warrior team*.

Doctor's Commentary

Unfortunately for the medical consumer, doctors are trained for the most part to maintain the status quo in delivery of medical services. There is very little incentive and even significant disincentive to change the current paradigm. For that reason, Wayne's doctors continued on the same venue of treatment with little modification and an ongoing static approach despite generalized poor outcomes. The impasse eventually led to a parting of ways, one might say, between Wayne's conventional physicians and his goal of health enhancement. It seems incredible that Wayne would be given the ultimatum to report to the hospital, almost against his own wishes and better judgment, to undergo a more toxic recipe of pharmacological therapies likely to produce even more toxic side effects, since none of the therapies to date worked effectively for him.

While pharmaceutical approaches may ultimately be necessary in many cases, Wayne's advocacy in exploring alternatives was self-guided without the support of his physician and specialists, even though the published data and information available in medical journals— that they should be reading—certainly offers significantly less toxic approaches than other options considered or advised for Wayne.

Another significant factor that Wayne alludes to is the concept of intuition. When Wayne notes that the nitrate drug ISMO seems to be addictive and causes his heart to crave it or that his circulatory status no longer needs this drug for support, Wayne is speaking from his gut (and heart). From the orthodox medical perspective, these comments will be viewed as non-scientific. It has certainly been my experience that often the patient knows best. Therefore, in all the approaches that we use therapeutically, it is always important, after considering the individual's clinical history, elements of physical examination, and in-depth functional laboratory assessment, and a review of the potential treatment approaches, that I ask the patient whether this makes sense to him or her, and whether this feels like the right choice. If that response is affirmative, we can assume that we are on the right track. If there is hesitancy, I ask the patient to think about it for a while and call me back. If the patient expresses the need for further investigation, this would be the best advice to follow.

Most patients encounter (like Wayne) that the medical establishment rarely has the time (or ideology) to address the individual's concerns. Consider the commentary on nutrition, when Wayne's physician stated that his nutrition was okay since it had been tested. One would argue that the very superficial, generic lab tests often used in primary care settings to look at mineral status are woefully inadequate. Unfortunately, the very tests that would have been most helpful for Wayne were not even recognized. Had Wayne undergone more thorough nutritional tests, one would have looked at levels of CoQ-10 in the serum or RBC mineral analysis for magnesium, which would produce results and a nutritional profile significantly more accurate.

Even the response to adjunctive procedures, such as biofeedback, as being "trickery" seems to go against the common sense of the average consumer. Today, the average consumer is very educated about and familiar with therapeutic approaches, such as biofeedback, acupuncture, and others. These therapies are no longer considered on the "fringe" and are well-established and commonplace medical avenues of therapy. However, it can take a good 20 to 30 years before the common practice of adjunctive therapies is incorporated into contemporary medical practice. However, the challenge for many patients (Wayne included) is that they do not have 20 or 30 years to wait for the mindset of modern medicine to catch up with the very therapies that could be most helpful to them.

Also, looking at the patient from a holistic or interconnected whole is very important. As stated to Wayne, his chronic infections and apparent immune system dysfunction had nothing to do with his heart symptoms, when in actuality it is quite the contrary. Chronic infections, particularly in the dental area, can be an ongoing co-contributor to heart rhythm abnormalities. In addition, heavy metals, toxins, and electrolyte imbalances also contribute. I would, therefore, state that the accusation of "being in denial," as Wayne heard from his physician, should be viewed as a prominent problem, not with the patient but rather with the modern medical establishment. Medical practice is often clearly in denial of supportive therapies that could indeed prove to be most helpful.

However, escaping that medical prison requires enormous self-advocacy, confidence, and courage. For most patients, the pontifications of their physicians still carry enormous weight, and it would be difficult for the average person to go against medical advice. It is our goal in the upcoming chapters to outline for the individual the steps needed and the resources required to self-confidently engage a more broad-based and efficacious treatment approach.

—Dale Guyer, M.D.

Chapter Eight
Winning the First Battle

Sunday, October 23, 1994, my sixty-second birthday. While still in bed, I make my final decision to discontinue one of the drugs in my drug therapy package, ISMO. This drug improves circulation; however, after one year of use, I believed I had become addicted to it. This medicine gave me a "buzz," and I felt that it was interfering with my nervous system. It was an important medicine initially, but now that my circulation has improved, I feel that ISMO is creating problems by contributing to the recent high heartbeat rates I was experiencing during atrial fibrillation that was putting my life in danger.

Each day for the past year, I have taken one ISMO pill at 6:00 A.M. and a second pill seven hours later at 1:00 P.M. I have carried in my right-front pants pocket an alarmed pillbox set to sound every day at 1:00 P.M. as a reminder to take this second pill. However, today will be different. I take the other four medicines prescribed by my cardiologist, but leave the ISMO pill in the alarmed pillbox and do not take it. Now that I have accepted the responsibility for my own health and with my five Christian Warriors praying, I feel that discontinuing ISMO is the right thing to do.

I shower at 6:30 A.M., eat breakfast, and attend the early 8:30 church service. I am relaxed, knowing that the church prayer team has been praying for me, along with others on the pastor's prayer list. During the prayer portion of the Sunday service, I ask God to place an obstacle in my path if it is not His will that I discontinue ISMO. After church, I return home to my informal birthday party attended by my son Greg and his family. After the party, Betty and Greg's family leave for a noontime Indianapolis Colts football game. I remain home alone, but with next-door neighbors nearby.

Relaxed, I lie down on the couch to watch the football game on TV. My heart is beating normally, and everything seems fine, when suddenly without warning my heart stops and then restarts with a series of kangaroo-like kick-beats, followed by a heartbeat rhythm similar to a pinball machine in action. I break out into a sweat. During the past year, I have experienced over ninety irregular heartbeat attacks, but this is by far the worst. There is no real pain, just a very high rate of body stress combined with tremors in the stomach and in my back, up between the shoulder blades. I feel additional pressure in the right side of my brain. I glance at my heart rate monitor. The digital readout is fluctuating between

190 and 205 bpm. I move to our bed. With the telephone nearby, I snuggle down between the sheets, take up a fetal position, and prepare to hang on, to ride out what I believe to be ISMO withdrawal symptoms. The stress is so great that tears start flowing down my cheeks. I began to pray and ask God for mercy.

Three hours go by without change. The first dose of CoQ-10, magnesium citrate, and Tums® is not effective, so I take an additional dose. Three more hours go by, and my irregular heartbeat is as wild as ever. My heart has now beaten irregularly for six hours. Betty returns from the Colts game and is not surprised to find me having withdrawal problems. Three more hours go by without change. It's 10:00 P.M. My heart has been at a high irregular rate for nine hours, a new record. I become concerned and call Dr. Walter Able, a long-time business associate. I explain what I am doing and ask for advice. Dr. Able instructs me to write down a list of symptoms, and if any one of them develops, I should call 911. We both agree: If the irregular heart rate does not begin converting back to normal within two hours (by midnight), I should go to emergency for treatment. Before hanging up, I ask Dr. Able if I could hurt myself by drinking large doses of magnesium citrate. I want to know because I have used it in the past, and it had helped me convert to normal rhythm. He replies that it is very unlikely it would cause harm because, when the body receives too much magnesium, it simply dumps it out the bowel.

I hang up the telephone, rush to my supply of magnesium citrate, and down two ten-ounce bottles, chew up six more Tums®, and go back to bed. Within twenty minutes, I can feel my heart muscles trying to create a tug-of-war for a better rhythm. An hour goes by, and the tug-of-war has not made much progress. Only one hour remains before the midnight deadline. I have been out-of-rhythm for ten hours.

Suddenly, a voice within my own mind shouts, "Drink salt water. Sodium is an essential heart electrolyte too!" I quickly prepare a twelve-ounce glass of warm water, stir in a teaspoon of sea salt, and drink it. Before I can get back to bed, my irregular heart rhythms are beginning to break up and new ones are trying to form. Excited, I rush back to the kitchen and down another twelve-ounce glass of salt water.

With twenty-four ounces of magnesium citrate, twenty-four ounces of salt water, 400mg of CoQ-10, and a handful of Tums® in my system, I remain in bed for the next four hours, cheering for the tug-of-war going on in my heart and giving praise to the Lord for the support His five Christian Warriors are providing me. Slowly, my heart begins to slow down to a normal beat. At 4:00 A.M., my heart slips back into a regular slow rhythm. It has been fifteen hours since it all began. I am dead tired, and so is my heart. I remove the heart rate monitor and roll over on my right side to prepare for sleep and suddenly discover that the pillowcase is wet. I then realize how great the trauma has been that God has guided me through. In the early stage, I was calling out for mercy and shedding tears of worship to a sovereign God. Later, I was giving tearful praise when I realized that God was in charge of the tug-of-war, and I was the recipient of His loving grace. I reverse the wet pillow to the dry side and go sound asleep.

Quietly, I wake up. It is 11:00 A.M., Monday, October 24, 1994. My heart has a nice steady rhythm. I become aware that my heart muscles are as sore as a pitcher's arm. But, I am extremely happy. I have fought the battle, and—by the grace of God—I have WON!

Little do I realize, however, that this is only a turning point. More battles lie ahead. Over the following two years, I will have an additional 120 atrial fibrillation attacks. None of these attacks, however, will rise above a 151-bpm level into the life-threatening area, and most attacks will be confined to the 100 to 130 level. I continue the drug therapy package my cardiologist had prescribed except for ISMO. Withdrawing from ISMO has proven to be a wise move.

Doctor's Commentary

Wayne makes reference to an anomaly typical of many patients, a gut-level sense that the medicine they are taking is probably no longer doing its job or is even toxic to their bodies and causing vague side effects or alterations to nervous system function. In my experience, this has been a common observation of many patients prescribed a variety of medicines or therapeutic nostrums. At some level, the whole process just does not make "sense." It has come to my attention over the years that this sense, however vague it might sound in academic terms, must certainly be noted, as it will guide the doctor-patient partnership unerringly toward a level of better health.

Wayne, of course, was at a medical disadvantage in that he did not at the time have a physician to work with, while opting to discontinue ISMO. A doctor looking at the situation from a functional perspective would have suggested that he use high doses of CoQ-10, perhaps injectable sources of magnesium, and EDTA simultaneously while discontinuing the prescribed medicine, so that the process would be much more comfortable and without prolonging the side effects that Wayne unfortunately endured.

Wayne's experience took enormous courage and a bit of luck. Certainly, the addition of the prayer service played a significant role. Today, the clinical "buzz" refers to this process as "non-local healing." There is a tendency for the academician to find comfort in describing a process that cannot be quantified scientifically, yet at the same time remain, at least from a descriptive standpoint, focused on reductionistic themes and hence the nomenclature, "non-local healing."

Another important observation, alluded to in Wayne's conversation with his friend Dr. Able, revolves around the concept of biochemical uniqueness. This functional concept really relates to the obvious fact that everyone is totally different. A drug dose or an approach that might work for one will not work for another, and even the types of medicines or supplements, combinations, timing of administration, and the enhanced artful inclusion of supportive therapies all have high degrees of variability from person to person and even the same person at different times of the day.

Wayne, for example, was taking fairly high levels of magnesium to help control an irregular heart rhythm. Most likely, an analysis of his intracellular levels of magnesium would have revealed a deficiency. Clinically, he would have had to consume enormous amounts of magnesium to help restore optimal cellular levels to help normalize his cardiac rhythm. If an average person, not plagued with Wayne's clinical or medical issues, consumed this large amount of magnesium, he or she would promptly experience explosive diarrhea, because the magnesium ingested would be far in excess of what the body needed at that time.

Keep in mind, however, that in Wayne's case, the magnesium did not completely succeed without adding the secondary electrolyte, sodium. If Wayne had been able to analyze his adrenal status at that time, it most likely would have exhibited subclinical deficiency. It certainly was subclinical when I did his initial evaluation. In any event, one must remember that nutrients, minerals, vitamins, antioxidants, and electrolytes all work in unison. That is, each has to be in balance—one relative to the other—much like all the instruments of a symphony, to produce a recognizable melody.

In our current medical approach, which is mostly reductionistic or so-called HMO medicine, the entire focus tends to be on a certain symptom and a certain drug to block that symptom, rather than on looking at a more comprehensive holistic evaluation. A holistic evaluation is an exploration of what systems may be out of balance and how they can be restored to their natural balance and what tools will be most efficacious to create that balance. Once balance is restored, the body will function very well on its own. This analysis is like viewing the body as a garden rather than a machine.

—Dale Guyer, M.D.

Chapter Nine
Taking Charge

Winning the first battle reinforced my confidence for "Getting Well." My goal now was to find the cause of my atrial fibrillation, a task the six-member cardiologist team at the hospital failed to accomplish. I had produced for a year EKG data for it to analyze every Monday, Wednesday, and Friday at the heart rehab center, along with detailed computerized recordings of my heart going in and out of atrial fibrillation and atrial flutter during normal daily activities. Even with unlimited access to laboratory testing, this highly paid team of doctors repeatedly *struck-out*, and without shame continued to utter, "We don't know the cause of your irregular heartbeat." At first, I interpreted the team's actions as incompetence, but then I realized that cardiologists, being specialists, sincerely believe they know everything there is to know about the heart and what is best for the patient. I found that my opinions and suggestions as a patient were not taken seriously, and if I did not respond to treatments they prescribed, then I was labeled as not cooperating.

I considered going to the Cleveland Clinic, but after talking on the telephone to one of its arrhythmic specialists, I soon realized that its primary approach would be to experiment with anti-arrhythmic drugs. I made it clear I was looking for a cure, not a quick cover-up fix with drugs. At no time did the specialist suggest how he would look for a cause, but he did make it clear that if I decided to see him I should bring $600 cash for the first appointment because, as he said, insurance companies normally will not pay for a second opinion concerning irregular heartbeat.

I called the National Hotline 800 number for Atrial Fibrillation. The recording advised me that "your life may be in danger—report to an emergency room and be examined by a cardiologist right away." The recording assured me that there was "a large assortment of drugs available to treat this medical condition—drugs you may have to take the rest of your life." After listening to the recording twice, I was convinced that this hotline message was sponsored by the drug industry.

I Began My Own Research

Dismayed with the medical industry's lack of knowledge concerning atrial fibrillation, I began reading medical literature searching for cures for atrial fibrillation. My sister Pat spent hours at the Cleveland Clinic medical library. Her close friend Jackie spent hours searching the Internet.

I researched the Indiana Medical School Library. I read medical books along with both old and current medical studies. After two months of research, we had only a handful of real cures. Five of the cures stood out. The patients had "silver fillings" removed from their teeth, and their atrial fibrillation attacks stopped.

I began to study the silver material used in teeth fillings. I was shocked to learn that silver filling is an *amalgam,* a mixture of fifty percent mercury and fifty-percent silver/copper/tin/zinc. They should be called "mercury fillings," a metal so toxic that no level in the human body is considered safe.

The toxicology books warn never to allow mercury to make direct contact with the human body because it can be absorbed through the skin and into the bloodstream. Once in the bloodstream, it can travel through the body and damage nerve and brain cells. Mercury not filtered out of the blood by the liver and kidneys is directed by the immune system to be stored in fat cells of organs like the brain, kidneys, and heart. I found this alarming and began wondering if mercury from my fourteen tooth fillings had leaked into my body and damaged the nerves in my heart, causing my atrial fibrillation.

I contacted the FDA through the Freedom of Information Act, and it replied that amalgams have been used for more than 100 years, and their safety was *grandfathered in as safe* in 1979 when Congress made the FDA responsible for the safety of all implants into the human body. Because of the low volume of health problems recorded by the American Dental Association (ADA) over the years, the FDA listed amalgams as a safe medical implant. However, it was quick to point out that the FDA had not conducted any scientific research that proves amalgams to be safe in the human body.

I researched the ADA to find that it is not a health organization. Instead it acts as the trade union solely for the benefit of member dentists. The ADA's commitment to dentists is the same as the United Auto Workers' commitment is to the people who build our cars. It finds ways to increase its members' annual income, lobby for laws favoring their trade, and protect its members from competition and legal challenges. There is nothing wrong with this. That is what trade organizations do. However, I believe we as patients should not be confused and think that the ADA has any real concern for our health. Its primary concern will always be for the welfare of the dentist.

My research reveals that the ADA has good, self-serving reasons for promoting, protecting, and certifying the safety of mercury amalgam as a tooth-cavity filling material. On pages 151-154 of the book *Elements of Danger*, the author, Dr. Morton, reports that the ADA holds patents to certain amalgam dental materials, indicating that it in the past received royalty income. The ADA produces additional income by selling the right to use its Official Logo of Approval to toothpaste and other dental manufacturers. I believe that this ADA-approval logo is only a marketing gimmick. The ADA is not certifying the performance or safety of the product to consumers. The manufacturer remains responsible for the product. True, the ADA certifies mercury amalgam material as safe. But, ADA certifications are to its member dentists only. Courts have ruled that the ADA responsibilities do not extend to consumers. The amalgam manufacturer, state dental licensing boards, and individual dentists remain responsible to the patient for the safety of amalgams.

I discovered that the primary reason the ADA fights so hard to defend the safety of mercury amalgams is that installing them is low cost to the patient and a very fast way for dentists to make a lot of money. Compared to white composite materials that require more skill and time to install and gold inlays that patients often judge as too expensive, mercury amalgam tooth-reconstructive materials remain the choice of most dentists. As I often read while I was researching amalgams, dentists like mercury amalgams because they are very fast to install and an easy way to make money. I agree. The way I see it, all they need to do is "**drill'm**, **fill'm**, and **bill'm**."

Because mercury amalgams are quick and easy to install, I believe we can expect dentists to continue installing mercury into the teeth of their patients for as long as the ADA continues to keep malpractice lawyers away from their doors.

I found a lot of research from medical studies from around the world indicating that mercury amalgams are causing a wide assortment of medical problems in the human body, including irregular heartbeat like mine. Most European countries have studies that associate health problems with mercury amalgams. Many countries are in the process of phasing out and banning mercury amalgams as a dental restoration material. During my investigation, I could not understand why our elected officials were not investigating this widespread threat to our basic health.

Later, I learned that the ADA is so rich, powerful, and aggressive that most dental schools bow down to anything it says, because it is through their good relationship with the ADA that schools maintain their certification to teach and graduate dentists. The FDA seems fearful of upsetting the ADA because the U.S. Congress always supports the ADA's position involving disputes. When a U.S. Congressional committee announces plans to hold hearings concerning the safety of mercury amalgams, I believe that an army of ADA lobbyists calls on the Congressmen involved and quiets them down with what appears to be generous contributions to their reelection accounts. I have never heard a U.S. President or any elected official, except Congressman Dan Burton, speak-out and question the safety of mercury amalgams, although they have received a lot of information from research scientists like Dr. Boyd E. Haley, Professor and Chair, Department of Chemistry, University of Kentucky, who has provided our elected officials with both sworn testimony and documented scientific evidence that mercury amalgams are contributing to serious health problems of many sick people. **I believe that lobbyists have developed ways to keep our elected officials quiet.**

The American Medical Association (AMA) and the ADA agreed long ago to stay out of each other's professional arenas. This leaves patients like me, made ill by the mercury in our tooth fillings, all alone without support from anybody in the medical industry or in government.

Dentists who make judgments on their own, without a patient's demand or a medical doctor's order to remove a patient's mercury amalgams for the sole purpose of improving a patient's health, may be charged with medical malpractice by the ADA Ethics Committee, which then can recommend that the dentist's state license to practice dentistry be revoked. That is why most dentists will not say anything negative about the safety of mercury amalgams when you question them. This is detailed in ADA Resolution 42H-1986, sometimes referred to as a "gag order" on dentists.

During the period when I was investigating mercury amalgams, by chance I found myself seated at lunch next to a General Motors metallurgist. I outlined to him the composition of metals making up the fourteen silver fillings in my mouth and asked what reactions would happen over time within this mixture. He was not surprised I had experienced electrical currents in my mouth when I rinsed with salt water because salt water, he said, "is a good electrolyte." He explained that an amalgam is a mixture of metals cold-bonded and held together by the fifty percent mercury. A mixture is not stable like an alloy that is fused together when melted at high critical temperatures. From the moment an amalgam mixture of metals is bonded together, each metal tries to separate from the mixture through a process known as electrolysis. Electrolysis creates low voltages called **galvanic electricity** that eventually separate the mixture. Copper and zinc, being the least noble metals, will be the first to be released from the mixture and absorbed into the human body. Silver and tin in the amalgam will then be released and absorbed. Mercury, being fifty percent of the mixture, is being released constantly as the other metals break their bond from the mercury. Mercury and tin are the most toxic to the human body and attack the nervous system as well as weaken the immune system.

Armed with this new information, I made an appointment with my cardiologist to discuss the possibility that the galvanic electricity being generated by the large amount of metals in my mouth was creating my atrial fibrillation along with the possibility that the toxic mercury and tin had damaged the nerves in the sinus node, the natural pacemaker in my heart. My cardiologist asked no questions, but instantly stated that my dental work was not affecting my heart's electrical problems in any way. To further strengthen his professional position, the next day he wrote a letter to my primary-care physician assuring him that the small amount of mercury entering my body was not causing my irregular heartbeat problem. Again, I realized I was up against a brick wall.

I Selected a New Family Doctor

After more than 100 exploratory telephone calls, I selected a new primary-care physician to replace Dr. Branden. I chose a young family-practice doctor who had finished additional nutritional studies and often prescribed vitamins and minerals along with prescription drugs. He promised to work very hard to help find the cause of my atrial fibrillation. My first appointment lasted three hours as he gave me a hands-on physical and recorded small details of my past health history, employment working conditions, and lifestyle. He asked a lot of questions and then sent me to the hospital for x-rays and lab work.

Three weeks later, all the lab work was back, and we met for my second appointment. It lasted two hours as we carefully reviewed every detail. In general, most of the test results fell outside the accepted range, indicating that I was in declining health. He showed me the letter he had received from my cardiologist, assuring him that mercury was not causing my heart-rhythm problems and adding that I was not being a very cooperative patient. This new doctor said that he too did not believe that my dental work was causing my atrial fibrillation based on what he had learned in medical school. However, based on sixteen years of my employment being in toxic environments, he suggested I make contact with Dr. Zimmer, who practiced environmental medicine, and be tested for **heavy metal deposits** in my body.

Doctor's Commentary

Wayne and many patients are assured that they have had unlimited access to laboratory tests and to the best, most well-educated, and capable physicians available to ascertain what is going on with their medical condition. Unfortunately, all efforts "struck-out" as Wayne wrote. In reality, however, the diagnostic testing and the treatment options available to the American public represent probably about ten percent of the options routinely used throughout the world. Many of the other 90 percent of available options tend to be the most efficacious and successful, in my own clinical experience.

However, as Wayne discovered, expanding the therapeutic options already offered to him was fairly limited and not a consideration. Even calling specialized centers, such as the Cleveland Clinic, did not provide additional encouragement, nor did contacting the National Hotline for Atrial Fibrillation. All too often organized support groups present the party line. The problem stems in part because many national organizations receive much-needed funding from pharmaceutical companies and political interests with a focus on maintaining status quo approaches. Seldom do professionals provide commentary on optional, alternative, complementary, or adjunctive therapies. In my experience, when the information is provided, it is often inaccurate. Many medical experts, consulted to provide opinions on some of these matters or therapies, have not had direct clinical experience or training, or reviewed original research on the matter. They simply repeat information that they may have overheard at medical meetings or express personal, often biased, opinions.

The toxicity of metal fillings is an illustration of this process. For example, some people develop potential toxicities from bioaccumulation of mercury in selective body tissues. However, mercury amalgam toxicity remains a political hotbed in the minds of many dentists and certainly the American Dental Association. The overall reasons are well-cited and outlined in Wayne's commentary. While recognizing all the political undertones that maintain business-as-usual medicine, it seems difficult not to at least recognize that potential toxicity in a sensitivity-prone individual may be a medical force that needs to be recognized. It is hard to imagine this possible health hazard is not taken seriously, if one simply looks at facts, such as:

- Any textbook addressing toxicology will note clearly the extensive potential toxicities of even minute levels of mercury. Dental fillings contain mercury. Dental fillings have been shown to leak mercury vapor gradually over the years that will accumulate in biological tissues.

- In addition, even the Environmental Protection Agency will not allow dentists to dispose of amalgam filling material in the environment, but the FDA accepts its use as a dental filling material for human beings. What is the logic? It does not take much scientific insight to ascertain that some people are going to be affected adversely by even minute levels of bio-accumulated mercury toxin exposure.

- One of the aspects that early in my career I found intriguing using complementary therapies such as chelation (which removes toxic heavy metals from the body), is that they tend to improve the well-being of almost every patient who undergoes the series of treatments. Rarely do I find an individual who does not feel significantly better after treatment. In the big picture, it would now be easy to understand. While chelation can be of benefit because of the inclusion of multi-nutrients, trace minerals, and antioxidants in the IV, the active ingredients, such as EDTA, are removing heavy metal toxins from the body. Most of us have accumulated a certain amount of toxic metals while living on this planet, some more than others depending on our individual exposures, genetics, and ability to clear toxins from our body. It is not surprising that, as people become detoxified, they start to function in a much healthier way. It is only recently, however, that many studies are emerging showing that there seems to be a direct link between high metal toxin levels in body tissues and the occurrence of diverse symptomatology and organic findings, such as heart disease, immune system dysfunction, and probably even neurodegenerative disorders such as Alzheimer's disease.

- However, the financial incentives to maintain the status quo, happily and succinctly stated as "drill'm, fill'm, and bill'm," will likely continue for some time. It will be only through the evolution engineered by advocacy groups and patient demand that the potentially toxic approaches to modern dentistry will be changed to more acceptable and less toxic approaches.

—Dale Guyer, M.D.

Chapter Ten
Discovery and Hope

I made an appointment with Dr. Zimmer, an environmental medical doctor, for heavy metals testing on February 2, 1995. At that time, I had been seriously ill for two years with chronic atrial fibrillation, along with twenty other symptoms (as described in Chapter 3) and a general body weakness from heart disease. My family, as they later told me, did not think I was going to live much longer because of my many health problems along with recent signs of losing weight and rapid aging.

Arriving at my home two weeks before my appointment was an extensive "New Patient Questionnaire" with instructions to fill out and return five days before my appointment date. At my first appointment, I spent one and one-half hours with Dr. Zimmer. I was surprised to find he had already studied my case and began asking specific questions from the questionnaire. He spent most of his time checking for weak areas of my body using a muscle testing technique he called "applied kinesiology." He said that muscle testing helped him decide the weak and strong areas of my body and the types of laboratory tests needed. He then sent me to a medical laboratory with prescriptions for a series of blood, urine, and saliva tests.

After lunch, I returned to Dr. Zimmer's clinic for the heavy metals test. A technician prepared a 500cc IV bag of a special medicine formula referred to as a *chelation preparation*. The primary active ingredient for this type of *provoking chelation* is a man-made, FDA-approved, synthetic amino acid called EDTA, a prescription product developed by Bristol-Myers. A nurse checked my temperature, heart rate, and blood pressure and then began drip-feeding the chelation formula through an IV catheter inserted into a vein of my left arm. Over three hours, the EDTA flowed slowly through my bloodstream and quietly made ion-exchange-type bonding with various toxic metals stored primarily in fat cells of my organs. After bonding, the EDTA, being attached to the heavy metals, was carried out of my body in the urine. I was given a large plastic 3,000ml jug with instructions to collect all my urine for the next twenty-four hours and to ship a sample overnight to a special laboratory for testing.

Interpreting the Test Results

Two weeks later after all tests were completed, I had my second appointment. Dr. Zimmer first reviewed the results of the twenty-four-hour heavy metals test. The first page of the test results listed the parts per million of the fifteen elements considered toxic to the human body. The toxic elements in my body that tested elevated—so high they were beyond the range of the testing scale—were aluminum, arsenic, cadmium, lead, mercury, and tin.

From Dr. Zimmer, I learned that my high level of aluminum probably came from my being around a lot of welding in my early thirties, underarm deodorants, soda cans, or eating food cooked in aluminum utensils. Dr. Zimmer said that high levels of aluminum are implicated with senile dementia and Alzheimer's disease. But in my case he thought it was contributing to my short-term memory loss problems.

Dr. Zimmer was not sure where my high level of arsenic came from, maybe from drinking well water because I lived out in the country, or from burning trash in my backyard. I learned that most paper contains small traces of arsenic used in its manufacture. If you smoke cigarettes, you can accumulate elevated levels from the paper. Also, some imported vegetables in our supermarkets have been reported to have high levels of arsenic. Regardless, I was advised that it must be removed because arsenic is a strong carcinogen associated with cancer of the digestive system. "Don't worry," Dr. Zimmer said. "Arsenic is easy to remove."

Cadmium is a different story, I was told by Dr. Zimmer, because it is somewhat difficult to remove from the body. I have since learned that cadmium is a strong carcinogen, too. Cadmium injections are sometimes used to give cancer to laboratory research animals. That's how powerful it is. At the time I became ill, I had quit smoking over twenty years before. However, some of the toxic cadmium I discovered in my body by testing in 1995 came from the cigarettes I smoked—not from the tobacco, but from a fungicide containing cadmium that was sprayed on the tobacco leaf to prevent mold forming during the curing process. I also received some of my cadmium from just being around so much welding during my late twenties and early thirties. In addition to provoking cancer, cadmium also destroys vitamin D, impairs cellular energy production, and creates neuropsychological problems such as mood swings and behavior changes. The presence of mercury or lead with cadmium dramatically increases their toxic effects. Each acts as an enhancer for the other. I believe that that situation was going on in my body when Dr. Zimmer began treating me.

Lead, I discovered, is a toxic heavy metal everybody thinks they know a lot about. As I began to read basic toxicity books like *Toxic Metal Syndrome*, I learned that almost every adult has some lead stored in his or her body and doesn't know it. It was ingested from breathing automobile exhaust fumes twenty-five years ago when lead was an anti-knock additive in gasoline or was in house paint, or when we had lead-soldered water pipes in older-type houses. Most of these lead sources have been outlawed, and many older houses have been updated, but adults older than thirty years may still have a lot of toxic lead stored in their bodies, and it will not show up with a simple blood test. When lead is absorbed into the bloodstream, the lead not excreted via the urine during the first three to six hours is directed by the immune system to be stored *out of harm's way* in the aorta walls, active liver cells, kidney fat cells, brain cells, heart muscles, adrenal glands, thyroid gland, bone marrow, or tooth dentin.

When I studied the scientific literature, I learned that lead is a broad-range toxin, and once it is introduced into the body it slowly continues to alter and destroy the healthy cells surrounding it. Often a conventional doctor is prescribing long-term drugs for a malfunctioning organ or gland, but does not know what is causing the problem. Based on my studies, I believe that, if the doctor would just take the time to properly remove all the heavy metals from the patient's body, the organ or gland, with proper nutrition, would usually heal itself and go back to being healthy.

I told Dr. Zimmer at this second appointment that I had this high level of toxic mercury in my body, because the mercury in my fourteen amalgam fillings had migrated throughout my body and damaged my immune and nervous system. I thought that toxic dental mercury was ravaging my body, and that was why I had chronic irregular heartbeat, muscle twitch, body tremors, brain fog, difficulty concentrating, short-term memory loss, sore tongue, bleeding gums, and red-rash blotches on my skin.

Dr. Zimmer scratched his head and informed me that the ADA said we get most of the toxic mercury detected in our body from the contaminated fish we eat and the polluted air we breathe, not from the small amount of mercury coming from our tooth fillings. I told him that research did not support the ADA's statements. Eskimos eat largely a seafood diet, and those without amalgams do not have high mercury levels. I believed there were a lot of people with high mercury levels all over the world in modern societies who did not eat fish at all. China, East Germany, and Russia have a much higher level of air polluted by coal-fired factories, steel mills, and power plants than the United States. The adults in these countries without mercury amalgam fillings do not have high mercury levels either. "Research also clearly shows," I reminded Dr. Zimmer, "that pregnant women transfer toxic mercury to their fetus in amounts directly related to the number of mercury amalgams they have in their teeth."

I believe that all the ADA and the FDA are trying to do is to send up a distracting smokescreen to keep mothers from knowing that their family dentist is installing pure metallic mercury two inches from the base of their little kid's brain and insisting this procedure is good medicine and that it will improve their children's health. The truth is: if all mothers were informed of the fifty-percent mercury content in silver teeth fillings and knew the true danger involved, every ADA-member dentist in its big powerful trade union might be sued for malpractice.

Dr. Zimmer seemed to agree I might be right about mercury. He preferred, however, to address the fact that we had to lower my mercury level before it would be safe for a dentist to remove my amalgams. He said that the process of removing amalgams would always increase the amount of mercury toxicity in my body, and that, if we didn't lower the toxic mercury level first, I risked doing additional damage to my immune and nervous system.

The lab report listed tin also at a sky-high level. I learned from the well-documented book *Elements of Danger* that tin is very difficult to remove because it has a strong affinity for nerve cells in the nervous system and is bound very tightly to them. Tin toxicity causes emotional upset with a sense of sadness, anxiety, and the dread of seeing people. These patients commonly complain of headaches in the temples and forehead, with motion causing the pain to worsen. To get relief, patients toxic with tin tend to sit quietly and remain motionless. In my case, I reported small spots of intense pain moving around my body I named "fifty-cent pain," as described in Chapter 3. I learned later that the pain was actually a nerve going through a brief spasm.

I learned that there are other symptoms associated with tin toxicity. Often a cramp-like colic is present around the navel, which is relieved only when hard pressure is placed against the abdomen. Typically, a tin-toxic patient will sleep with one leg drawn up and the other stretched out straight. Spasmodic twitching of the muscles of the forearm and hand are common; fingers often jerk when holding a pen. Patients have difficulty holding on to objects; they begin to drop things. When tin migrates to the nerves in the lungs, mucus congestion often develops, resulting in difficulty clearing the throat. Taste is affected, and the smell of food cooking sometimes causes vomiting. The sweat of an individual with dental-generated tin toxicity is smelly and musty—really offensive to someone standing nearby. Women have reported an unexplained pain in the vagina that extends upward and backward to the spine and a white vaginal discharge. So, as you can see, any location in the body containing nerves is an area in which tin can create pain and unusual health problems.

Referring to my heavy metals test report, Dr. Zimmer pointed out that my test showed that my toxic nickel level was not off the chart but was reported as "very elevated." The source of nickel toxicity for most people is the dental nickel commonly used by dentists in partial plates and braces. But, in my case, I believe that elevated levels of toxic nickel came from breathing arc-welding fumes every day at the manufacturing factory where I worked for ten years. High-strength welding rods contain large amounts of nickel to assist fusing of unlike metals.

Scanning the test results in Dr. Zimmer's clinic that day produced some good news, too. The eight remaining heavy metals regarded as toxic to the human body—antimony, beryllium, bismuth, platinum, thallium, thorium, tungsten, and uranium—all tested within the reference range as safe.

Flipping to the second page of the twenty-four-hour urine test, "Elements Expected to Be Seen in Usual Specimens," Dr. Zimmer said he also tested the levels of good elements that should be present in my body because they are needed for good health. The six essential elements that tested in my body exactly at the correct level were potassium, phosphorus, copper, iron, iodine, and lithium. The five essential elements that tested on the high side were calcium, magnesium, zinc, sulfur, and manganese. But, none of them was high enough to cause a problem. However, the report showed there were seven essential elements that tested too low: chromium, selenium, boron, molybdenum, silicon, strontium, and vanadium. I learned that we needed to get these essential elements up to their proper levels because they were affecting my blood sugar control and my body's ability to fight infection.

Dr. Zimmer laid the twenty-four-hour urine test aside and without comment handed me my copy of the four-page laboratory report listing the results of my blood, urine, and saliva tests from the medical laboratory. He pointed out that the first thing wrong was that my cholesterol was way-too low. My cholesterol was below 130 and normal is 200.

According to Uffe Ravnskov, M.D., Ph.D., a highly respected cholesterol researcher, with a cholesterol level as low as mine, my risk of cancer had increased five times, and also this low level invited inflammation into my cardiovascular system, which contributed to my heart disease. Eating organ meat and red meat again was recommended to raise my cholesterol back to the normal range. Dr. Zimmer advised me that there are some important enzymes in red meat that are not available from other foods. I was beginning to understand I was not going to get well with this low cholesterol reading I had maintained during the twenty previous years I had slowly developed heart disease.

Dr. Zimmer was really concerned about my immune system. The performance of my immune system tested so low that the medical doctor at the lab reviewing my test results had called Dr. Zimmer. The lab doctor reported my T-cell count looked like the early stage of an HIV/AIDS patient. Dr. Zimmer said the reason I had lost so much weight during the past year was that my digestive tract was contaminated with Candida, a massive yeast infection. The lab test indicated there was so much yeast growing in my body that it had blocked most of the receptors that transfer nutrients into my bloodstream. The nutrition needed to support a healthy body was not being made available to my cells. Even with three good meals a day along with vitamins and minerals, I was starving, because of the Candida infection. I had other problems too, but Dr. Zimmer elected not to address them until we cleared up the yeast and fungus infections so that good nutrition could start rebuilding my immune system. The large volumes of antibiotics I had taken in preceding years had weakened my immune system slowly, and then my immune system was practically destroyed when mercury and other heavy metals accumulated in my body.

My First Plan for "Getting Well"

Knowing that the toxic heavy metals and their *free-radical effects* on my body were creating a chemical and electrical imbalance to the point where my immune system was no longer effective, and the nutrition needed to keep me healthy was not being absorbed, the first thing we concentrated on was removing the heavy metals from my body. This was my plan: Every Monday and Wednesday for the next five weeks, I was scheduled for a chelation-therapy treatment to begin the process of removing all those toxic heavy metals. Then, every Friday I visited the clinic for a nutritional IV treatment. These treatments created the process of correcting the chemical and electrical imbalances in my body and at the same time feeding a high level of nutrition directly into my bloodstream to jumpstart the rebuilding process of my immune system. Once the toxic burden was removed from my body and new enhanced nutrition kicked in, my immune system could bounce back to full power, and then the twenty illness symptoms I had developed over the past thirty-five years would start, one at a time, to be eliminated. I would then have a chance to become completely well again.

Dr. Zimmer said that the second ingredient of my plan was for me, as a patient, to learn my part in making the treatment plan work. He recommended three books that I should read and understand. The first book was *The Yeast Connection*, by Dr. William Crook. Dr. Crook teaches how to change your diet and cure the yeast infection growing in your digestive system that is blocking nutritional absorption into your bloodstream. By following Dr. Crook's proven plan, I learned how to cure my Candida in about two months, and then my nutritional plan could be switched from the Friday nutritional IV to the daily use of conventional vitamins and minerals. To help speed up the elimination of the yeast infection, Dr. Zimmer prescribed nystatin, a drug that kills the fungus that supports a broad range of yeast infections. The second book Dr. Zimmer wanted me to read was *Love, Medicine & Miracles*, by Dr. Bernie Siegel. This book teaches the characteristics and attitude found in patients who have the very best chance of "Getting Well." The third book, *Your Body Doesn't Lie*, by Dr. John Diamond, explains the *applied kinesiology* Dr. Zimmer used to detect the strong and weak areas of my body. In 1979, Dr. Diamond refined this scientific testing method so we as patients could understand it.

My plan called for another twenty-four-hour urine test in six weeks, along with some additional blood tests to check the progress we were making in removing the toxic heavy metals, stopping the yeast infections, increasing nutritional absorption, and our effectiveness in boosting my immune system.

On the way home, I stopped at the Georgetown Health Food Store on the west side of Indianapolis and purchased the books *The Yeast Connection* and *Love, Medicine & Miracles* from the shelf, but had to order *Your Body Doesn't Lie*. Another book caught my eye, *Forty Something Forever, A Consumer's Guide to Chelation Therapy*, so I bought it, too.

Overwhelmed by what I had learned that day, I began immediately to make hand-written notes in my personal journal. I summarized my notes with four reminders: #1, Remove all toxic heavy metals from my body; #2, Improve the nutritional absorption into my body; #3, Learn to be an exceptional patient with a determination to get completely well; and, my #4 reminder, Continue to challenge my body and mind with daily exercise.

Doctor's Commentary

Wayne describes a situation similar to so many other frustrated patients. "Walking wounded" is a phrase used by one of the smartest men I have had the pleasure to meet, Jeffrey Bland, Ph.D. The term refers to individuals like Wayne for whom, by the time a detailed evaluation is done, practically every system in the body is exhausted, out of balance, and dysfunctional. Although the causes can be easily traced in Wayne's and many others' cases to toxin exposures, ongoing stress, and environmental factors wedded to genetic potential, they are far-removed from the potential help of HMO-style medicine—namely, a simple treatment for a simple symptom. This approach works very well for some problems, such as strep throat that responds rapidly to antibiotic intervention.

However, for Wayne and others like him, the process of "Getting Well" is more akin to the proverbial layers of the onion, pulling back one layer at a time to gradually return to a more pristine state of biochemical balance, in which all systems work in harmony. To achieve that harmony, many patients require aggressive nutritional supplementation, herbal medicine, chelation therapy, and many other therapies generally labeled as alternative or integrative.

To be successful in treating these individuals, doctors must undergo extensive postgraduate training and develop this new practice approach into an art form. Part of that approach requires extensive details of the patient's history. The initial questionnaire is the first encounter that attempts to acquire a level of detail that to date was unexplored even in complex cases of patients who have gone to well-known tertiary referral centers for evaluation. Unique types of medicinal testing are used, looking in detail at hormone levels, metabolism, bowel ecology, neural-transmitter synthesis, and the ability of the body to detoxify chemical toxins.

This diagnostic approach always provides a more comprehensive understanding of the interplay of the person's unique biochemistry. Once imbalances are determined, appropriate treatments can be applied to restore the body to its optimal state of health. High levels of toxic or heavy metals, such as aluminum, arsenic, cadmium, lead, mercury, and tin, severe problems for Wayne, are now associated with immune system dysfunction, various types of heart disease, rhythm disturbances, and even neural cognitive dementia, such as Alzheimer's.

The problem is that we are all exposed to these toxic compounds through many avenues, some from vocational environments and others from amalgam fillings. We all have varying degrees of efficiency in how our bodies are able to eliminate toxins. In those of us who are biochemically inefficient, these toxins will gradually bio-accumulate—a process that will eventually lead to wide-scale dysfunction.

Toxic exposures may have occurred many years ago. Patients boast proudly that they have had all of their mercury-containing dental amalgams removed 12 years ago so; therefore, they are now "mercury free." However, what they fail to realize is that, while they have removed a potential source of chronic mercury exposure, they have not done anything to remove the level of toxic mercury that might have accumulated in the tissues of the body over those many years during which the fillings were in place. Additionally, even the process of removing fillings—even in the most skilled dental hands—may add more toxic burden of mercury to the body, as the fillings are drilled out. Also, toxin exposure from vocational sources, even in patients who have retired or changed jobs decades ago, can remain in the body, continuing to erode their overall health.

So-called normal levels of lead or other toxins in the environment should not be referred to as "normal" at all. These levels should probably be called "usual" levels of lead or other toxins. It would arguably not be normal for the human body to contain any amount of toxic metal such as arsenic, lead, or mercury. However, because our world has become so toxic, it becomes usual in laboratory analysis to find small amounts of many toxic compounds. The point is that no level is normal. And some individuals can be so sensitive to even small amounts that exposure may create a lot of toxicity for their bodies. As Wayne mentioned, certain tissues of the body, such as the bone marrow, the immune system, the adrenal glands, the muscles, and bones, actively accumulate these toxins, and they are often the first areas of the body whose function is adversely affected.

The politics of toxicity needs to be addressed, particularly mercury. According to some sources and data published by the World Health Organization, the majority of tissue mercury occurs from the out-gassing of mercury-containing dental amalgams. The American Dental Association has adamantly stated that these background levels of potential toxins do not cause any medical problems. The ongoing and fierce debate would fill an entire textbook.

With scientific-based studies that any scientifically-minded individual would agree upon, it is amazing that we cannot take the next logical step and acknowledge the fact that some people may be affected adversely by the mercury toxins that inevitably leach into body tissues. I have seen case after case of significant physical and medical improvement in many individuals after these toxins are removed from their bodies using chelation therapy. In essence, the process seems rather logical to this clinician, who has seen these often-incredible changes with his own eyes. However, it admittedly remains an elusive and hotly debated item within medical orthodoxy and certainly more than the mainstream opinion of the American Dental Association.

In Wayne's initial medical evaluation, a broad range of abnormalities is noted—chronic deficiency states of essential minerals—such as magnesium, zinc, manganese, and sulfur; a dysfunctionally low cholesterol level; yeast overgrowth in the digestive tract; and severe impairment of the immune system. All are fairly common long-term consequences seen with chronic toxicity. Generally, removing chronic toxins from the body will improve these levels of function dramatically.

The other component most important to focus on in this chapter concerns a proverbial "fork in the road." Wayne was recommended to read the book *Love, Medicine & Miracles* by Dr. Bernie Siegel. This book introduces the concept of the "exceptional patient." Exceptional patients are individuals who become self-advocates. They consider what physicians and specialists have to offer diagnostically and therapeutically. They do their research, compare notes, and make their own decisions about how to engage their medical care. This is an entirely new approach to being a patient, as advocacy is rare, empowerment is low, and attitudes of entitlement often run high.

We are a society conditioned to expect near-miraculous overnight successes from medical therapies, totally underwritten by the government or a health maintenance organization. The reality is that we Americans are offered only a small number from the vast array of medical therapies available throughout the world. Many therapies, often 50 or more years old, have proven to work better than those widely available and covered by HMO systems in our country. For that reason, many people find themselves in a role of working outside of the insurance safety net to reacquire their health.

In addition to attitudes of entitlement, it is important to recognize the role that the individual's emotional state plays in his or her overall health. I observed over the years a chronic response to negative thinking and how it leads to and creates negative health issues. Even traumatic emotional events seem to center in various anatomic areas of the body, leading in time to bona fide medical symptoms and bodily dysfunction. In essence, to be an exceptional patient with the highest expectation of regaining vibrant health, one must do an honest assessment of one's emotional state and honestly answer two very difficult questions:

- What intentions and thoughts are creating roadblocks to my reacquiring a more vibrant state of health?
- What beliefs about entitlement dictate that I should expect the world to restore and maintain my health rather than that I should co-create it for myself?

—Dale Guyer, M.D.

Chapter Eleven
Learning about "Getting Well"

You, too, will be excited like me when that *new-type medical doctor* you select presents your personal plan for "Getting Well." Dr. Zimmer's approach to practicing medicine was so different that it took me a few days to absorb everything he had said at my second appointment. Rolling around in my mind were his words, "As a medical doctor, I cannot cure your illnesses, but what I can do is to help you prepare your body and place it into an environment suitable for healing itself." I found Dr. Zimmer to be a humble man, but at the same time very secure and confident in the way he practiced medicine. His father, an orthopedic surgeon, was hopeful his son would join his private practice. But, as Dr. Zimmer told me, "After medical school, I worked as a trauma doctor at a major hospital, but continued advanced nutrition and environmental medicine studies. Later, I opened my private practice. I selected Indianapolis in 1990," he said, "because it was a major city and did not have a certified environmental doctor in practice at that time."

My IV treatments at Dr. Zimmer's clinic began the third week of February 1995. I began each Monday, Wednesday, and Friday morning at 7:00 by exercising one hour in the same heart rehab program where I began in 1993. After exercise and breakfast at the hospital's cafeteria, I reported to Dr. Zimmer's clinic by 9:30 A.M. The chelation IV treatments on Monday and Wednesday, to remove heavy metals, required a slow three-hour drip, necessary to give EDTA time to bond with the toxic metals. On Fridays, the nutritional IV was fed into my bloodstream in less than thirty minutes. It gave an immediate energy boost that usually lasted through the weekend. On Tuesday, Thursday, and Saturday, I exercised at home on my treadmill and Airdyne bike. As I made progress, I found that the daily exercise was a very important ingredient in my "Getting-Well" program.

A Good Beginning

During my first six weeks of treatment, I began listening carefully to "Getting-Well" stories told by heart patients exercising at the heart rehab center and patients at Dr. Zimmer's Environmental Clinic. Their personal stories of progress gave me great encouragement and reinforced my hope for "Getting Well."

I remember a local medical doctor we called "Dr. Bob" who exercised with us every morning at rehab. Dr. Bob was one of the first patients to survive open-heart bypass surgery in the state of Indiana. Daily exercise, he claimed, had kept him alive. His grandparents, father, mother, brothers, sisters, and cousins had all died from heart disease before age fifty. He had elected not to have children because of this gene defect and had no known blood relatives living. Dr. Bob was approaching age sixty with sixteen years dedicated to heart rehab-type exercise. He was an inspiration to all us beginners.

But, the most inspirational activity at the heart rehab center was observing new rehab patients taking small, slow baby steps on the treadmill, often with a frightened look on their faces, as a specially trained nurse grasped their arms and gave instructions of encouragement. Over just a few weeks, I watched their daily workouts progress to a normal gait, and a confident smile would return. Observing other patients' progress gave me great inspiration to exercise. That is why I remained in the heart rehab program for over three years.

Learning from Other Patients

My real education for "Getting Well" began developing during the Monday, Wednesday, and Friday mornings while I received treatment at Dr. Zimmer's clinic. About twelve patients receiving IV therapy were seated in a U-shaped pattern facing each other while three nurses provided the medical treatments. During the three-hour treatment period, new patients would arrive just as other patients were finishing. As a result, I had the opportunity to talk to ten or more people each day. Most of the patients had a chronic medical condition their family doctors, and in many cases specialists, had failed to cure. They had come to Dr. Zimmer as a last-ditch effort.

I met several patients like John who drove over 100 miles every other week for an EDTA chelation treatment. A year earlier, John was faced with heart bypass surgery for the second time. Instead he elected chelation therapy. After thirty treatments, he said, "I feel like a new man. Best I have felt in years. Wished I had never had bypass the first time." Other patients had severe food allergies and chemical sensitivity. Most were young to middle-age women, and I could tell they were really feeling miserable. Their family doctors in many cases had run a lot of tests that often revealed that nothing was wrong and then would suggest that their illness was "all in their head." Typically, allergy patients were completely well with six to twelve months of treatments. Chelation therapy was used to remove the toxins from their bodies that had created the allergy in the first place. Nutritional IVs were used to build up their immune systems, and diet changes along with prescription medicines were used to kill the yeast infections in their digestive systems. Most allergies were eliminated, and these patients ended up vigorously healthy, active "soccer moms" again.

Some of Dr. Zimmer's patients were elderly and chronically ill just like me. Many came to him after receiving disappointing medical treatments at large, famous, well-staffed clinics. In every elderly case that I observed during the two years I received treatment at Dr. Zimmer's clinic, all were greatly improved or made completely well by removing from their body the toxic heavy metals that had accumulated over many years, followed up with a vitamin and mineral supplement program. It's worth noting that none of the large, famous, expensive clinics offers treatments for removing heavy metal toxins or vitamin and mineral consultation. The reason, I believe, is that neither chelation therapy nor nutritional therapy has proven as profitable for the medical industry as surgery and drug treatments.

Not all medical people are negative about chelation therapy and nutritional supplements. I met a seventy-eight-year-old registered nurse who was still working. She said that most people guessed her age to be under sixty, and the reason was she had taken over 300 chelation and nutritional therapy treatments during the past thirty years. "Just like Zsa Zsa Gabor does," she said.

I twice sat next to a retired orthopedic surgeon receiving an IV of chelation therapy. He said he had received regular treatments over the past thirty-five years as a preventive medicine measure, to which he gave much of the credit for his excellent health. Interesting, I thought, for this doctor to be practicing medicine at a large major hospital and yet be forbidden by the Hospital Board of Governors to recommend chelation therapy to his patients, which he admitted to me could have relieved some of their arthritic pain.

Kathy, a forty-eight-year-old R.N. and amateur competitive runner whom I met at Dr. Zimmer's clinic, was forced to quit work in early 1994 because of low energy resulting in muscle weakness. Her husband, a medical doctor, had sent her to every specialist he knew in the Indianapolis area, and all had reported they could not find anything wrong with her. Her husband then advised her that the doctors had agreed collectively her problem was being created by delayed menopause and was not physical but instead mainly mental. She said she didn't say much, but at Christmas she became so weak while shopping that her husband on one side of her and her son, home from medical school, on the other side had to pick her up at the elbows and carry her across the wide downtown Indianapolis streets before the stoplights changed. She elected to spend Christmas Day in bed and realized her illness was not mental. She remembered some nurse friends talking about Dr. Zimmer, so she made an appointment for the first week of 1995.

By the time I met Kathy, she had completed over four months of chelation and nutritional therapy. She was back to running a mile each day and had taken up golf again. She said everything about her body was responding to treatment except her thymus gland, and Dr. Zimmer wanted to treat it with "live cell" therapy shots. "The thymus vaccine," she said, "is made from the thymus gland of an unborn, healthy beef calf, and when it is received overnight from California, it is frozen in a plastic vial suitable for treating six patients." She was looking for five other patients to take shots with her because the thymus cells had to be injected alive just as the frozen contents of the plastic package thawed. I agreed to be one of the patients receiving the live cells, after Dr. Zimmer approved me for trying it.

Six of us were scheduled for the live-cell injections at noon each Friday for six weeks. While waiting for the vaccine to thaw, we would stand around in the lab room and exchange stories. Kathy said that her husband, a medical doctor, referred to Dr. Zimmer as "a quack" and asked that she not tell her friends where she was receiving medical treatment, because, should the word get out, it might degrade his professional reputation. We asked her if she had told him about the live-cell thymus injections. She held her hand over her mouth but managed to muffle a long, drawn-out no-o-o-o!! During our fourth Friday noon meeting, Kathy told us that she was in big-time trouble with her husband. He had received her Visa charge card invoice and was upset she had spent over $1,500 with Dr. Zimmer in the past month alone. "My husband said I was spending money faster than he was making it, and that, if I didn't slow down my spending, he might be forced into bankruptcy. I asked him, 'What is more important, my health or your money?' and, you know, he didn't answer me," she added.

At our fifth meeting, I asked Kathy if her husband was still on her case about spending so much money on her health treatments. She surprised me by saying, "No, he is back to his usual loving self."

I asked, "What caused the big change?"

She said, "It was simple. I made a list of all our assets, and then walked in his office in the middle of his day and informed him I was on my way to see Larry, his lawyer. 'Why?' he asked. I then laid the list of our assets on his desk and said, 'I am going to ask Larry to divide everything down the middle. This will prevent you from going bankrupt, and I can spend my half any way I want and for anything I think might help me get completely well."

"What happened," I asked anxiously.

"He immediately requested I not see Larry. He canceled his appointments, and we spent the afternoon at his private club talking. He told me how proud he was that I had made such great progress during the past six months "Getting Well." He said he was amazed that I was now running over a mile each day and playing golf twice a week. He told me how nice and healthy I looked. We had wine and dinner at his club, and when we returned home a large bouquet of fresh flowers greeted me."

"That's a nice story," I replied. "But, please don't let my wife find out what you did." With that, everyone in the room had a good laugh.

Our sixth and final Friday meeting did not take place. On Wednesday, we each received a telephone call to our homes informing us that the frozen live-cell thymus would not be shipped from California on Thursday to arrive overnight on Friday morning, so our Friday noon appointment had been canceled. It seemed that the FDA decided to withdraw approval of all live-cell treatments because the research supporting the safety of this type treatment had been conducted in Europe, and from that moment the FDA was requiring that new acceptance research be conducted here in the United States.

I Was Never Sure about Live-Cell Therapy

I was never sure how effective these live-cell thymus shots were. Kathy said that every time she received an injection her golf score improved. Two of the six patients receiving live-cell shots were in wheelchairs at the beginning, but walked into the lab room on their own for the fifth shot. I have always wondered how much of the treatment created a placebo effect and how much was real medicine at work. However, live-cell injections are widely used throughout Europe. I will never know because I took the live-cell injections during the same five-week period during which I received two chelations and one nutritional IV each week. As my first six weeks of treatments progressed, I gained noticeable strength and began to feel better. I was unsure if any one treatment was causing my improvement, but I suspected it was the combination.

At the end of my first six weeks of treatments, I really didn't care which treatment was doing the best job because I had developed an inner feeling of confidence. My body seemed aware that "Getting Well" was going to happen. I was still having the same number of atrial fibrillation attacks, but the irregular heartbeats were at a lower rate and less stressful.

Dr. Zimmer gave me a two-week break from any type of treatment while he studied the results of my second round of urine and blood tests.

A Big Change in My Treatment Plan

My blood profile was beginning to improve at the end of my first six weeks of treatment. The blood test showed more functions of my body closer to normal, but my thyroid gland was under-performing, so after additional thyroid tests, Dr. Zimmer added a prescription called Armour® Thyroid, an FDA-approved natural medicine made from beef and pork thyroid. Candida, the yeast infection in my digestive tract, was less, but still tested positive, so he switched me to the prescription drug Sporanox®. Much to Dr. Zimmer's dismay, my cholesterol level continued to test below normal at 130. He insisted I was going to die from cancer if I didn't get my cholesterol up. The seven essential elements that tested low before—chromium, selenium, boron, molybdenum, silicon, strontium, and vanadium—had improved but needed help, so I was placed on a rather long list of vitamins and minerals balanced to my needs, based on blood tests, urine tests, and applied-kinesiology muscle testing.

After two weeks on these food supplements, Dr. Zimmer said, "It will no longer be necessary for you to have a nutritional IV every Friday. In the future, should your energy seem low, just call in, and the R.N. will schedule you for a nutritional booster IV. What I really want to accomplish during the next two months is to determine the exact balance of vitamins and minerals your body needs to rebuild your immune system and to provide every cell in your body the nutrition required for sustainable good health. To accomplish this, it is necessary to continue removing the toxins and heavy metals that have your body's chemical and electrical balances in such turmoil. In addition, I want you to schedule a B-12 shot and a testosterone shot rotated every other week." Dr. Zimmer expected me, the patient, to be actively involved and to make sure his instructions were carried out.

Handing me a copy of the new twenty-four-hour urine test, Dr. Zimmer pointed to the six elevated toxic elements—aluminum, arsenic, cadmium, lead, mercury, tin, and nickel—and then commented, "The aluminum, arsenic, and cadmium have each dropped a little, but the lead, mercury, tin, and nickel have not started down at all. In fact, the lead level tested higher on this second test than the first test. This means you have a lot of old lead deposits in your body that may be very difficult to break down and remove.

"I want to stop chelation therapy," Dr. Zimmer said, "for two or three weeks while we do a detailed evaluation of the effect your dental work may be having on your health. So, next Thursday, you are to be examined at 1:00 P.M. by Dr. Maklin, a mercury-free dentist I use as an advisor. He will make a report back to me, and then you and I will discuss where we go from there. In the meantime, I want to continue the process of removing the toxin burden from your body. Starting tomorrow, begin taking a 1,000mg dose of powered vitamin C four times a day, a dose at each meal with the fourth dose at bedtime. After your body accepts this level of vitamin C, begin gradually increasing the dose until your daily intake reaches 14,000mg. Vitamin C at a high level is a good chelator. It is very good at removing chemicals used in food processing, chemicals ingested from household cleaners, pest sprays, paints, traffic fumes, and common toxic chemicals found in industrial pollution circulating in the air around the world. We will continue using high levels of vitamin C even when we start chelation therapy again in three weeks. From now on, high levels of vitamin C will be important to your 'Getting Well.'"

My Visit with a New-Type Dentist

My visit with Dr. Maklin, a mercury-free dentist, was very informative. My first question was, "What is a mercury-free dentist?"

He said, "A dentist who has elected not to use silver filling materials, which contain fifty percent mercury, to fill dental cavities. Instead, I use the white non-metal composite materials from the plastic industry."

"Why have you elected to be a mercury-free dentist?" was my next question.

"Twelve years ago," Dr. Maklin said, "my right hand developed a slight tremor. I knew that my career as a dentist would soon end unless the tremor was eliminated. At first, the medical doctors were sure I was developing a brain tumor. But, after a long series of tests, they gave up as to what was causing it. Shortly after the tests failed to identify the probable cause of my hand tremor, I attended a dental convention and met a sixty-year-old mercury-free dentist from California who suggested I have my six silver fillings replaced with composite materials to see what might happen. I did and immediately the tremor stopped and has not returned. That same day, I made the promise not to install anything in my patients' mouths that I would not permit in my own mouth. It took me two years to make that promise good while I sought additional training to develop the skills required to install composites that were as strong and durable as mercury amalgams. Eventually, I acquired the skills, and today I am proud

95

to say that I have not installed a filling material containing mercury for over ten years."

"I happened to notice down the hallway," I said, "that there is a lady dentist who specializes in treating children. Does she use mercury amalgam filling materials to fill cavities in kids' teeth?"

Dr. Maklin leaned forward, placed my dental chart, which he had in his right hand, to the right side of his mouth, and whispered, "Yes, she does."

I replied, "Does that mean that mothers of those little kids do not know that mercury, a toxic metal considered too dangerous for anybody to touch with their bare hand, is routinely being installed less than two inches from the base of their children's brains? Are you sure the ADA considers this to be a healthy medical practice?" Dr. Maklin continued to write on my dental chart but did not respond to my two questions.

"Your present dentist has provided me with a complete set of your old dental records," Dr. Maklin said, "and this will make my job today a lot easier. You might be interested to know that your dentist was my instructor when I attended dental school eighteen years ago. I can see from the x-rays that your dental work, especially the construction of the three posts supporting one end of each of your gold bridges, is exactly according to the book. As an instructor, your dentist taught by the book and demanded the highest of standards for his students."

"That's nice to hear," I replied.

"Before you arrived today, I reviewed your old dental records and a listing of your current health problems sent to me last week by Dr. Zimmer. On your new x-rays taken today, I can count fourteen amalgams. Seven are out in the open in individual teeth, and seven are listed as hidden under the gold dental work on your old charts. You have five missing teeth that are covered by three gold bridges, and two teeth have gold crowns. Five teeth have root canals, and they all look okay except the one at tooth number nineteen, which has some inflammation developing. Dr. Zimmer says that your mercury and tin levels are elevated, so, using a small video camera, I will record a close-up picture of each tooth that has an amalgam implanted. Later, I will blow the pictures up to about the size of a baseball on this special screen and examine each tooth for cracks. A small crack through the tooth and the amalgam can greatly increase the amount of tooth restoration materials that can transfer out of the tooth." Using a *galvanometer*, Dr. Maklin then measured and recorded the galvanic electricity present in some of my teeth.

He ended our one-hour appointment by saying, "Within two weeks, I will inform Dr. Zimmer of my findings, but please understand that my advice will not include whether your amalgams should be removed. I am providing professional dental information only. If having your amalgams removed is a health issue, only you and your medical doctor can decide what is best for you." Dr. Maklin shook my hand and thanked me for my business. He then handed me a small book, *Dentistry without Mercury*, written by Sam Ziff and his son, Michael F. Ziff, D.D.S., a dentist practicing in Orlando. Alfred V. Zamm, M.D., F.A.C.A., F.A.C.P, introduced the book.

Doctor's Commentary

Wayne addresses some particularly salient characteristics of patients guided to pursue a personal path to a more optimal state of wellness. He describes the approach of a more comprehensive medical evaluation with a more defined approach to gain better understanding. It is lamentable that many patients live in a chronic state of the "walking wounded." They feel terrible most of the time, though most of the standard superficial testing always yields so-called "normal results." They go from doctor to doctor only to get the same response—"We cannot find anything wrong with you"—a result of the reductionistic approach common in modern medicine.

If you have a strep infection, a simple shot of penicillin will usually clear it up. For many chronic patients, like those described in this chapter, typical approaches that are not cause-focused will not help that patient achieve an optimal state of wellness, nor will taking a reductionistic approach of merely looking at one symptom cluster or one area, such as the heart, lung, or thyroid. On the contrary, the approach must be comprehensive or holistic, addressing each body system scientifically and objectively to understand what types of biochemical parameters are out of balance. Then, appropriate therapeutic strategies must be put in place to restore the balance.

In addition, doctors who use these therapies share common strategies. They usually see only ten to twelve patients a day, spending much more dedicated time with each patient. It takes a commitment beyond the three-minute HMO office visit model to really understand what is going on with these patients, who are much more complex and have been to several clinics prior to arriving at the doors of what Wayne calls an "advanced medical doctor." Many of these clinics or offices use adjunctive therapies with a decades-long track record and that are often unheard-of in conventional medicine, e.g., chelation therapy, intravenous vitamin therapy, and live cell injections. Some consider all of these therapies to be alternative or experimental, but often the therapies have been around for decades.

These are the adjunctive treatments, in my experience, that offer a "care group" of therapies that really assist patients in getting well. I must say that I, like other doctors who practice similarly, never learned about any of these treatments in medical school. Yet, we find that they work better in nine cases out of ten than most of the standard drug prescriptions currently available as tools in conventional clinical practice. I am mystified why this current political situation exists in medicine.

Why is it that therapies that have been available for decades are not more routinely used when they have a very successful track record? Very early in my clinical training, a wise fellow resident observed that anytime you need to determine the motivations of a complicated question, always look at the money trail. Everything became clearer. A person only needs to look at the lavish surroundings of most hospitals and insurance companies with large quantities of marble, exotic wood veneers, and lavish original and expensive art. But when you go to the average holistic doctor's office, the décor is generally simple.

Also, there is not that much profit in nutritional or natural therapies. Therapies, such as chelation, live cell treatments, nutritional supplementation, acupuncture, and herbal medicines, generate significantly less profits than surgical procedures, invasive modalities, or prescription drugs. Ultimately, there is very little incentive to change the status quo. Many of the most effective therapies are unavailable to average consumers, except those who can afford to pay for them out of pocket, because many insurance companies do not cover these approaches. Additionally, many doctors in the large major hospital systems must be on-guard. They may be familiar with or even have direct experience with alternative therapies, yet are precluded from offering a patient beneficial advice.

There are exceptions. Remember from Chapter 6 that a staff cardiologist at a major clinic, at great risk to his career, unofficially suggested to a patient that noninvasive chelation therapy might be the treatment to try first to address his diagnosis of coronary artery disease, chronic angina, and poor peripheral vascular circulation, thereby possibly avoiding open heart bypass surgery.

With that information, the patient promptly located in Indiana a doctor who offered chelation treatment. After 20 treatments, he felt completely cured, and all of his symptoms resolved. His primary doctor did follow-up testing, and he was advised that no abnormalities were detected. By the time he came to see me, it had been several years since he had done the chelation therapy, but he was still doing very well clinically, aside from the low-back pain, which he had strained while installing a door in his house. I thought how open-minded his cardiologist at this clinic was to suggest to him the treatment that would make the biggest difference in his life. I found it terrible that my profession at large did not have the political permission to speak the truth and recommend chelation therapy. Unfortunately, this is a common daily experience that I am sure many of my peers would note as well.

—Dale Guyer, M.D.

Chapter Twelve
Principles for "Getting Well"

During my first six weeks of treatment at Dr. Zimmer's clinic, I met a constant flow of new patients arriving for treatment. Most suffered from a chronic illness and had exhausted all hope that conventional doctors would ever find the cause of their illness so they could be treated. Many had multiple symptoms from a long list of typical ailments like:

• allergies	• anxiety
• apathys	• chronic body pain
• chronic fatigue	• chronic headaches
• circulatory problems	• cold hands and feet
• depression	• dizziness
• gastrointestinal problems	• insomnia
• irregular heartbeat	• irritability
• lack of concentration	• loss of memory
• muscle ache	• muscle tremor
• muscle weakness	• nervousness
• numbness	• skin lesions
• skin rashes	

As I became acquainted with these new patients, I was surprised to find that most were well-educated white collar workers, school teachers, artists, musicians, business owners, chemists, engineers, farmers, executives, and, yes, even dentists and medical doctors. All expressed disappointment that their family doctors, and in many cases specialist doctors that their family doctors had referred them to, had not diagnosed the cause of their illnesses. Some had suffered for years. Most were on prescription drugs. Many expressed an angered determination to get completely well and were willing to try any safe treatment that might work.

During those same six months, I spent hours chatting with determined patients in the process of "Getting Well," and almost daily a patient would step out of Dr. Zimmer's office with a big smile on his or her face, wave goodbye, and say, "I won't be seeing you again. I am completely well! The doctor says to come back in a year for a checkup." This little ceremony always added to my confidence that I, too, would get completely well.

Occasionally, a patient under treatment who was not completely well would also wave goodbye and say, "I have made some progress, but I won't be seeing you any anymore because I have run out of money." Some of the cost for treatments prescribed by Dr. Zimmer usually had to be paid by the patient because most insurance companies would deny part of the claim.

Dr. Zimmer was a board-certified medical doctor in Indiana like any other M.D. in good standing, however some of the treatments he used to make people well were not on most insurance companies' approved list. It appears to me that insurance companies basically pay only for treatments that have been approved by the AMA, the trade union for medical doctors. And, it seems to me that the AMA usually selects from the FDA-approved list those treatments medical doctors can make good money performing, and those treatments least likely to attract medical malpractice lawyers. Insurance companies, I believe, select the lowest-cost treatments from the AMA list and try to convince us it is good medical care. This, I find, leaves some FDA-approved procedures and treatments that insurance companies will not cover. Chelation therapy is a good example. This excellent treatment that will help many sick people get well is approved by the FDA, but is not on the AMA's approved list because it takes about three hours of clinic time for a typical $120 chelation treatment. The AMA, being a trade union, I would judge, sees this as too low-paying for their dues-paying doctors. Again, we chronically ill patients are left without support from our government, our insurance industry, or the medical industry. I believe that big money usually controls, not patients' health.

Doctors practicing medicine like Dr. Zimmer also use treatments developed and approved in Europe. These treatments are never on an insurance company's approved list because nobody has spent the millions of dollars necessary for FDA approval. U.S. citizens for the most part are isolated from the many good medical treatments developed and used successfully in Europe.

During my first six weeks of treatment, I learned from dozens of Dr. Zimmer's patients what had caused their chronic illness and the treatments being used to heal them. I began to recognize a common thread connecting the cause of their illnesses and the similarity in the treatments each was receiving that was making them well. By combining my knowledge obtained from these patients with the knowledge I learned reading books like *The Yeast Connection, Love, Medicine & Miracles, Your Body Doesn't Lie, Dentistry without Mercury, A Consumer's Guide to Chelation Therapy*, and *A Physician's Handbook of Nutrition*, I was able to outline **The Four Basic Principles for "Getting Well"** I used as the *Master Template* of my own plan for "Getting Well."

The Four Basic Principles for "Getting Well"

Principle #1 All toxins and heavy metals must be removed from your body before healing can take place. These toxic foreign substances cause chemical and electrical imbalances that weaken your immune system, interfere with nutritional absorption, render body hormones less active, cause false symptoms, disrupt nerve path messages that control body functions, interfere with the effectiveness of prescription drugs, and make it impossible for your body to return to complete wellness.

Principle #2 Remember, the body is a complex organism that has the ability to heal itself, provided we make available to each of its parts high concentrations of certain nutrients when needed. Establishing a well-balanced, highly nutritional diet is the first step toward "Getting Well," but recognize that it is impossible for food alone to provide all the vitamins and minerals needed by an ill person trying to get well. Complete wellness requires the physician to identify lack of nutrients in the sick human body and prescribe food supplements along with prescription drugs. Failure on the part of the physician to address nutrition will result in reoccurrence of the illness or a domino effect, creating additional sick body parts.

Principle #3 Learn to become, as Dr. Bernie Siegel says, a responsible participant and an "Exceptional Patient" who refuses to be a victim. Educate yourself and become a specialist in your own care with a goal of finding the cause of your illness and participating with your doctor in directing a complete cure. Gain internal healing strength by trusting the "inner focus of control" within you, supported by your faith in God's divine power.

Principle #4 Exercise is absolutely essential to "Getting Well." It is the master catalyst that energizes all healing actions of the human body. The other three principles will not be as effective without exercise. Without exercise, you may make small improvements in your health, but you will not get completely well. Learn to exercise correctly. Join a fitness club that provides a personal trainer to its members. People who do not exercise will never experience life's excitement that permits the exceptional patient to stay in good health to age ninety years and beyond.

Later in this book, as you read Chapter 16, "Toxins Everywhere, Including Your Body," you will gain a better understanding as to why following Principle #1 is mandatory for "Getting Well." Reading

Chapter 17, "Why Food Supplements Are Necessary," and Chapter 18, "Understanding Longevity," will make the case for including vitamins and minerals in your *getting-well program*. Principle #4 will be explored in Chapter 19, "Exercise, the Miracle Drug."

Learning to Be an Exceptional Patient

For the remainder of this chapter, I will address *Principle #3* and discuss the changes we as chronically ill patients must make to reach our goal of getting completely well. To accomplish this, I will conduct a book review of *Love, Medicine & Miracles*, which is a summary of the unique knowledge Dr. Bernie Siegel learned from his patients, about patients, over his forty years as a general surgeon practicing in New Haven, Connecticut.

As a young surgeon, Bernie, which he prefers to be called, began interviewing each patient before surgery and holding group meetings after surgery for recovering patients. Bernie discovered that he as the surgeon was not in control as to who lived and who died, but instead he found that the patient was in charge.

As Bernie continued to conduct pre-surgery interviews and post-surgery group meetings, he began to understand keenly what patients were really like and discovered by their individual actions that they fell within three distinct patient groups.

I learned from Bernie's book that about fifteen to twenty percent of all seriously ill patients welcome their illness with open arms because they have already made up their minds that they are tired of living and are looking for a respectable way to die. When their doctors explain the seriousness of their illness, they seem unconcerned and say they are "fine" and that "nothing" is troubling them. They often cancel appointments with their doctors and do not always take their prescriptions or follow their doctors' treatment plans. While their doctors work hard trying to make them well, this type of patient has a strong desire to die and get it over with.

I also learned that the largest group, sixty to seventy percent of all seriously ill patients, strives very hard to please doctors by doing everything the doctors say to do. These patients take medicines exactly as prescribed. Their actions caused Dr. Siegel to describe them as "actors auditioning for a part." They show up for all appointments and let their doctors make all decisions and would not consider learning enough about their illness to make even minor changes to their treatment plans on their own. Their greatest fear is that their doctors might prescribe lifestyle changes. This group of seriously ill patients will elect a quick-fix surgical operation rather than make lifestyle changes to overcome the cause of their illness.

The remaining fifteen to twenty percent of all seriously ill people are what Dr. Siegel refers to as "exceptional patients." I first read Dr. Siegel's book in 1995 and realized quickly that, if I were to get completely well, it would be necessary for me to get over the idea that I was a victim, to accept full responsibility for my illness, to educate myself, and to become a specialist in my own care. I immediately expanded my doctor's role to that of being my teacher. From that moment on, for each doctor's appointment, I always prepared a list of questions I wanted answered. A ten-minute office call often grew to thirty minutes. One week before an appointment with my cardiologist, I would send him a schedule of subjects I requested he be prepared to discuss. I read a lot of medical books and became capable of discussing my illness at a medical doctor's level. I also developed a survivor's personality typical of an "exceptional patient"!

It's Your Decision

Of all the chronically ill patients diagnosed at this very moment, we now know statistically that only two out of ten will become completely well. An additional two will die soon because they want to die, and the remaining six will barely survive for a while by taking an assortment of prescription drugs in an attempt to suppress their aches, pains, and other symptoms, trying to please their doctors.

If you are chronically ill, it is important that you decide which of the three patient categories you occupy right now and which one you would like to select for the future. Becoming an exceptional patient requires desire, knowledge, courage, hard work, and dedication. But, I personally have found it to be more than worth it. Today my quality of life is excellent, and my doctors expect it to remain that way for another twenty years or so, to age ninety and perhaps beyond.

If becoming an exceptional patient is your decision, then you will be pleased to know that the first change you may want to make is presented in Chapter 15, "Selecting a New-Type Medical Doctor."

Doctor's Commentary

Wayne continues the theme of essential elements of an individual's journey to wellness, especially patients with chronic illness. For me, you must make an honest assessment of your emotional and psychological perspective on your present situation. Often, patients consciously or unconsciously gain a lot of "value" in remaining sick and codependent. While this is not meant to place all blame on a patient for his or her medical maladies, it has become quite clear to me over the years that one cannot separate unhealthy emotional attitudes and psychological thoughts from contributing to, exacerbating, and supporting chronic physical unwellness. Therefore, the most important decision one can make is to pursue health in an honest and direct fashion. After that, things start to fall in place.

People are often led to practitioners and other individuals who offer the right advice and direction to help them better structure a path toward optimum wellness. As Wayne described, many of these patients currently exist as the "walking wounded." They have many vague symptoms and others that Wayne mentions, including chronic pain, headaches, fatigue, anxiety, allergies, heart irregularity, digestive problems, memory deficits, or concentration problems—a mixed bag of global dysfunctions. Unfortunately, symptoms rarely match a neat diagnostic label, except perhaps chronic fatigue syndrome and fibromyalgia. For that reason, patients are often shuttled from physician to physician and from clinic to clinic, receiving myriad pharmaceutical interventions, none of which is able to restore the patient's wellness.

For the average consumer, much of this process is changing with education and self-advocacy, particularly with the advent of the Internet. Most of the patients I now see are well-educated. They have done an enormous amount of work and research on the Web, read related textbook materials, and come better educated about their medical concerns than the average physician. Second, I have seen those outside the realm of so-called alternative medicine, mostly physicians, speculate that those who dabble in herbal medicine, acupuncture, natural hormone therapy, or other so-called unproven remedies are really uneducated with marginal medical understanding.

Contrary to this widely held belief, clinical studies have shown that those individuals and consumers who incorporate nutritional supplementation and alternative medical approaches are among the most highly educated—a group that includes engineers, accountants, pharmacists, and physicians.

Once the decision to embark upon a more holistic direction in health restoration is made, one must also accept some of the pitfalls that Wayne described. One can be financial. Many of the therapies that are well researched and performed routinely throughout the world and our country are not often covered by health insurance plans. As a matter of fact, it is generally the standard method of operation for health insurance plans to deny a high percentage of most claims categorically based on any marginal irregularity that can be identified. This is a business maneuver. I am told that 80 percent of people will elect not to follow up on a claim that has been denied by their insurance company and will pay for it themselves. Since insurance companies are well aware of this statistical likelihood, it is in their best financial interest to return most claims unpaid. However, of the 20 percent who respond and pursue their claims, it is my understanding that about 80 percent receive reimbursement.

Another challenge that the consumer falls prey to is the lack of interest and knowledge on the part of the medical delivery in our country about more broad-scale therapies, such as chelation, that Wayne mentioned. The reasons that our medical delivery services have evolved to this position are broad. However, one must remember that physicians are not necessarily selected into medical school because of open-mindedness. More often, they are picked because they have the capacity to remember a vast amount of information rather efficiently and then to spit it back verbatim on a standardized test. Second, they are able to get high marks in college. Also, the status quo tends to keep a tight rein on medical practice style. A physician's peers will usually look down their noses if a partner or a fellow member of their group begins the audacious practice of recommending nutritional supplements, engaging in consultation about natural hormone therapy, or, Heaven forbid, including chelation therapy into practice. Since this is atypical and not recognized by the AMA, the physician is likely to be excommunicated from the respect of his or her peers. Third, most physicians who work within the tight constraints of the insurance world will not be able, as Wayne mentions, to engage in nutritional consultation, because it is not a covered service. Fourth, insurance companies often will prohibit physicians from ordering an array of diagnostic laboratory tests to get to the core issues regarding a person's health.

The tightly woven web continues, and, unfortunately, the patients themselves suffer from lack of accessibility to the very therapies that may be the most helpful to them. Therefore, individuals embracing Wayne's Four Basic Principles for "Getting Well" will find that almost every type of physical malady for which they might suffer will tend to improve or resolve. An example is Principle #1, which focuses on toxins and heavy metals in the body, with Wayne's commentary and description of positive results with chelation therapy. After reviewing thousands of tests on heavy metals and detoxification issues from patients, I felt that almost everyone in our country has some degree of toxicity present, obviously some more than others. Invariably, as they are able to work on supporting their detoxification mechanism and undergoing therapy, such as chelation, that helps remove toxins, they start to feel functionally improved.

I have witnessed just about every physical symptom somehow improved with chelation therapy. Often, hair will become darker if white. I have seen improvements in digestive symptoms. The propensity toward chronic infection tends to go away. The list is endless. Although, in an initial consultation with an individual, a physician may not have assumed that just doing chelation therapy would have treated someone's dysfunctional immune system, for example. However, when laboratory testing indicates high levels of lead in the body and appropriate treatment is engaged, it is not surprising that the rest of the body starts to function in an improved fashion as well.

Another major component that Wayne highlights is exercise. Working with a capable trainer to help an individual develop a program suited to his or her goals and body's needs is essential. In my experience, this is one of the most important—let's call it "icing on the cake"—remedies. Still, it is one of the few optimal aspects of healing not yet regulated by the FDA and not yet offered through the pharmaceutical venue. Exercise is something completely free of charge, apart from the cost of gym membership, in which anyone can participate. As everyone knows, exercise has decidedly broad-scale benefit, improving the function of almost every aspect of the body.

Ultimately, as Wayne concludes, it is your decision, but a lot of that decision requires accountability. You must decide the relative value of looking at your life/health as your most precious asset and define its value, as some of the therapeutic interventions may not be provided free of charge, i.e., covered by your insurance company policy. Additionally, some of the most helpful and health-supportive processes that you can engage in, such as emotional and psychological maturation, self-introspection, and exercise therapy, require effort and work.

I have found that many will choose a different path, but, of course, we all know where that leads. Those who want to embrace health have to make the decision to embrace accountability on all levels.

—Dale Guyer, M.D.

Chapter Thirteen
Applying Principles #1 & #2 for "Getting Well"

By mid-April 1995, Dr. Zimmer had received the results of my dental examination from Dr. Maklin. Based on Dr. Maklin's report and the knowledge I had acquired quickly by reading *Dentistry without Mercury*, Dr. Zimmer and I agreed that my toxic mercury amalgams should be removed before my body could overcome the harmful effects of mercury and gain enough strength to begin the process of "Getting Well." I made my decision to have my amalgams removed out of desperation based on very little knowledge about mercury. I trusted primarily Dr. Zimmer and the information Dr. Ziff had written in his books.

My frequent attacks of high-intensity atrial fibrillation and other chaotic heart rhythms along with my increasing brain fog were creating an uncontrolled monster within me. My wife Betty did not waver, but insisted we stay within a thirty-minute drive of our hospital. As a result, we did not leave town for over two years. We did not have dental insurance, and we had already paid from our savings about $3,000 to Dr. Zimmer for medical services not covered by our health plan. Based on Dr. Maklin's estimate for amalgam removal and complete restoration, including composite fillings, gold crowns, and gold bridges, along with Dr. Zimmer's estimate for detoxification and nutritional therapy, we were faced with a cash outlay of $20,000-25,000. Betty quickly voted yes to spending the money and volunteered not to buy a new car to replace her twelve-year-old 1983 240D Mercedes until I got well. We both agreed to spend up to $100,000 from my I.R.A. if necessary, searching for a doctor who was smart enough to find the cause of my irregular heartbeat problems and cure me. We knew that if we spent $100,000 from our retirement funds, it would probably be necessary to sell our "dream home." This thought did not upset Betty. She said, "Our first home was a twenty-seven-foot house trailer at a military base. We were very happy then, and if we have to downsize to a house trailer again, I don't see any reason why we can't continue to live a happy life." With this kind of support, I made a firm commitment to get completely well.

Preparation for Amalgam Removal

Dr. Zimmer recommended we do about six more weeks of EDTA chelations and nutritional IVs before Dr. Maklin started the amalgam removal process. In addition, Dr. Ziff's book suggested that DMPS IVs would be a good way to speed up the removal of the active mercury in my body generated by the removal process. DMPS is a powerful chemical chelator, used throughout Australia, Europe, Japan, China, and Russia, developed specifically to remove mercury from the human body. The brand name Dr. Zimmer used to treat me was "Dimaval®," trademarked and manufactured by the Heyl Company of Germany.

Our Government Is Not Concerned

It is my opinion that the FDA sees no need to approve a DMPS-type drug because our entire government is so politically controlled by the very rich and powerful ADA that claims that the amount of mercury being transferred from our amalgams to our bloodstream is harmless. The political contributions made by the wealthy ADA dentists create a universal "we agree with ADA" by our elected officials. In the spring of 2003, I heard Congressman Dan Burton say on WIBC morning radio in Indianapolis that he believed that the mercury in amalgams is causing widespread serious illnesses, and he planned to introduce a bill to outlaw amalgams, like some European countries have done. I called his office to offer my support and was told by his staff the bill couldn't possibly be introduced for three years because of the preparation time needed to defeat the strong opposition. I believe the primary reason that Congressman Burton made that negative comment about silver/mercury amalgams on WIBC was to draw the attention of the ADA, knowing that its lobbyists would beat a path to his Washington office door in an attempt to settle him down by contributing to his reelection war chest. I came to this conclusion after I offered the Burton staff FDA documents I possessed, and they showed no interest in receiving them.

Written information I received concerning the "safety of dental amalgams" from the FDA through Senator Richard Lugar reveals that millions of taxpayer dollars were made available to the FDA in 1993 to study the health effects of mercury amalgams, but most of the research has been terminated by the FDA and labeled as "inconclusive." This indicates to me that the FDA doesn't want to know the truth or to be the bureaucracy that interferes with the long-standing campaign-funds deal our U.S. Congress has with the ADA and its wealthy dentists. Senator Lugar has remained very quiet over the years about the public safety issue of mercury amalgams. Because of the FDA documents his office provided me under the Freedom of Information Act, I know that his staff is aware that hundreds of hard-working, tax-paying citizens like me have reported to the FDA that their tooth fillings, which contain fifty percent mercury, have made them seriously ill. Senator Lugar's office sent me 981 FDA-documented cases of dental amalgams causing health problems in year 1991 alone.

The FDA and our elected officials, I believe, have banded together under a "code of blue"-type moral ethic that says: As long as we do not admit officially that the mercury entering the human body from dental amalgams is dangerous, then we can keep the common ordinary man in the dark and can continue to collect our normal government agency approval fees for new dental products, and Congress can continue to collect generous "please don't talk about it"-type, political reelection contributions. I contend that, by keeping secret the simple fact that amalgams contain fifty percent harmful mercury, our elected officials help their friends at the ADA and its wealthy dentist members avoid the massive medical malpractice lawsuits that might erupt if the general public knew the real truth about their silver tooth fillings.

Removal of My Amalgams Begins

Actual removal of my fourteen mercury amalgams began the first week of June 1995. During the previous three months of treatment, Dr. Zimmer had administered twenty EDTA chelations to lower the overall burden of toxic heavy metals, five DMPS chelations to lower the toxic mercury level, and ten nutritional IVs to help boost my immune system.

My coordinated amalgam-removal plan called for four three-hour sessions scheduled one month apart with Dr. Maklin removing the old mercury amalgams in a quadrant of my mouth and at the same time replacing the silver/mercury fillings with new white plastic composite materials. Upon completion of each dental appointment, I would go directly to Dr. Zimmer's clinic and receive both an EDTA chelation and a DMPS IV, and this would be followed up with nutritional IVs combined with more EDTA and DMPS treatments dictated by lab tests. Some areas of my mouth required gold crowns and bridges to be removed to expose the mercury amalgams. This meant that impressions for new gold crowns and bridges had to be completed that same day. Dr. Zimmer limited Dr. Maklin's dental work to a single session no longer than three hours because the new mercury entering the bloodstream generated by the removal process would be absorbed from my bloodstream into my organ cells within four to six hours. Dr. Zimmer wanted to capture this newly generated mercury with DMPS and lead it out through the kidneys before it started doing more damage to the cells of my body's organs.

Doctor Maklin Takes Special Precautions

Mercury-free dentists like Dr. Maklin, who remove a lot of mercury amalgams, employ special procedures to protect the patient, the dentist, and the dental assistant. First, the dentist's and the assistant's upper body is covered with a hooded garment, long-cuff surgical gloves, a facemask, and a face shield. They look similar to astronauts; you can see only their eyes. As a patient, my chest, both arms, and my hands were covered. A rubber dam was placed in my mouth to prevent small pieces of amalgam grindings from migrating down my throat. Attached to my nose was a hose that connected to an air purification breathing machine located next door in a sealed-off room. As an extra precaution, fresh purified incoming air passed over and around my face and was then exhausted out a vent in the ceiling directly above me. The dental assistant controlled an extra-large water hose nozzle and an extra-large evacuator tube in my mouth that provided an extra-large volume of water directly on the extra-fast, high-speed cutting drill to minimize the mercury vapor being generated by the removal process. These extra precautions reduced the amount of mercury vapor that was passing directly through the roof of my mouth into my brain tissue located less than two inches away from the cutting drill. Dr. Maklin worked very fast and was extremely well coordinated with his assistant.

Four Ways to Remove Mercury Trapped in Your Body

I learned that mercury trapped in my bloodstream and organ tissue could be removed in four different ways. The #1 way: Some of the mercury circulating in the bloodstream is filtered by the liver, mixed with gall, and injected into the digestive system, scheduled to be eliminated from the body with the feces. A slow-acting colon, however, will permit some of the mercury to be re-absorbed into the bloodstream. The #2 way: Some of the mercury circulating in the bloodstream is also filtered out via the kidneys and discharged with the urine. After the mercury has been in the bloodstream three to six hours, the mercury not filtered out by either the liver or kidneys is directed by the immune system to be stored, out of harm's way, in the fat cells of the body. Common storage places are the brain, the pancreas, the heart, the liver, and the kidneys. Also mercury is often found in the various glands like the prostate, gonads, and ovaries.

Breast tissue and the fat cells of chest muscles surrounding the heart are favorite locations, too. Stored mercury masquerades as a super-nutrient that immediately attracts the healthy cells surrounding it and slowly begins changing the cells' characteristics and ability to function. Cell mutations and inability to function create many of our chronic diseases for which doctors have difficulty finding causes. The #3 way to eliminate mercury from the body can take place weeks, months, or even years after it is stored. Mercury is eliminated by the actions of sauna baths, steam rooms, or vigorous exercise that creates a sustained flow of body sweat. During the sweating period, the body converts fat cells to glucose that releases the stored mercury, and it is then escorted out of the body by the fluids flowing throughout our body in our lymph system. Please remember that our body is two-thirds water and only one-third elements or tissue. Of the two-thirds water, ten percent is blood and about ninety percent is lymph-type fluids. The #4 way is a medical procedure: Your doctor connects a vein in your arm to a 200cc bag of DMPS that slowly drips over two hours into your bloodstream. The DMPS searches specifically for mercury that is active in your bloodstream or stored for years in the fat cells of your organs. Once contact is made, the DMPS activates an ion-exchange bond with the mercury and escorts it out of your body via your urine.

I Began Experiencing Improvement Immediately

At my first appointment, June 1995, Dr. Maklin was to remove all the mercury-amalgam fillings in my teeth located in the upper-right quadrant of my mouth and replace them with a white plastic composite material. When the numbness in my gums faded that afternoon while I was receiving a DMPS IV treatment at Dr. Zimmer's clinic, I immediately felt calmness in the entire upper-right side of my head that did not exist in the remaining three quadrants of my head. After three days of being a couch potato, drinking a lot of distilled water to help the DMPS work, and taking a shower every four hours the first day and every six hours the next two days to remove the mercury being carried out of my body in my mild sweating, I began to feel changes taking place in my body. My first feeling when I arrived home that first day was elation. I felt like taking a five-mile walk or going shopping at the mall. I am glad I didn't because exercise can interrupt the chelating action of DMPS and EDTA and can actually make you sick because toxic metals are starting to break loose. After three hours on the couch, I started to feel like I was catching the flu. These flu-like symptoms persisted for about twenty-four hours and then began to fade. At the end of the three-day couch period, I was left with a new feeling of well-being. It seemed like I had boarded a bus that was headed in the right direction. I continued to have those same soul-wrenching periods of atrial fibrillation, chaotic heart rhythms, and fifty-cent pain, but the brain fog seemed a little less dense. I could not yet see the light at the end of the tunnel, but I sensed it was there.

The Second Period of Amalgam Removal Was a Mini-Nightmare

My July 1995 appointment was a tough assignment for Dr. Maklin. With a small cutting burr, he had to remove a three-tooth gold bridge to expose the mercury fillings in my lower left jaw area. The bridge was anchored on tooth number seventeen, which had a root canal in it, and then after spanning missing tooth number eighteen, the bridge was anchored forward on tooth number nineteen. Removing the gold bridge exposed a big mess at tooth number nineteen that had a large mercury filling implanted thirty years ago that had expanded and cracked the tooth in half. A gold crown had been added fifteen years ago to hold the tooth together and to act as a bridge anchor. Remember back in Chapter 3 that this was the tooth that became enraged with infection in 1992 and transferred so much mercury into my bloodstream that it made my immune system so severely depleted I was launched down the road toward serious illness.

Now with the gold crown completely removed, raw infection started spewing out into my mouth. The dental assistant began flushing and suction evacuating without being told. Dr. Maklin said he wanted to extract number nineteen, but first he had to clean the mercury amalgam material from root canal tooth number seventeen and then prepare tooth numbers twenty and twenty-one as an anchor abutment for a new five-tooth bridge he would later make and install in this lower-left jaw area.

Extracting tooth number nineteen was a piece of cake. Dr. Maklin lifted this old jaw tooth from its pus-laden socket with little effort. He must have spent an hour removing discolored gum tissue and deteriorating jawbone. After declaring this large tooth socket clean enough to heal properly, he packed it with medicated cotton and took an impression of that entire area in preparation for the construction of the new five-tooth bridge. After installing a temporary plastic bridge to protect the area, I was released to Dr. Zimmer's clinic for EDTA chelation, a DMPS IV, and nutritional therapy treatment.

When I arrived home that Thursday evening, I fully expected to become ill sometime during the scheduled three-day couch time because we assumed that a lot of raw infection had entered my bloodstream from tooth socket number nineteen. Much to my surprise, I did not get ill. After twenty-four hours of feeling like I was catching the flu and of several sweating periods and hot showers, I felt fine. However, late Saturday afternoon I began to feel pressure and mild pain in the tooth socket number nineteen under the temporary bridge. I asked Betty to examine it. She could see a big ball of infection that looked like it was trying to push up the plastic temporary bridge. I called Dr. Maklin's home at 7:00 P.M. that Saturday, and he agreed to see me at his office right away. He removed the temporary bridge, and much to his amazement, with a set of tweezers, he lifted three neatly packaged pea-sized sacs of infection from the tooth socket. Suddenly, we both realized that the nutritional therapy Dr. Zimmer used to build up my immune system during the past three months was paying off. The immune system had prevented this very harmful mercury-saturated infection from entering my bloodstream in a natural way by collecting it in tough little sacs. Amazing, Dr. Maklin and I thought that Saturday night, what a healthy body can do to keep us from danger if we just support it in a way that nature intended. Later the next week, he removed two more little sacs of infected debris from number nineteen.

Taking a Rest

Dr. Zimmer, my chelation/nutritional doctor, stopped Dr. Maklin, my dentist, from additional dental amalgam removal work until he was sure that new live healthy tissue was growing and filling in the socket at number nineteen. This took two months. My prescribed vitamin C daily intake was 14,000mg, and, in addition to EDTA and DMPS mercury-removing IVs weekly, I was also receiving an immune supporting nutritional IV directly into my bloodstream along with B-12 shots and an assortment of food supplements.

When Dr. Zimmer finally released me for more mercury amalgam removal, my health was beginning to improve rapidly. I had gained five pounds and felt much stronger. My atrial fibrillation and irregular heartbeat attacks were less frequent and less intense. Irregular heart rates were not exceeding 120 bpm. Most were around 100 beats. I still had fifty-cent pain. The medical staff over at the heart rehab center where I exercised three days a week had cut my blood pressure medicine to half doses. I definitely had made progress, and the nurses at the center had noticed.

My next appointment with Dr. Maklin was the first week of September 1995 to remove the mercury amalgam fillings from the teeth in the area of my lower-right jaw. It was necessary for Dr. Maklin to destroy two perfectly good gold crowns by removing them so that the large mercury amalgams in these two teeth could be exposed. He drilled out the two mercury fillings, plus mercury fillings in two additional teeth without crowns, and filled the four cavities with the white composite material. He took impressions for making new gold crowns and installed temporary plastic protective crowns. My reaction to this third mercury amalgam removal period was similar to, though less intense than, the other two periods, but I rested quietly on the couch for three days anyway.

We Fell behind Our Schedule

At this third amalgam removal period, we were a month behind schedule because of the extra waiting time for the socket healing at tooth site number nineteen in July. Dr. Maklin suggested we consider not removing the old three-tooth gold bridge located in my upper left jaw because the new x-rays did not show any silver mercury fillings in that area, nor did my old dental records indicate that any fillings had been implanted over the years in that area. Dr. Maklin pointed out that, by not removing it, we would be back on schedule, and by not making a new gold bridge, I could save $2,000. I agreed quickly not to touch this fourth and final quadrant of my mouth. However, two weeks later I called Dr. Maklin and requested an appointment to have this gold bridge removed. Dr. Maklin asked me why I wanted it removed.

I replied, "Because the other three areas where you removed the mercury amalgams have left three-fourths of my face and head feeling very calm, but the upper-left side of my face and head is not calm. I think there might be some mercury under that old gold bridge."

Dr. Maklin didn't think so. But, if I wanted to come in at 5:00 P.M. the next day, he would take a look.

In five minutes, the gold bridge was removed, and much to Dr. Maklin's surprise a silver/mercury filling was in tooth number fourteen, the rear bridge anchor. Only a small piece of the amalgam remained; most had dissolved and had darkened the gum tissue surrounding it. Although tooth number fourteen was still alive, Dr. Maklin extracted it immediately, trimmed away the mercury-saturated gum tissue, and cleaned the socket in preparation for good healing. Dr. Maklin then prepared this area for a new four-tooth bridge, took impressions, and covered it with a temporary plastic protector. A few days later, this upper-left area was as calm as the rest of my face and head. Because my immune system was in top working order, the gum and socket area at number fourteen healed very fast.

Doctor Maklin Completes My Dental Work

By October 1995, all silver mercury amalgam fillings had been removed from my teeth, and the dental lab was given the order to make three new gold bridges and two gold crowns. The weekly EDTA and DMPS chelations to remove mercury and other toxic heavy metals continued at Dr. Zimmer's clinic along with weekly nutritional IVs to sustain my immune system. By December 1995, my body tested free of mercury and all other toxic heavy metals except lead, which now was at a low level, and tin, still at a very high level. After a physical inspection of the gum tissue healing that had taken place, Dr. Zimmer gave the okay for Dr. Maklin to install permanently the three new gold bridges and two gold crowns. Dr. Maklin's dental work was finished and his bill was $9,000, and Dr. Zimmer's medical treatments, not covered by insurance, were also $9,000. I now know that it was the best investment I have ever made. The results speak for themselves.

What One Year of Good Medical Treatment Can Do

Before I list for you the health problems I no longer have, please remember that the **only medical treatments** I received during the one-year period that cured these problems were:

#1   removal of my silver mercury amalgam tooth fillings and their replacement with white natural-looking plastic composite materials

#2   the removal of the toxic heavy metals burden that had accumulated over many years in my body, through the use of EDTA chelation for heavy metals and DMPS IVs for removing the mercury

#3   the building of my natural immune system to peak performance with vitamin and mineral food supplements, along with weekly nutritional IVs

#4   daily exercise, along with three days each week of cardiovascular exercise, monitored by the professionals at the heart rehab center

I began the one-year treatment with Dr. Zimmer, taking high doses of four prescription drugs for blood pressure and heart rhythm problems. I ended the treatment eliminating the need for drugs, but elected to continue one aspirin daily along with a small dose (0.125mg) of Lanoxin® daily until I was sure my heart had adjusted to drug withdrawal.

After only one year of treatment, at 5' 9" tall, I weighed 165 pounds with eighteen percent body fat and could sustain a 4-mph walk speed for one hour. The floor exercises I had learned reshaped the contour of my body to that of a much younger man than my sixty-four years. I could feel it, and my friends could see it.

Most of My Twenty Health Problems Listed in Chapter 3 Vanished

- The atrial fibrillation monster was captured, caged, and sent back to its mercury-laden home. I was free at last of unexpected high-rate irregular heartbeat attacks. My wife and I could go on vacation without that monster insisting that he go too. I had experienced heart rhythm problems for three years. Now, I was cured, something six cardiologists were unable to accomplish.
- My infected sinuses were completely clear. I had had sinus problems for thirty-eight years beginning at my workplace at age twenty-six, breathing that terribly polluted factory air.
- My thirty-four years of weight gain problems became history. My overall nutrition was now so complete that my body no longer craved more vitamins and minerals. Learning that weight control was a matter of complete nutrition, not discipline, was a relief. I found great joy knowing that my body no longer produced food cravings that commanded me to overeat.
- After taking blood pressure medicine for twenty-six years, I no longer needed any. Typical blood pressure now is 126/76. Small amounts of amalgam mercury vapor entering my body each day over the years had caused high blood pressure. Large amounts caused low blood pressure. During the summer of 1995 when large amounts of mercury were entering my body because of the amalgam removal process, my blood pressures recorded at the heart rehab center were typically 90/60.
- Now that my sweat no longer contained heavy metal toxins, red streaks on my face and rashes on my chest, underarms, groin area, and feet all disappeared.
- Twenty-three years ago at age forty-one, I began having anxiety attacks. During the past three years of about 200 atrial fibrillation attacks, my anxiety symptoms were high also, but now my body has become very quiet. Never in my life have I experienced such a calm mind, body, and spirit as now. I am confident that when your body is free of mercury, you, too, will have a quiet body, just like mine.

- I experienced dental problems most my life. At last, I am free of the metallic taste that silver/mercury amalgams create. Now, ordinary food has an exciting new taste, and I can again smell the food. There are no more sensations of electricity jumping around between my teeth and creating stress. Upon removal of the mercury, the stressful activities going on in my mouth transferred to a peace and joy in the rest of my body beyond all dreams.

- The single most exciting improvement I experienced after my body became mercury-free was the lifting of fog in my brain. At age sixty-four, my ability to concentrate returned quickly to very close to the level I experienced at age twenty-four as a military pilot. Now when I relax in bed at night, often a new thought will be revealed to me that I did not know was there. By concentrating on that thought for the moment, a roll of facts and pictures begins appearing in my mind. Suddenly, I realize that this new thought isn't new at all; it really happened to me, and I had completely forgotten about it, but now it is as clear as yesterday. What happened yesterday and the day before and last month now is easy for my mind to recall, too. There is no need to write down the ten things I have to do tomorrow. I need only to ask my brain to remind me. My body became free of mercury and other toxic heavy metals at age sixty-four. Today at age seventy-two, I am writing this book. With the fog gone, my brain has not only become healthy again, but it has continued to grow and develop to a much higher level than imaginable. I have developed new skills I did not have as a young man. Don't take my word for it. Read the rest of this book and decide for yourself.

- My gallbladder was removed nineteen years ago. I now know that the operation was not needed. Advanced-thinking medical doctors now believe that the body decides to form gallstones because it becomes fearful that the liver cannot produce enough cholesterol to keep the body healthy. When the body's cholesterol is forced to a low level like my 130 to 160 readings and held there for several years, it reacts by attempting to hoard it for a rainy day by forming solids in the gallbladder, made up of cholesterol. I believe that my health would be even better today if I still had my gallbladder.

- I became a type-2 diabetic just nine months after my gallbladder was removed. I have always felt that there was a connection, but have not learned what it is. I have discovered that a good low-carbohydrate diet supported with selected vitamins and minerals, combined with dedicated daily exercise, is more effective than the best diabetes drugs available. Now that my ability to read and comprehend books has escalated, I find that current advanced medical research indicates that diabetes may be caused by a low-level infection created by fungi, much like the discovery of stomach ulcers being caused by bacteria.

- I believe that, if there was a concentrated effort to remove the mercury from the teeth and brains of our medical researchers, we might be amazed what their unshackled minds could discover to improve our health.

- My family doctor always said that a lot of people have muscle twitch. Nothing to worry about. Maybe not, but I no longer have that annoying problem. I don't know for sure which heavy metal we removed was causing it, but I would guess mercury or tin.

- Years of discomfort of my sore tongue have come to an end. It is without question mercury vapor emitted from my fourteen amalgams was causing this tongue irritation.

- My big toe pain is now history. I had the problem for years. With my body clean of toxic heavy metals, I can now sleep all night without being awakened with pain in my big toe.

- When my dental work was completed, I continued to have those small spots of intense fifty-cent pain around my body that lasted only two or three seconds. But, I also had high levels of tin that had not been removed by EDTA chelation. To address this problem, Dr. Zimmer changed the plan. He prescribed a deep muscle massage to help release the tin from my fat cells the evening before my scheduled chelation. Without a massage, a single chelation would remove 300 parts per million of tin. With a massage, the amount of tin removed was around 900 parts per million. With weekly massages and a revised EDTA chelation formula, the large deposits of tin were removed during the first three months of 1996. My fifty-cent pain stopped when all the tin was gone. Tin, when present, proved to be very toxic to the nerves throughout my body. No question about it, tin was causing my nerve pain.

- After my body became mercury-free, one of the first changes I noticed was that my driving became much more courteous. In the past I was usually in a hurry, short-fused, and easily agitated. Now, I enjoy driving in heavy traffic and receive real satisfaction letting drivers in a hurry cut in front of me. I know I am a safer driver now because the cells in my brain are clean and eager to stay alert.

- As I walked down the busy sidewalks of Indianapolis, I began to notice how much more friendly the people were. People began nodding their head and saying good morning or hello or just simply nodding and smiling. Occasionally a stranger would surprise me by saying, "You have a nice smile today," or "A smile like yours is contagious." I soon realized that my body was so overjoyed without toxic mercury interfering with my mental attitude that it wanted the whole world to know, by offering a perpetual smile. Amazing!

- My hearing grew noticeably keener, and my eyes have become sharper each year since the broad spectrum of toxins was removed from my body. The fact is, with toxins removed from my body, I can now absorb much higher levels of nutrition. As a result, my body requires fewer calories, and my weight is stable naturally.

- My energy level began a steep increase when I began having my silver/mercury amalgams removed. I went back to shoveling snow in the winter and mowing grass with a walk-behind mower in the summer. At age sixty-five, my body again enjoyed sustained exercise and a good sweat. If you don't sweat freely, it could be heavy metal toxins blocking the normal, healthy action of your sweat glands, which by the way is a primary basic function our body uses to remove disease-causing toxins from itself.

- When 1995 ended, my dental work was completed, and mercury was completely removed from my body. However, I continued to have a reaction to certain foods. As a result, Dr. Zimmer began treating me with special allergy shots formulated especially for me, and seven months later, by July 1996, I was cured of the eighteen allergies. Today, I can eat any food without an allergic reaction. Many people I meet say that they have taken allergy shots for years and have not been cured. I believe they could be cured if their physician would prescribe chelation therapy first. Once our bodies are made free of mercury and other toxic metals, the doctor's prescribed medicines can be much more effective. Good medicines do their job by creating good chemical reactions in our sick bodies, and toxic heavy metals interfere with good medicines by creating bad chemical/electrical reactions. From experience, I found this to be the simple fact.

- Aging: When I was fifty-five, people guessed me to be sixty-five. When I was sixty, most thought I was closer to seventy-five. Now that I am seventy-two, people believe me to be only seventy. That two-year advantage I now enjoy seems very valuable for some reason.

I Became Very Confused and Angry

On one hand, I was elated and overwhelmed that only sixteen months of advanced alternative medical treatment had made me so completely well. Years of chronic illnesses seemed to have vanished from my body. I felt blessed by God and let Him know the great joy I felt in my heart for this great gift of restored wellness.

On the other hand, I was an angry man. I thought about the many times over the years I had sat in a dental chair when not one single dentist had hinted that the silver filling material he was using contained fifty percent mercury. I was convinced that most of my past health problems were caused by the mercury from my dental work. All I could think about was getting even with dentists. I imagined locating each one of them, and then walking into their office unannounced and smashing them in the face with a big cream-filled pie or letting the air out of their tires and then sticking around and videotaping their reaction. My lawyer said that I didn't have enough money to go up against the powerful ADA, so a lawsuit could not be considered.

To help calm my rage, I wrote a two-page letter addressed "To My Friends." I informed them that their silver tooth fillings contained fifty percent toxic mercury. I described how mercury from my fillings had made me very ill. I stated strongly that I knew this to be true because my silver fillings containing mercury had been removed, and I was now completely well again. This letter helped calm my anger. I was getting even by presenting the truth. The truth I discovered could set me free of rage and anger.

The very first person I handed a copy of my letter to was my good Christian friend Bill Mutz. He read my letter and then, with a puzzled expression, looked at me and said, "I didn't know that silver dental fillings contained fifty percent mercury. Wayne, are you sure that this information you have about mercury is correct?"

"I am absolutely sure," I replied.

"I know how very ill you were three years ago, and I have watched your health recover, but do you really think your dental work caused it?" Bill asked.

"I really think so, Bill."

Bill then said, "Let's find out. I have a very close friend who is a dentist. He is a strong Christian man. I have worked with him on church projects. I know he will tell us the truth." Bill quickly scribbled a note on a fax header page and sent my two-page letter to his dentist friend.

The next day Bill handed me the fax reply from the dentist. I have saved this fax, and I have it in my hand at this moment. This is what it says:

Bill

This is bad stuff. [This was his opening comment concerning my two-page letter. Then his fax said that he had attached an article from *ADA News* about Hal Huggins, an outspoken dentist in Colorado who was being prosecuted for saying that mercury in dental amalgams was causing a host of illnesses. Then, he continued to respond to my letter.]

There is no question that mercury is bad—I think in rare occasions some patients could be affected. My experience has been that once they feel that their fillings are hurting them—you cannot convince them otherwise.

Bottom line…there may be some validity…it would not be a major item…. A little knowledge is a dangerous thing. Love you

Signed_____

As soon as I read this fax, a smile came on my face, and my rage of anger began to fade. I knew there was a problem with the safety of dental amalgams and that what I needed to do was to launch an investigation seeking out the truth. The next chapter, "Mercury, No Safe Level," contains the highlights of my one-year investigation.

Doctor's Commentary

Wayne highlights an absolutely essential element in an individual's wellness journey, i.e., the support of family and friends. Wayne was fortunate to have a strong prayer group and an enormously supportive spouse. Wayne is rare among medical consumers. Instead of complaining that his insurance would not cover certain medical procedures or dental amalgam removal, he opted to take a different approach and invest in his own health regeneration through procedures that would cure him of his complicated medical issues. More often than not, the average consumer, even if he or she lived in a lavish home and drove expensive cars, would balk at investing in their most precious health more than the ten or twenty dollar co-pay. While everyone likes to save money and be financially responsible and frugal when necessary, it seems paradoxical that we would spend huge amounts on homes, cars, vacations, boats, and other luxuries, but be unwilling to invest nominal amounts in our most precious possession—health.

The other paradox is that, if one added up all of Wayne's out-of-pocket expenses that led to a cure over many years, it would still be less than the cost of one coronary artery bypass surgery. Of course, his insurance company would have readily paid for the bypass procedure, given Wayne's completely occluded heart arteries. It is obvious that the procedure would have done nothing to change the underlying cause of Wayne's problems (toxins, hormone imbalances, and so on). Inevitably, he would emerge from surgery no better off from the circulatory standpoint, because he already had ample collateral circulation and would still possess the same problems that drove him there in the first place. Such is often the plight of the medically wounded. I hope that in the future insurance companies will develop an interest in greater fiscal responsibility and seriously look at results-oriented medical approaches versus the constant reflex action of shoveling vast sums of money into procedures and therapies that may not deliver benefit and may actually be a detriment to the patient's overall health.

Relationships are an integral key to one's wellness. If the affected individual struggling with chronic and complex medical issues lacks the support of his family, friends, coworkers, and others important to his or her life, the healing journey can be an enormous challenge or even a detriment in codependent relationships, where the unhealthy individual needs constant rescue attempts from the healthy partner. Second, the healthy member will often want to maintain control, perpetuating the unwellness of the spouse or significant other.

Government positions and/or politics are a significant barrier. Even with the hotly debated topic of the potential adverse health consequences of mercury-containing dental amalgams, it remains a daunting task to arrive at any relative truth. The government's position has always been that there is little inherent danger to the mercury contained in dental amalgams. However, in speaking with decision-makers in the political arena, it seems obvious that most lack even a modest understanding of the basic chemistry of toxicology at play.

When we look at the enormous number of reports to the FDA on toxic reactions to dental fillings and subsequent symptom improvement upon removal, remember that these reports are probably less than 1 percent of the total of the potential problem, i.e., most people who experience some toxic setback from dental amalgams do not report it to the FDA or, for that matter, even their dentist. Instead, they suffer in quiet obscurity, and their outcome is never added to the statistics that might provide momentum to help sway public opinion.

A third challenge relating to mercury amalgams is finding a dentist to attend to these problems. Wayne was fortunate in being able to work very closely with a well-respected and capable mercury-free, or biological, dentist. As Wayne clearly writes, most dentists strongly oppose any notion that mercury-containing fillings would pose any health detriments. That issue has already been discussed and will be addressed in more detail in the next chapter. Also, even though most dentists are not aware of the potential mercury toxicity or do not believe in it, they are also ill-equipped and untrained to remove mercury-containing dental fillings without inducing further biological toxicity to the individual. Ideally, the patient would work closely with a trained physician that helps support the body's detoxification process as Wayne did. A number of patients have read books about mercury toxicity and decided to have their dental fillings removed by a local dentist, who would gladly do the procedure because it is expensive and generates substantial profits. Unfortunately, these unsuspecting patients underwent the removal in an unsupported way and eventually developed significantly greater levels of toxicity.

It is also important to discuss chronic dental infections. I have seen numerous patients with chronic jaw, gum, and localized infections, such as root canals. Infections release ongoing toxins into the body and disrupt normal biological functions. Testing for these infections is not always 100 percent accurate, i.e., a panoramic x-ray may not always detect cavitational-type infections. Regulation thermography and similar devices may show infectious tendencies, but are not always conclusive. Bone scans, if not read by an endodontist familiar with NICO or cavitational lesions, will be unlikely to detect these problems. Therefore, careful history, careful clinical exam, and correlation with the best diagnostic testing, along with an evaluation by a well-trained dentist or endodontist are highly important. When patients work with all of these professionals together, I have seen consistently dramatic results. Wayne highlights personal changes in this chapter. While the positive results may sound dramatic, I would add that these clinical observations are fairly typical. Truth exists somewhere in the middle, but collectively we have not been able to define truth well, as it is being shuffled through a complex array of political and financial machinery and outright closed-mindedness.

—Dale Guyer, M.D.

Chapter Fourteen
Mercury, No Safe Level

Highlights of My Investigation

I spent much of 1996 thinking about, reading about, and investigating how and why toxic mercury entered my body. Convinced that mercury was the primary cause of my illness, I wanted to determine how possibly that could have happened to me. Had I been careless? Or, had my government's protection agencies knowingly or negligently failed to warn me of this danger? As you follow the highlights of my investigation in this chapter, please decide for yourself.

Mercury Is Extremely Dangerous to the Human Body

Read any toxicity reference book, ask any metallurgist, or consult with any medical doctor schooled in the effects of toxic heavy metals on the human body, and you will learn that there is no amount of mercury considered safe for contact with the human body. Mercury was demonstrated scientifically more than 100 years ago to cause cell mutations and damage and eventually to destroy healthy live human cells in a process creating an assortment of disease symptoms especially in the nervous system and brain.

When the practice of mixing mercury, commonly called "quicksilver," with other metals and creating a mixture to fill teeth started, the American Society of Dental Surgeons (ASDS) investigated the safety of mercury making contact with the human body. As a result of its investigation, beginning in 1848, the ASDS required all member dentists to sign a pledge promising not to use mercury in the filling of cavities.

Some dentists refused to sign the pledge because they were making a lot of money installing *low-cost silver/mercury fillings* that created a larger group of patients who could afford to have their decayed teeth restored instead of having them extracted or filled with expensive gold inlays. Subsequently, these dentists were suspended from the ASDS for persisting in their pursuit of *malpractice by using silver/mercury fillings.*

Because there were no government agencies regulating the safety of dental filling materials, dentists were legally free in 1848 to use any substance they wanted, including mercury mixed with other metals, for filling decayed teeth. Because of the low cost of this fast method of filling teeth, dentists electing to use mercury amalgams attracted a much larger group of patients, resulting in a much higher income level for the dentists. ASDS dentists not installing mercury amalgams began noticing that this fast "drill'm, fill'm, and bill'm" method of filling decayed teeth with mercury amalgam material was cheap and was making their fellow dentists very wealthy. As a result, more and more ASDS dentists withdrew their pledge not to *poison their patients with mercury* and joined their wealthy peers installing poisonous mercury into children, pregnant women, and healthy adults.

August 1859, the ADA Is Founded

It seems clear to me the primary purpose of forming this new dental association was to assure the general public and government officials that the mercury amalgam tooth filling material was not poisonous to the human body as claimed by its predecessor, the ASDS. Proving that mercury amalgam *silver filling* material containing fifty percent mercury was safe in humans was impossible because all scientific evidence at that time revealed clearly that mercury was unquestionably poisonous to humans and all animals.

Overcoming scientific facts did not seem to be a problem for this new trade organization. Without a government agency to monitor it, the ADA simply conducted its own testing, with its own people, and produced the test results it wanted. For the past 144 years, the ADA has continued its closely controlled testing and has produced documents continually showing that the mercury that makes up fifty percent of a silver tooth filling is completely harmless to human beings, even little children and unborn babies. At no time did my investigation reveal a government agency seriously challenging the ADA's claim that the mercury in our silver fillings is harmless. I could find no serious challenges from the FDA, Environmental Protection Agency (EPA), National Institutes of Health (NIH), Surgeon General, U.S. House of Representatives, U.S. Senate, or President of the United States. I could find no evidence that any of these government agencies or elected officials has conducted scientific testing on its own showing mercury amalgams to be safe.

Instead, our government agencies have reviewed and agreed with the test results controlled and produced by the ADA. The ADA is not a health organization responsible to the American people; instead, it is a trade organization responsible only to its membership. As I pointed out in Chapter 9, the ADA is the trade union for dentists, the same as the United Auto Workers (UAW) is the trade union for the people who build our cars. You can't sue the UAW for defective workmanship in your automobile, and you can't sue the ADA for a serious illness caused by the mercury in your tooth fillings. The only people who can challenge the actions of unions are their members and government officials. You and I are helpless in a court of law.

A Lawsuit Is Filed against the ADA

On August 14, 1992, retired California businessman William H. Tolhurst filed a lawsuit against five defendants, claiming they were involved in his personal injuries resulting from mercury toxicity through exposure to his mercury amalgam fillings. The five defendants in the Superior Court of the State of California were:

- the ADA, which claimed that the small amount of mercury being emitted from his amalgams was harmless
- Johnson & Johnson Consumer Products, Inc., which manufactured the dental amalgam
- Englehard Corporation, packager of the amalgam dispenser system
- ABE Dental, Inc., distributor of the amalgam system to the dentist
- Thomas Fitzgerald, D.D.S., Mr. Tolhurst's dentist

The first thing the attorney for the defendants, Robert S. Luff, did was to file a demurrer saying: "**The ADA owes no legal duty of care to protect the public from allegedly dangerous products used by dentists. The ADA's only alleged involvement in the product (amalgam) was to provide information regarding its use. Dissemination of information relating to the practice of dentistry does not create a duty of care to protect the public from potential injury.**" Judge Read Ambler agreed and dismissed the charges against the ADA.

Without any support from the government agencies—the FDA, EPA, or NIH—created to protect him, Mr. Tolhurst eventually lost his case. A number of similar cases have been filed since, but I could find none ruled in favor of the plaintiff. Now you can see why my lawyer in 1996 advised me that it is impossible to sue the ADA. I believe the ADA maintains its enormous power not through its legal position, but through its strong political lobbying position made possible by its wealthy dentist membership's generous contributions to our elected officials' reelection war chests.

129

The ADA Brags about Its Legal Success in *ADA News*

ADA News posted 8/13/2003 on the Internet informs its membership that thirty-two lawsuits have been filed against the ADA since June 2001, concerning amalgam-related complaints, and the courts across the country have in every case dismissed all charges against the ADA and state dental societies.

The ADA, like other trade unions, has special legal privileges the rest of us don't have. The only people who can sue a trade union are its membership or the federal government, as witnessed by Judge Ambler ruling in the Tolhurst lawsuit.

The ADA Files Lawsuits against Others

Although the ADA is exempt from the general public suing it, it continues to sue others. Unable to find state laws to support its claim that health plans operated by large insurance companies did not adequately compensate ADA dentists, the ADA sued three major insurance companies under the federal RICO Act.

It is common knowledge that Congress passed the RICO Act for the sole purpose of investigating gangster-type organizations. Suing under RICO implies that the ADA is charging that these three insurance companies operate in a Mafia-like manner, making and breaking contracts by illegal threats.

On 5/20/2003, *ADA News* informed its readership that the ADA had indeed filed RICO-type charges against three major insurance companies:

- **Cigna Corp., its subsidiary, Cigna Dental Health, Inc., and Cigna affiliate Connecticut General Life Insurance Co.**
- **Metrolife, Inc., and its subsidiary, Metropolitan Life Insurance Co.**
- **Mutual of Omaha Insurance Co.**

The ADA Also Brags about Its Power to Control States' Laws

ADA News, 5/30/2003, informed ADA members that the Arizona Dental Association had acted as a powerful catalyst in defeating HB 2467 and SB 1146, which had been introduced by an anti-amalgam Arizona state lawmaker. HB 2467 would have banned amalgams in children, nursing mothers, and pregnant women. SB 1146 required dentists to warn patients that amalgams contained harmful mercury and to offer non-mercury alternatives.

You Be the Judge

I include this information about the ADA so you can better understand what type of organization the ADA really is. Please don't forget that it is not a government health agency; instead it is a trade union for dentists, and, as judges have ruled in over thirty-two cases, the ADA has no responsibility to patients or the general public. Its sole purpose for existing is to serve the needs of dentists who support the ADA with their annual union dues.

Why Did This Happen to Me?

On one hand, in 1996 I was very happy because, by the simple act of removing the mercury amalgams from my teeth and detoxifying my body, twenty illnesses had been eliminated, including that terrible monster atrial fibrillation. On the other hand, why didn't my dentist warn me over the years that illness could develop from mercury in my tooth fillings?

In mid-1995 while consulting on the telephone with Dr. Ziff, a mercury-free dentist in Orlando, he told me that the FDA had accumulated hundreds of records showing the health improvements of patients when they had their amalgams removed.

Under the Freedom of Information Act, I filed through Senator Dick Lugar's office for these patient records, and I also asked the FDA for proof that dental amalgams had been tested as safe. I received 981 FDA patient reports accumulated in 1991 by the FDA, a 200-page, two-year dental amalgam study conducted by the U.S. Public Health Service in 1991/1992, signed by the Assistant Secretary of Health in 1993, and a two-page letter directed to me by an official at the FDA that stated, "**Amalgam fillings release small amounts of mercury vapor that the body can absorb that could cause allergic reactions in a few persons but that...there is scant evidence...health...is compromised...there is no scientific justification...for having them removed.**"

The 200-page Public Health Service study I received was signed in January 1993 by the Assistant Secretary of Health with a summary statement: "**There are no data to compel a change in the current use of dental amalgams.**" However, in his closing statement, the Assistant Secretary said, "**Adverse health effects resulting from the use of dental amalgams cannot be fully discounted based on available scientific evidence.**" He then recommended that more research concerning the safety of amalgams be done. That was more than ten years ago. To date, Congress has not funded that recommendation. In fact, the Department of Health & Human Services, which includes the FDA, has no convincing FDA-approved studies on file showing amalgams to be safe.

Following are four typical FDA 1991 patient reports from the 981 I received:

Patient m22958

Pt, age 37 yrs. Sex female, experienced the following symptoms: confusion, lack of clarity, headaches, allergies, arthritic pain and fatigue. Pt was sick for 6 years before fillings were removed. Pt's condition improved by 90% after removal. Pt was able to stop/reduce drug intake.

Patient m23060

Pt, age 36 yrs. Sex male, experienced the following symptoms: chronic fatigue, numbness of hands and feet, recurring intestinal Candida and parasitic infections, depression, low libido, poor circulation, tightness in chest and universal reactive/massive allergies. Pt was sick for 9 years and 10 months before fillings were removed. Pt's condition improved by 50% after removal. Pt was not on any continuous medication.

Patient m23050

Pt, age 34 yrs. Sex female, experienced the following symptoms: bleeding gums, blisters in mouth, ear problems (snapping, crackling, ringing, feelings as if fluid-filled), blurred vision (left and right) once for an hr, nausea, diarrhea, weight loss, muscle aches, extreme fatigue, anxiety attacks, memory loss, twitching, shaking and trembling in arms, legs, neck, suicidal thoughts, fear and depression. Pt was sick for 20-25 yrs before fillings were removed, pt's condition improved by 100% after removal. Pt was able to stop/reduce drug intake. Pt was ill from the first installation, then symptoms came and went and became chronic.

Patient m22953

Pt, age 58 yrs, sex male, experienced the following symptoms: metallic taste, a lot of tension. Pt was sick for 20 yrs before filling was removed. Pt's condition improved by 100%. Pt was able to stop/reduce drug intake.

In the 200-page *Dental Amalgams* report I received from the Department of Health & Human Services, there was a workgroup of doctors who worked two years studying what patients like me had reported about the effects that mercury amalgams had on their health. This workgroup said that patients like me who thought that their mercury dental amalgams were causing illness have mental problems and need psychological care. Its contributing summary to the 200-page report stated:

Dental amalgams contain 40 to 50 percent mercury that is released in minute amounts over the lifetime of the restoration. Small amounts of mercury are absorbed and distributed throughout the body accumulating primarily in the brain and kidney. However, the significance of this accumulation is unknown.

The focus on the amalgam problem may give these patients an immediate and transient relief from their anxiety and depression. However, such patients need a thorough medical, oral, psychological and social examination and counseling to address the core problems of their lives.

These statements come from the best medical doctors who our Department of Health & Human Services employs. They spent two years studying the safety of dental amalgams containing mercury, and, to me, their statements do not support their conclusions. To conclude that a small amount of mercury accumulating throughout our bodies with the highest levels in our brain and kidneys is safe and will not cause illnesses seems intentionally deceptive. Every book I have read has stated that **there are no safe levels of mercury in the human body**. I believe there is something seriously wrong with our Department of Health & Human Service's assessment of mercury amalgams. I think Congress should investigate and appoint non-government and non-ADA scientists to conduct studies and determine the safety of dental amalgams. We Americans deserve to know the truth, and I believe that some people are unknowingly falling victim to illnesses from their mercury amalgams every day because we are not receiving the truth.

My Review of the 981 FDA Patient Reports I Received

In the 981 FDA patient reports I received, a few patients showed improvement of zero to thirty percent. Most patients improved 50-100 percent. As I reviewed each case history, I made a list of the most common ailments that were either improved or cured when their amalgams were removed. This is my list:

allergies	anxiety	bloating
blood pressure problems	chest pain	depression
dizziness	fatigue	gastrointestinal problems
gum problems	headaches	insomnia
irregular heartbeat	irritability	lack of concentration
lack of energy	metallic taste	muscle tremor
nervousness	numbness anywhere	skin disturbance
sores in oral cavity	sore throat	tachycardia
thyroid problems	urinary tract problems	vision problems

Now that I have presented to you a list of illnesses the FDA's patients' reports say were cured or improved when the mercury dental amalgams were removed from patients' teeth, please select the illnesses you would ask your dentist to treat. Your answer of course would be "none." You would instead take these-type medical problems to your family doctor. The point is that, when the FDA asked the ADA for a list of negative patient reactions to mercury amalgams, the dentists checked their records and replied, "Less than one percent." Because we as patients do not suspect that our tooth fillings have caused our illnesses, we don't report these-type medical problems to our dentists.

When we go to our family medical doctor with any of the above-listed illnesses, he or she does not suspect that our dental work is causing the problems because medical doctors have no training in diagnosing the symptoms caused by dental amalgams. Our doctors are told in medical school that mercury does not leak into the human body from dental amalgams. In fact, most medical doctors I asked did not know that silver tooth fillings contain fifty percent mercury. As a result, there are no medical records anywhere in the United States documenting the illnesses caused by dental amalgams containing mercury; yet, these illnesses caused by mercury are occurring every day.

You can call it medical malpractice, medical incompetence, or just plain-old medical doctor complacency, but the fact remains that there are no medical records for the FDA to examine showing the results of mercury leaking from the one billion dental fillings implanted in the mouths of 200 million Americans that are causing illnesses at this very moment. However, we must not forget that hundreds, and perhaps thousands, of ill patients have taken the time to file a report with the FDA stating what happened to their illnesses when their dental amalgams were removed. So, the FDA is not completely in the dark, but refuses, I believe for political reasons, to investigate mercury amalgams and conduct acceptance tests.

What Does This Mean?

I believe that, if we examine the list above carefully, it becomes obvious that this is a normal set of illnesses the average family-practice doctor treats every day. Perhaps fifty percent of the doctor's time is spent trying to calm with drugs some of the symptoms created by these illnesses. If this is true, it seems to me that our medical expenses in the United States could be quickly cut by at least forty percent or perhaps more if the 200 million people with implanted dental amalgams had their amalgams replaced with white non-metal composite material and had the mercury along with other heavy metals removed from their bodies. I would think that the FDA could conduct a good test in less than twenty-four months by selecting, say, 200,000 ordinary, hard-working citizens diagnosed with illnesses from the above list, and by replacing their amalgams and detoxifying their bodies, the FDA would then have a pretty good idea of what to do next and wouldn't have to mumble constantly its unyielding position: "There are no data to compel a change in the current use of dental amalgams."

If you want to know more about the hazards of mercury in dental amalgams, there are books I have read on the subject listed in the back of this book. Or, just enter the words "dental amalgams" in a search engine, and there are volumes of articles to read. You also might consider calling your two Senators and telling them how you feel about toxic mercury being in tooth-filling materials used in your family's teeth. Your Senator's telephone number is listed in most telephone books in the white pages or in the blue pages, under government offices.

My Closing Statement

We need to do something fast about the toxic mercury in our environment. Most experts believe that eighty percent of all the mercury man has mined from deep in the earth and brought to the surface continues to recycle in our environment and is a larger amount each year. The central recycling mechanism is the human body. The largest burden of mercury enters our body from our amalgams every day. Mercury also enters our body from the air we breathe, from the meat/fish, fruits, and vegetables we eat, and from the water we drink. I learned that a healthy body will store in its tissue about ten percent of the mercury that enters it each day and will discharge the remaining ninety percent through the liver, kidneys, and sweat glands. The mercury in the sweat is washed down the shower drain. If the mercury from sweat is deposited in our clothing, it is washed down the washing machine drain. The mercury filtered by the liver is mixed with our feces. Our kidneys filter out the mercury into the urine. Regardless of the source, this large discharge of mercury from our body each day is sent to our local sewage disposal plants.

At the disposal plant, the liquids are separated, treated with chemicals, and discharged into a local natural stream. With the mercury still present, the liquid discharge mixes with natural flowing water into larger and larger rivers until some of the mercury ends up in our oceans. But, most of the mercury remains in our riverbeds temporarily to eventually contaminate fish, lakes, flooded farmland, and underground freshwater supplies.

If the sewage solids separated from the liquid are burned, mercury is vaporized into the air and made available for man and all animals to breathe. If the solid sludge is applied to farm fields as fertilizer, then the mercury enters the crops eaten by man or animals. Eventually the mercury stored in farm animals ends up in the meat we eat. Mercury not processed into the food supply migrates to our pure underground aquifers, which carry the mercury to our food supply through crop irrigation or directly to our drinking water.

Regardless, much of the mercury, whether in the air, in the water, or in our food supply, eventually reenters our bodies and is recycled to one of the thousands of sewage disposal plants to start this toxic environmental cycle again.

There are a lot of professional people concerned, but not our elected officials. I believe they see little reelection money in it for themselves. If they were concerned about the health of the American people, they would outlaw mercury dental amalgams immediately, which is the largest source of mercury to the human body. Removing the amalgams from all Americans would be the fastest way of reducing by fifty to sixty percent the mercury recycling in our environment.

Warning

Do not under any circumstances have your mercury dental amalgams removed without first contacting a medical doctor who has the training and experience to guide the dental removal process, followed-up with mandatory body detoxification to remove the mercury from your organs and tissues. Dentists do not have the training to safely remove dental amalgams and detoxify your body. Failure to follow a medical doctor's advice could result in disability or death.

Reader Alert: Please note that the very next chapter, "Selecting a New-Type Medical Doctor," will tell you how I found qualified medical doctors trained in the correct dental amalgam removal process and effective mercury detoxification procedures.

Doctor's Commentary

We have, in modern society, a bit of a conundrum, similar to ongoing discussions about the relative safety and effectiveness of childhood vaccinations. The issue relates, of course, to Wayne's concern—mercury and its inherent toxicity. In one sense, a consortium of government agencies assures us that mercury-containing dental amalgams pose no toxicity to the general public. At the other end of the spectrum, practitioners, physicians, and dentists among others see patients whose health has declined in myriad ways following the placement of mercury-containing dental amalgams. We also witness their subsequent improvement, consistent with the cases filed with the FDA that Wayne obtained under the Freedom of Information Act, with amalgam removal.

I have observed many cases of patients who demonstrated elevated levels of mercury in the body by RBC Membrane Toxic Metal analysis and urine analysis with provocation. When patients are given medicines to treat elevated mercury levels by removing the toxic metal from the body, subsequent testing shows a diminution of the toxicity threshold with dramatically improved symptoms. Yet, we are all assured that mercury-containing amalgams are not toxic. This assurance makes getting at the truth even more difficult. It is intriguing historically, of course, that, as Wayne concluded his research, he noted that the American Society of Dental Surgeons initially requested a ban on mercury-containing dental amalgams. Only when the more politically muscular American Dental Association came into power did mercury-amalgam placement become standard and acceptable practice. It seems not to have changed since.

I have often wondered whether, if mercury-containing dental amalgams were brought to the market today and subjected to the intense scrutiny of FDA toxicology testing, they would ever be approved as a restorative option in dental practice. I certainly have my doubts. However, the political issue remains a significant hurdle even for dentists who are friends and very aware that some patients can suffer complications from mercury-containing fillings. They are not at liberty to discuss the issue openly with patients. Most of their patients, of course, are well-informed, well-read, and well-educated. They request that their amalgams be removed because they understand mercury's toxicity. However, even in this situation, my dentist friends cannot state openly that there may be a toxic association, but may agree, for example, that the amalgams are aging and should probably be replaced with a composite or nonmetallic product.

In the face of mounting evidence that mercury-containing fillings may indeed impart toxicity to at least some individuals, I anticipate that this dilemma will play out for several more decades before it is finally resolved. Like the political powerhouses of the tobacco industry, huge corporations can do much to ensure the continued sluggish pace of change. I suspect that in the future the evolutionary trend would be that the ADA would recommend standard composite fillings, in lieu of mercury-containing dental amalgams. That would enable the ADA to take a position less in favor of using mercury-containing amalgams and to suggest instead safer, nontoxic composites. However, the presupposition is that the newer composites are more attractive and at least as strong as the metallic amalgams. I doubt that there will be an admission that the amalgams caused toxicity problems in individuals for decades. We will all have to wait and see the outcome, even though the question of toxicity seems inherently obvious.

—Dale Guyer, M.D.

Chapter Fifteen
Selecting a New-Type Medical Doctor

If we are injured in an accident, we usually do not have the opportunity to select the medical doctor who treats us. Fortunately in the United States, the medical industry has developed the very best lifesaving trauma treatment system in the world. The system places great emphasis on 911 dispatch of emergency medical service vehicles and helicopters with highly trained emergency medical technicians (EMTs) aboard to stabilize the traumatized victim on the way to the hospital emergency room (ER). Actual lifesaving treatment usually begins during the trip to the hospital because of the excellent communications taking place between the emergency doctor on duty at the hospital and the EMTs in the emergency vehicle. By the time you arrive at the hospital, a team of doctors and nurses has already learned the details of your injuries or illness and has organized an action plan just for you. Anyone making a 911 call can cause the on-duty emergency service to be available immediately to every man, woman, and child, twenty-four hours a day, anyplace in the United States without reference to their ability to pay. It is the very best system in the world.

Another area in which we usually do not select our own medical doctor is when we need surgery. In most cases we need a certain type of surgery, and we have no idea which surgeon is best for us. We frequently let our family doctor make the selection. Again, fortunately for us, the U.S. medical industry over the years has developed the very best surgeons and surgical procedures in the world. Our medical doctors have studied and understand in great detail how the human body works mechanically. Whether it's repairing or reattaching the twisted broken bones and body tissue of a person evacuated from a serious accident, correcting a birth defect, delicately entering the brain, or bypassing or transplanting a heart, surgeons literally bring thousands of victims back from the brink of death every day. Our surgeons, through careful planning, can correct almost any defect in our body and make us like new. The outstanding skills of our surgeons are recognized all over the world. That is why so many people come to United States for their difficult and delicate surgery. We have the very best. We are indeed fortunate.

However, only about twenty percent of our doctors work full time as surgeons or professional trauma doctors. The remaining eighty percent work full time as family practice doctors or specialists. Within this eighty percent group, we patients have difficulty selecting a good doctor.

True, most of these family-practice doctors are very good at diagnosing, and often curing or placing into remission, common diseases they studied in medical school. Diseases that have been around for decades include diabetes, pneumonia, blood pressure problems, ulcers, bladder and all other types of bacterial infections, prostate cancer and many other forms of cancers, pinworm, and mononucleosis, along with bone and muscle problems of all types. These common illnesses make up about half of a family doctor's daily workload. By working with specialists or surgeons, our family doctors do a good job treating illnesses diagnosed from lab tests or x-rays since the cause is usually already known, making treatment routine.

Based on my own experience, it is my opinion that the other half of a family-practice doctor's daily workload is treating disease symptoms with drugs without regard to the underlying cause of the illness.

In 2003, I began to have some swelling in my feet. I saw two different cardiologists who said that the circulation in my legs was okay and not causing the swellings. Each spent four to five minutes examining me, and each wrote a prescription for a diuretic drug. I then saw two different foot doctors. Each spent three minutes checking the pulse in my feet, and each wrote a prescription for a diuretic drug. I then took all this information to my family doctor. He did not touch my feet, spent two minutes with me, and said he didn't know why my feet were swelling, but wrote a prescription for another diuretic drug anyway. I began taking one of the water pills each day for thirty days, and the swelling came and went like it always had. One day, I opened up my medical guide and discovered that there are eighteen different causes for swelling of the feet. None of these five doctors attempted to determine the cause of my feet swelling by placing these eighteen causes on a check-off list, but instead wrote a quick prescription and sent me on my way.

Patients talk to each other, and I, over the years, have heard numerous stories similar to mine. In Chapter 20, I reveal how Dr. Guyer determined the cause of my foot swelling and treated me.

I believe that automatic drug treatment of certain symptoms happens for several reasons. Most family practice doctors I know are trying to see forty-five or more patients each working day and have insufficient time with a patient to determine the cause of his or her illness. The quick solution for the doctor is to write a prescription and see what happens. At least half of the symptoms I reported to my family doctor over the years could not be connected to a cause because they were symptoms, as I learned later, created by my toxic environment, which caused an imbalance in my body that seemed to me to be too complicated for my doctors to understand. Then, when the toxins began affecting my heart rhythm, nervous system, immune system, and digestive system, my doctors, I could tell, became confused. Yet, they did not investigate the possibility that toxins in my body were causing my illness symptoms. When they began saying, "We don't know what is causing your medical problems," and I confirmed later that the removing of toxins from my body cured my illnesses, I became convinced that family-practice medical doctors and cardiologists do not learn in medical school to test for and remove toxic heavy metals and other toxins from the human body.

Although all of my family doctors over the years acted very professionally, none of them recognized my symptoms caused by pollution entering my body or lack of my nutrition being absorbed, nor found the cause of my symptoms before they developed into a serious illness. Listed below are typical symptoms caused by toxins or lack of proper nutrition that often develop into serious illnesses. Usually not taking or having the time to determine the underlying cause, family doctors spend half their time every day trying unsuccessfully to cure these common patient symptoms. They include:

allergies	anxiety	chills
depression	dizziness	drowsiness
excitability and anger	fatigue	fearfulness
gastrointestinal problems	gum and tongue soreness	hallucinations
headaches	inability to concentrate	indecision
insomnia	irregular gait	irregular heartbeat
irritability	joint pain	loss of energy
loss of memory	low blood sugar	metallic taste
muscle tremors	nausea	nervousness
numbness	shaking	skin disturbances
tachycardia	thyroid problems	tremors, hands & eyelid
twitches, small areas	urinary tract problems	vision problems

Conventional Doctors' Approach to Treatment

Based on thirty-four years of seeing medical doctors on a regular schedule, I am of the opinion that the most common way conventional doctors treat symptoms on the above list is with prescription drugs. If the patient has more than one symptom, then the doctor usually writes a prescription for each symptom. Often one of the ailments is so pronounced that it requires more than one drug to calm it down.

The drugs may relieve the symptom, but drugs also may cover up an advanced alert that serious illness is developing, and, by the time the underlying problem is identified, it is often too late for a complete cure because serious, irreversible damage may have already taken place. Agreed, drug therapy is a fast way to control symptoms, but once started, the drug usually must be used for the remainder of the patient's life or until the cause of the symptom evolves into an advanced disease the conventional doctor can recognize from standard medical school training. After progressing to the highest dose allowed for the drug and the drug becoming ineffective, your family doctor usually refers you to a specialist or a surgeon.

Most doctors agree that increased pollution in our environment and chemicals in our food chain are causing cell mutations and diseases that are difficult to diagnose and cure. In my opinion, the reason these medical problems cannot be cured is because our very best medical schools do not teach doctors how to test for and remove the accumulation of toxic heavy metals and other toxins found in the human body; nor do they teach our doctors how to use proper nutrition to either prevent or treat the causes of chronic illness and disease.

In November 1994 when I began looking for a new primary-care physician, I telephoned, from the yellow pages listing, 100 doctor offices. I asked, "Does Doctor _____ sometimes prescribe vitamins and minerals to his patients along with prescription drugs?" I received ninety-eight noes and two yeses. I made an appointment with both "yes" doctors and selected the one who agreed to see me at the end of his day. We talked about my medical problems, and he, after a complete physical exam, suggested that heavy toxic metals might be causing my irregular heart rhythm problems and that chelation therapy might be what I needed. This young medical doctor, with only five years of experience, in January 1995 directed me down the path of complete wellness.

For those of you who believe I am wrong about medical schools not teaching our doctors how to properly test and remove toxic heavy metals and other dangerous toxins from our bodies, call your local medical association and ask for a list of local medical doctors certified to test for and remove toxic heavy metals and other dangerous toxins from a human body and see for yourself how many medical doctors have been trained and certified.

Why Doctors Add Complementary Medicine to Their Medical Practice

I have, over the years, talked to several complementary/alternative medical doctors and have found that, when they were conventional medical doctors, they became disappointed in the cure rate of their patients. Instead of blaming their patients, they went back to school and learned additional treatments needed to improve their cure rates. They discovered that these new skills filled the void of healing knowledge not learned in medical school.

They told me that a good first step in becoming a better M.D. is to enroll in the American College for Advancement in Medicine (ACAM), to study and become certified in chelation therapy, a process for safely removing toxic heavy metals and other toxins from the human body. They also learned nutritional therapy, a process of testing the patient for vitamin and mineral deficiencies and correcting these with nutritional IVs administered directly into the bloodstream or with food supplements from the local health food store. After conventional medical doctors have completed their advanced medicine studies, they are then usually referred to as complementary medicine doctors or alternative medicine doctors.

After certification, complementary medicine doctors have upgraded their nutritional knowledge to a level where their patient cure rates are greatly increased. Most conventional medical doctors don't offer nutritional treatments because they received almost no nutritional training, even in our highest-rated medical schools.

On TV, I heard Andrew Weil, M.D., author of the best-selling book *Spontaneous Healing* and many other medical books, telling Larry King that he could explain to Larry in just thirty minutes everything he had learned about nutrition after graduating from Harvard Medical School. After becoming an M.D., Dr. Weil said he studied nutrition for two additional years before feeling confident enough to actually cure most diseases.

Other Reasons Why Doctors Take Advanced Training after Medical School

There are other reasons why conventional doctors upgrade their medical practice after graduating from medical school. Often they begin wondering why so many patient illnesses they treat with drugs do not progress to being completely cured. They sometimes observe some of their patients taking the same prescription for years, and if they stop taking the drug, the illness symptoms reappear. Or, the medical doctors themselves become ill, or a loved one of the doctor's family becomes seriously ill, and the doctor cannot find a cure for the illness. This is tough on their medical confidence, especially after they contact other doctors, and they can't seem to find a cure either. Although often dismayed, smart doctors begin to reach out for help. By word-of-mouth, the doctor hears about a different type of medical doctor and decides to investigate. This investigation often acts as the catalyst that motivates the ordinary conventional doctor to take advanced medical training and upgrade his or her medical practice to that of an alternative medicine doctor. These doctors continue to use conventional treatments that work, but enhance marginal treatments with complementary/alternative treatments not taught in typical medical schools.

A typical story was reported in *The Indianapolis Star* about three years ago when a well-known, highly respected alternative medicine doctor retired after forty years of private practice. The *Star* newspaper reporter asked him why he practiced alternative medicine. He said that after he graduated from medical school and set up his own private conventional medical practice, one of his first patients was his own mother. She checked out healthy, but had an irregular heartbeat most of the time. Every medicine he tried failed to cure the problem. He then accompanied her to see several cardiologists and to be examined by more experienced general practice doctors. None could find the cause of his mother's irregular heartbeat.

With no place to turn, he began asking anyone he met for ideas. Then someone told him about an old-time doctor of osteopathy in a small Indiana town, who had a good reputation for curing irregular heartbeats. He said he watched with great curiosity as this doctor mixed a 500cc bag of medicine, containing prescription EDTA, along with other medicines, vitamins, and minerals. During the three-hour period it took the 500cc bag of chelation mixture to drip intravenously into his mother's arm, the young Indianapolis doctor received from the older doctor some advanced medical knowledge he had not learned in medical school. The treatment was known as chelation therapy, approved by the FDA to remove lead from a human body, but it also removes nearly all other unwanted toxic heavy metals. The small-town doctor gave this young M.D.'s mother a series of chelation therapy treatments and placed her on a prescribed list of daily vitamins and minerals. His mother's irregular heartbeat was permanently cured in less than ninety days.

This experience caused the young Indianapolis doctor to question the completeness of his medical school education. After extensive advanced medicine and nutritional training at ACAM and other schools, he developed into an alternative medicine doctor. He told the *Star* reporter he has enjoyed over forty years of private practice treating and curing thousands of chronically ill patients of many medical problems. I believe some of the problems he cured are on the list above.

How I Helped a Medical Doctor Advance to the Complementary-Medicine Level

On an August 1995 morning, while I was receiving an EDTA chelation IV treatment at Dr. Zimmer's clinic, a very handsome, athletic, dark curly headed, youthful-looking forty-one-year-old anesthesiologist was seated next to me. He said he was waiting for his first appointment to see Dr. Zimmer, my complementary medicine doctor.

I commented that I could not understand why he needed to see a doctor because he looked so healthy. He seemed eager to tell me his story, and I indicated that I was eager to hear it.

For the past fourteen years, he had worked as an anesthesiologist with a surgical team doing major general surgery. Most patients were first-time patients to him, which meant that, since every patient is different, he often had to experiment with four or five different drugs to keep the patient stabilized during surgery.

He said that about a year earlier his problem began when he would sometimes forget the combination of drugs that was working the best and would become confused concerning the additional amounts of drugs needed as the surgery progressed. He said that it was standard practice to record the amount of drugs used, but the problem was that, even with his notes, he would sometimes become confused. To help the situation, he added an additional notebook to write additional data to help prevent the confusion. He found the extra notebook detracted from the time needed to measure and observe the patient's vital signs. Fearing for his patients' safety, he banned himself from the operating room and explained his problem in detail to the supervisory board of doctors.

The board immediately placed him on paid disability and began three months of tests and a series of evaluations. They suspected a brain tumor or nervous system problems. With test after test, followed by being seen by the very best doctors available, they could find no medical explanation for his mental confusion.

After the three-month period was up, he was told his problem was not medical, but instead emotional. The doctors had all agreed that he and his wife should have personal professional counseling to get their marriage and family life straightened out. The doctor panel recommended that his disability insurance be extended one additional year to allow the time needed to make changes in their family's lifestyle.

From that day on, he found that his wife and he were excluded from social life with most of their medical doctor friends. This made him very angry, but not his wife. She gained great pleasure telling others how unprofessional this group of medical doctors was to diagnose a medical problem as a family emotional problem without first visiting and interviewing her, a stay-at-home-mother working full time caring for the five very well-adjusted children whom they had parented and were successfully raising.

After he finished his story, I looked him straight in the eyes and told him I knew exactly what was wrong with his health.

Looking quite startled, he wanted to know if I was a medical doctor.

I replied, "No, but I am a patient who has the same memory-loss problems you describe, and I know the exact cause, and I am responding to treatment very well right now, so I see no reason why you shouldn't whip this problem too."

I then described each of the twenty other symptoms I experienced, like muscle twitch/tremor, fifty-cent pain, rashes, big toe pain, sore tongue, sweats, and irregular heartbeat. As I related some of my twenty symptoms, I noticed several times that the doctor would knowingly nod his head. When I told him about my mental confusion being so bad that I would sometimes forget my grandsons' names or would get lost driving in Indianapolis, he interrupted me and asked me to get to the cause of my memory problems.

I borrowed a flashlight from one of the nurses and asked the doctor to open his mouth. I counted eight big silver/mercury tooth fillings and two gold crowns. I then told the doctor, "I think, with your being an anesthesiologist, you have been absorbing and accumulating in your body drugs and chemicals commonly used in the operating room each working day. These toxins could have entered your body by inhaling the vapors or through direct contact with your skin. These drugs are designed to sedate the nerves and brain, so a fifteen-year accumulation in your body could be part of your problem." I also told the doctor, "You have eight amalgam fillings out in the open and two mercury fillings under the gold crowns that are leaking mercury vapor all the time through the roof of your mouth directly to your brain cells. In addition, when you chew food, the mercury vapor generated triples the amount of mercury vapor because of the chewing action and is mixed with your food in your digestive system, potentially weakening your immune system, which can then invite additional disease." I told him, "Your memory problem could be an advance notice that a serious disease is developing right now, but has not yet arrived."

I talked again with the doctor about a month later. He and Dr. Zimmer had conducted a series of tests, and then had laid out a "Getting-Well" plan that included removal of his mercury amalgams and detoxification of his body. I also received a telephone call from the doctor's wife thanking me for talking with her husband. She said, "After talking to you, I saw an immediate change in him. He is now very confident he will get completely well."

Three months later in late November 1995, the doctor called my home to tell me that his lawyer had obtained a two-year extension on his disability insurance payments and that he had enrolled in additional medical training that would last about two years. He said that removing his dental amalgams was only half-finished and had made him very ill, so they were removing them more slowly over a longer period of time. He was still having low-level unexpected anxiety attacks, and he was scheduled for two weeks of medical training in Texas. He requested that I accompany him and care for him should he become unstable and need assistance during the two weeks of training.

I wanted to go, but my wife Betty said, "No way. We are not sure yet if you are completely free of irregular heartbeat attacks. You trying to take care of the doctor would be like the lame caring for the lame." The doctor was very disappointed in Betty's veto, but he called me at the end of his two weeks training and was very excited. He had not required medical attention while at school.

After two years of additional medical training, the former anesthesiologist/M.D. today is in private practice as a family practice physician with specialties in chelation and nutritional therapy. He is listed in the telephone book with all the other physicians in good standing, and occasionally I see his name listed nationally as a qualified complementary medicine doctor along with listings of certifications he has completed in advanced medical treatments...treatments not normally taught to conventional medical doctors at ordinary medical schools.

Now you know why a few hundred medical doctors each year upgrade their respective medical practices to the complementary medicine level. These doctors combine the best treatments of the conventional medical world with the advanced treatments used in the complementary medicine world, and, as a result, patient cure rates are greatly improved, and the chronically ill patient, like me, has a chance to be made completely well again.

Locating an M.D. Who Has Upgraded to a Complementary-Medicine Level

Please remember, I have always felt I needed a primary-care family physician who practices in the conventional, politically correct medical world. My family doctor offers only medical treatments Medicare or my insurance will pay. He is the only person in the conventional medical system who can authorize me to see a specialist or a surgeon. So, if I develop an illness symptom, I first make an appointment with my family doctor knowing that Medicare and my insurance company's willingness-to-pay strictly control his practice. I see my conventional doctor first, trying to gain a return on the premium payments I make to both Medicare and my supplemental insurance company each month.

When my family doctor admits he does not know what is causing my illness symptoms, I have found from past experience that his chances of curing me are slim-to-none. That is when I make an appointment with my complementary medicine doctor who has upgraded his medical practice and is dedicated to finding and treating the cause of my illness. I do this because over the years I have found that most of my illnesses have been caused by the accumulation of toxic heavy metals/toxins in my body or lack of proper nutrition being absorbed effectively into my precious cells. Although everybody knows what is causing my illness, my family doctor is not permitted to address these types of medical problems. This is probably a political problem I cannot solve alone.

Both my government and my insurance companies have in the past believed that toxins in my body or lack of proper nutritional absorption were not connected to my illnesses, so they have denied claims for treatment. As a result, to get well, I had no choice but to reach out, then reach down in my own pocket, and buy medical treatment that would make me well again. If I had not done this, I would be dead by now—sad, but oh-so-very true. I observe that most elderly people do not die from old age. Instead they die from their toxic bodies' inability to absorb proper nutrition. Some of my life-long friends are gone already. A few were quite young.

So, if you are plagued with chronic illnesses for which your conventional medical doctors have not found the cause, then you might want to consider investing into a better, healthier, happier future and again be able to live your life to the fullest. If this is your goal, then pick up the telephone and call toll-free 1-800-532-3688 and ask the American College for Advancement in Medicine for a listing of medical doctors in your area who are certified in advanced medicine, along with the medical specialties in which they practice. You can also obtain a listing of doctors and their medical specialties from ACAM's Web site, www.acam.org.

A New Class of Advanced Medical Doctors Is Emerging

After practicing complementary medicine for a few years, some doctors have so many chronically ill people wanting to become new patients that they often limit their medical practice to treatments not taught in ordinary U.S. medical schools. This change of practice usually eliminates the need for them to join local medical societies or have hospital privileges. The reason these elite doctors limit their medical practice is that they discover that some medical treatments used in other regions, namely Europe, China, India, Russia, Brazil, and Mexico, cure diseases much better than some of the conventional treatments used in the United States. When these doctors make these discoveries, they often travel to foreign countries, take training, and bring these new, superior methods of treating disease back to the United States.

There is only a handful (probably around 100) of medical doctors who presently travel worldwide to learn the best medical treatments available. These advanced medicine doctors often cure patients other doctors have failed. They are truly a doctor's doctor and, in my opinion, advanced above all other doctors. The problem, as you might expect, is that they are difficult to locate because it is not necessary for them to advertise for new patients in the yellow pages or local newspapers like conventional doctors often do.

Personally, I only know of one doctor whom I feel qualifies as an advanced medical doctor. His name is Dale Guyer, M.D. I first met this Indiana University School of Medicine graduate at Dr. Zimmer's clinic during the fall of 1995. Dr. Guyer was employed as a complementary medicine doctor at a local hospital. The Hospital Board of Directors prohibited chelation therapy treatments and greatly restricted patients being treated with nutritional therapy. As a result, during periods when Dr. Guyer was not scheduled to see patients at the hospital, he treated, at Dr. Zimmer's clinic, patients needing toxic heavy metals removed from their bodies with chelation therapy and also treated patients with dysfunctional immune systems using nutritional IVs and food supplements.

How to Find an Advanced Medicine Doctor

I have learned that finding one of these advanced medicine doctors must be by word-of-mouth. They never hurt for patients, so they have no need to advertise. During the eighteen months when I was a patient of Dr.

Zimmer, I also was a heart-rehab patient at a local heart rehab center. This gave me an opportunity to query the nursing staff about the reputation of Dr. Guyer who worked part time at Dr. Zimmer's clinic and full time at the hospital as a complementary medicine doctor. Every R.N. I talked with gave Dr. Guyer two thumbs up and usually followed up with a story about Dr. Guyer healing a patient whom other doctors had failed.

After Dr. Zimmer restored my health in the summer of 1996, I decided to get my first six-month checkup with Dr. Guyer. But the hospital where he worked would not give me an appointment, saying he was not taking new patients. The R.N.s told me that everybody at that time was trying to become a patient of Dr. Guyer. I did not schedule a six-month checkup with any doctor because I was feeling so good and didn't think I needed it, but in October 1997 my heart began skipping a few beats occasionally. By then, Dr. Guyer was in private practice, so I made an appointment, and he fixed my skipped-beat problem. I have continued to report back to him every six months for a tune-up. That is why, at seventy-two years old, I have zero aches and pains and have high energy levels all the time. And, of course, my once decrepit mind has recovered well enough to write this book.

The best thing for you, as a reader, to do right now is to absorb everything Dr. Guyer writes at the end of each chapter in this book. I feel sure that after you finish reading *Getting Well* and have considered carefully how Dr. Guyer approaches the healing process, you will become so familiar with how an advanced medicine doctor thinks that you will recognize this rare new-type doctor by just listening to a patient who has experienced these unique healing treatments advanced medicine doctors offer. Some of these treatments will be described in Chapter 20.

If you feel like you need to contact an advanced medicine doctor like Dr. Guyer right now, you might consider finding out where your local doctors and nurses go when they themselves are faced with a life-threatening illness. I say this because over the years I have met several doctors and nurses taking treatments at Dr. Guyer's Advanced Medical Clinic. I remember several nurses with chronic fatigue syndrome and fibromyalgia being treated by Dr. Guyer because conventional medicine, as they explained to me, had failed them.

I can clearly remember a fifty-four-year-old cardiologist taking a nutritional IV seated across from me and talking about his experience being treated with Dr. Guyer's method of combining chemotherapy with nutritional therapy, both before and after he had colon cancer surgery.

With tears running down his cheeks, I also remember a forty-two-year-old dentist telling me that he was so mentally ill he could practice dentistry only one day a week, and he was about to lose his business, his home, and maybe even his wife and two children because he was on the verge of bankruptcy. I told him to cheer up, that I knew exactly what it felt like to be mentally ill from mercury poisoning. I told him that Dr. Guyer could remove the mercury and guide him back to practicing dentistry full time within six months. I assured him that everything would be okay, but he was having great difficulty believing that his illness was caused by the mercury vapor he breathed while implanting hundreds of silver tooth fillings in his patients' mouths over the previous sixteen years. He thought he had played it safe because he never permitted dental amalgams to be installed in his own mouth. He told me he had only safe gold inlays, and that he just couldn't understand what went wrong.

I could go on and on about the real life stories Dr. Guyer's patients have related to me. I will never forget in 2002 the sad look on the faces of the grandfather and grandmother from California holding their very sick fourteen-year-old grandson on their lap waiting for the first appointment with Dr. Guyer. The grandfather told me they had traveled for a year from one major health clinic to another, trying to find out why their grandson was so physically weak and seemed unable to learn in school. The family would stay at a hotel in Indianapolis a week to two weeks while Dr. Guyer treated their grandson and would then fly back to California. For eighteen months, they made these trips. The last time I had contact with the grandson was October 2003. He had turned sixteen and was at Dr. Guyer's clinic for a six-month checkup. He had a big smile and looked strong and healthy like a teenager should. He said with pride that he was almost caught up in schoolwork and was playing on the soccer team.

My Final Story for Now

My final story also happened in October 2003. Every six months I make an appointment with Dr. Guyer, and we run heavy metal tests and a battery of lab tests tailored to watch the weak areas of my body. If we find something not testing within the normal brackets, Dr. Guyer makes changes in my nutritional plan or at times gives me special treatments to cure the medical problem in the early stages. My goal is to stay healthy and active for another twenty years to age ninety or perhaps beyond. This, of course, seems like the ultimate in practicing preventive medicine, but all we are really doing is following The Four Basic Principles for "Getting Well" presented in Chapter 12.

Now, for my final story: During the last week of October 2003, I was seated in a U-shaped arrangement with several other patients in the IV treatment room at Dr. Guyer's Advanced Medical Clinic. Each of us had a bag of medicine hanging high above our head with a long plastic tube connected to a butterfly needle inserted into a vein in our arm, back of our hand, or sometimes a foot vein. I was receiving an extra nutritional IV just before departing the cold winter weather common in Indiana and heading, with my wife Betty, to Florida for the winter. I was telling the group a story about the bad medical attention my friend was getting from his under-trained, run-of-the-mill, conventional medical doctor. Everyone was listening, and some were nodding their heads in agreement concerning my negative comments about doctors, when all at once this beautiful—I'm guessing thirty-eight-year-old—brunette, Elizabeth Taylor look-a-like who was receiving a nutritional IV, just like me, spoke up and said that the type of doctor-conduct I was describing did not happen in her office. Instantly the clock on the wall stood still! I broke the silence by asking her if she was a medical doctor. She replied that she indeed was. I said, "Doctor, you look very healthy. Why are you taking a nutritional treatment in the middle of the day here at Dr. Guyer's clinic?"

She laid down the book she was reading, and, while all eyes in the room focused on her, she told us her story. One year earlier, she had received the worst possible news a person could receive from a group of oncologists who diagnosed her health problem as a very rare form of cancer, with more than ninety percent diagnosed with this type of cancer dead within six months. Less than ten percent survive, and doctors don't know why they survive. Naturally, her whole world was immediately turned upside down. Her faith in God had supported her, but she really did not know what to do except immediately to start the large doses of radiation and chemotherapy her doctors recommended.

As she tried to regain her bearings, she thought of Dr. Guyer, whom she had heard about when he was a complementary medicine doctor at the hospital. She received an appointment right away. Dr. Guyer agreed she should take the radiation and chemo her oncologists recommended. However, he asked that they delay the start of these treatments for six weeks while he provided other treatments to build up her immune system to a maximum level. After she completed this run of Dr. Guyer's immune-support therapy, she started the radiation followed by chemo, being treated weekly during the following year. But, at the same time, Dr. Guyer continued to give her treatments that kept her immune system in top working order.

When she told us her story, she had completed her radiation and chemo treatments, but she intended to continue nutritional therapy. Her cancer had disappeared about eight months earlier, when she first started the radiation, and had not recurred. She said that the truly amazing thing to her oncologists was that she maintained the strength through all this to see her own patients every week while taking treatments herself.

I told her I could not understand why she did not get weak and lose her hair like other people do when they take large doses of radiation and chemo.

She gave credit to Dr. Guyer's nutritional therapy that had made it possible for her to work every day and continue to look strong and healthy. She smiled and said, "Even my own patients had not suspected I was ill."

I asked her what her group of oncologists said about this.

"They were absolutely amazed," she said. "Never had they heard of a patient beating this type of cancer like I had." As a result, they had written several papers on her bout with this deadly disease and had circulated them in the medical news.

I asked, "Since you got along so well, are there any other patients whom your group of oncologists have referred to Dr. Guyer for immune system treatment while taking radiation and chemo treatments?"

She said she didn't know of any. "What a shame!" I thought.

Doctor's Commentary

One of my favorite physicians in the United States is Ralph Golan, M.D., who has a primary-care practice with a holistic focus in the Seattle area. Ralph wrote the now famous book *Optimal Wellness* some years ago. I heard Dr. Golan speak many years ago, prior to my starting medical school, and a quotation from the speech is particularly memorable. He said that, if he were in a car accident and broke his leg, his initial response would not be to go to the nearest health food store to purchase herbal tea. Obviously, the immediate response would be to be transported to the emergency room for prompt treatment, and then to employ complementary or herbal approaches supportively later. The point is that modern medicine's ability to handle crisis management is topnotch. However, as Ralph also pointed out, the management of chronic illness is primarily focused on symptom relief, an approach referred to as "anti-treatment." For example, patients who struggle with depression are given antidepressants. Patients with chronic pain issues are given anti-inflammatories. The list goes on and on. Unfortunately, while these medicines can be beneficial in selective cases, none addresses the cause of illness. Some long-term may worsen the underlying condition that they are purportedly treating. For example, anti-inflammatory drugs used for osteoarthritis may hasten the progression of the joint destruction, even though they tend to help control pain. The problem is a primary focus on symptom relief rather than addressing underlying cause.

Individuals, like you or someone you know for example, may not feel well. Many factors that they encounter day to day may limit their ability to engage in general activities of daily living. However, most of their laboratory results in a general, generic, and superficial sense appear normal. Therefore, they are given various psycho-emotional labels along with prescriptions for antidepressants before their doctors exit the exam room. However, if these individuals had the luxury of a deeper, more broad-based diagnostic analysis and the opportunity to participate in broader-based therapies available throughout the world, they would often find the successful results they seek.

Unfortunately, most of this training is not available in conventional medical schools. I remember a conversation I had some years ago with a patient, acknowledging that the most effective treatments I use daily in my own office are not therapies I learned about in medical school. Doctors are not introduced to the avenues by which most people can regain their overall health. If lucky, physicians are introduced to these options after several years in private practice. They have seen good results either on a personal level or with patients who have been a catalyst to greater exploration.

The day-to-day practice of medicine, as Wayne points out, is a high-volume, HMO-style encounter in which the patient receives only two to three minutes of the physician's time, then participates in the ritual of scribbles on a prescription pad while the physician exits the room so that he or she may embark upon yet another avenue of symptom management and symptom cover-up. Unfortunately, the status quo is slow to evolve in a more favorable direction, and the motivation is generally high for all parties concerned to maintain the status quo. Pharmaceutical companies make enormous profits from drugs that do not often cure, so there is little motivation to support nutritional, alternative, or herbal approaches, even though they may be superior therapies. Often the mark-up on a prescription drug exceeds 500,000 percent. That is why pharmaceutical companies are among the top companies generating the highest profits in our country.

In addition, physicians themselves are often placed in a precarious position in that they are unable to make any effective changes regarding the typical practice of medicine. They are asked by insurance companies to see more and more patients, often for less and less reimbursement, and to generate prescriptions for more and more pharmaceuticals, which supports the system as it exists. It has always been a mystery to me why insurance companies, which of course like other companies would be focused on ongoing profits, would continue to pay for therapies that do not work and disregard those that do.

It seems a ridiculous notion. All of us would acknowledge that, if we took our automobile in for repair, we would not keep taking it to the same mechanic week after week, year after year, for a repair that clearly did not work, while the automobile's condition kept declining. Yet, such is the case in standard medicine. One reason, as Dr. Andrew Weil pointed out, is that education in medical schools about nutrition is rare. Dr. Weil's personal experience with nutrition education in medical school was very similar to mine. In four years, I basically received a 30-minute lecture on nutrition from a professor who brought in a paper bag full of junk foods that included Ding Dongs, candy bars, and Twinkies. He passed them out to all the students and said, "This stuff is bad. Fruits and vegetables are good. None of this will be on a test, but enjoy the snacks." Everybody had a good laugh. No one took notes, of course, since none of the information would be on a test. Then, the lecture proceeded with esoteric discourses on biochemical pathways that we all had to remember, at least for the test. Of course, the biochemical pathway information proved highly important for physicians who focus on nutritional and complementary avenues of healing. And to this day, I use the information to better understand the biochemical idiosyncrasies of unique patients.

—Dale Guyer, M.D.

Chapter Sixteen
Toxins Everywhere, Including Your Body

Over the years, I found that bacteria, viruses, or fungi did not cause most of my illnesses. Instead, toxins, accumulating in my body and creating chemical and electrical imbalances, caused them. These basic imbalances weakened my immune system, interfered with nutritional absorption, rendered my body hormones less active, caused false illness symptoms, disrupted nerve path messages that controlled my body functions, interfered with the effectiveness of prescription drugs, and made it impossible for my body to produce the energy needed to support the active healthy lifestyle I desired.

I am devoting an entire chapter to toxins because I believe that most conventional medical doctors have not been trained to consider the accumulation of toxins in our bodies as a major cause of illnesses. Doctors who treated me over a thirty-eight-year period not once investigated for and treated the presence of toxic heavy metals and other toxins that were accumulating in my body. Instead they treated my illness symptoms, which I now know were caused by toxins, with a treasure chest of cover-up-type drugs. I now believe I would have needed to take these drugs for the rest of my life, while I sat around and waited until my covered-up symptoms developed into raging diseases that my doctors could have recognized from their standard medical school training.

If it is your goal to get completely well, like I did from chronic illness symptoms, then you will need to learn on your own how toxins entering your body are causing your illness, because most conventional family-practice doctors I have met are devoid of this knowledge and cannot discuss it intelligently.

Once you have a basic understanding of how toxic elements in our world are causing your illness, then you can select a complementary/alternative medicine doctor and have these toxins safely removed from your body so you can experience your best chance for wellness again.

What Are Toxins, Where Do They Come from, and Where Do They Go?

The textbook says, "A toxin is basically anything that causes an irritation in the body or has a harmful effect on it." My medical dictionary refers to a "toxin" as "a colloidal proteinaceous poisonous substance... notably toxic when introduced into the body tissues and typically capable of inducing antibody formations."

I like to think of toxins as anything that enters the human body our immune system does not recognize. When the immune system does not recognize the toxins, it forms antibodies in an attempt to fight and destroy them. If our immune system is not capable of destroying the actions of the toxic substance, then it attempts to remove the substance from our body through our liver, which deposits the toxins in our fecal discharge or through our kidneys' urine discharge. If we exercise regularly, some toxic substances will be removed with our sweat.

The very moment when our toxin intake is greater than our immune system can destroy or eliminate, our weakened immune system, in a last-ditch effort, begins storing the toxins out of harm's way in the fat cells of our body. The storing of toxins can happen to a child during periods when his or her little immune system is giving maximum attention to illness or to a middle-aged adult consuming a bad diet and with a work-commitment candle lighted at both ends or to a senior citizen with a weakened immune system due to poor nutritional absorption.

Once the toxins are stored in our body, they are very difficult to remove. Usually they accumulate, continue to increase their contact with healthy cells surrounding them, and begin to create illness symptoms that eventually develop into a full-blown illness. The EPA has documented many of these events.

Natural Toxins in Our Food Supply

When toxins are discussed, government officials from the Food Standards Agency are fond of pointing out that some of our good, healthy foods contain substances that are harmful. For example, they say that dried red kidney beans contain a natural toxicant called lectin that can cause stomachaches and vomiting. Potatoes contain a natural toxicant called glycoalkaloid found in the green sprouting part of the potato which if eaten can be poisonous. They talk about the bruised areas on apples containing a dangerous mycotoxin called patulin and shellfish sometimes containing dangerous "algal toxins" formed by algae in the sea.

These are not the type of toxins I am concerned with, because we as consumers can control them. However, I believe that our government agencies go on and on about the natural toxins in our food for two reasons. One is that they often try to impress us with their knowledge. They do not realize, however, that our parents and grandparents have handed most of these common-sense food preparation precautions down through many generations of our families. For example, to handle the toxins in red beans, we were taught to "parboil" the beans, discard the water containing the toxin, and then add new, fresh water and finish cooking. We cut away the green areas in potatoes before cooking and the brown spots in apples before eating. Most natural toxins in food are made inactive with normal cooking anyway. The government's second reason, I believe, is to draw our attention away from the real problem, the long list (over 10,000) of FDA-approved chemical food additives in our highly processed supermarket food. Most food additives are toxins that are approved by the FDA for the benefit of the food grower and the food processor with few consumer nutritional benefits.

Food Additives, in General, Are Indigestible Chemicals

Many food additives are made from petroleum or coal-tar products! The largest food additive group is synthetic, artificial food flavorings, followed by synthetic coloring. But the list doesn't stop there. Other food additives include preservatives, bleaching agents, emulsifiers, texturizers, humectants, and ripening agents such as ethylene gas that is sprayed on bananas to make them ripen faster.

Artificial flavoring ingredients are not derived from natural sources, such as spices, fruit or fruit juices, vegetable juices, edible yeast, herbs, bark, buds, roots, leaves or similar plant material, meat, seafood, poultry, eggs, dairy products, or fermentation products. Instead, they are made from various chemicals controlled by expert chemists who study the chemical composition of natural flavors and experiment to duplicate the composition with low-cost synthetic chemicals. They come close, but natural flavors are usually judged to taste best; however, natural flavors are always more expensive. Food processors prefer artificial flavors because they are a lot cheaper and give their product a much longer shelf life because synthetic chemicals do not become rancid as quickly as natural food flavorings tend to do.

Read the Labels

If you don't recognize the name of an ingredient, your immune system probably won't either. Everything that enters your digestive system must be evaluated by your immune system. Your immune system must decide whether this is good nutrition to feed to your cells or whether this substance should be rejected down the colon as unusable food structure.

Chapter Sixteen

The Digestive System's Battle with Food Additives

This process begins when our food enters our mouth and we start to chew and break it down. Our saliva mixes with the food and then notifies our stomach and digestive support system what complex natural chemicals and enzymes are needed to digest the type food entering our mouth at that time. Each time our meal being consumed changes from a bite of salad to cooked vegetables with perhaps cheese, followed by a bite of meat and eventually dessert, the natural chemical makeup of digestive compounds in our stomach must rapidly change too. As the digestive breakdown of our meal continues in the stomach, the small intestines are being lined with millions of carefully selected digestive bacteria needed to prepare the nutrients for absorption through nutrient receptors into our bloodstream to nourish our cells and keep them active and healthy.

This rapidly changing chemical process is so complex that scientists cannot duplicate it or completely understand it. However, one thing is known for sure. Synthetic chemical food additives can disrupt the natural digestive process and sometimes kill on contact the critical bacterial flora lining the small intestines resulting in less good nutrition being made available to our delicate cells.

When our food contains additives consisting of artificial flavorings created from manmade chemical compounds or synthetic coloring with a petroleum base or off-the-shelf chemical preservatives, our immune system will not recognize these foreign substances as food. Instead, it immediately slows down the digestive process in an attempt to separate the indigestible, toxic food additives from the nutrition in our food so it can discharge the toxins through our colon. This usually results in a slower-responding and less-alert metabolism. This slowed-down digestive action causes some of the good nutrition to travel right past the nutrient receptors and exit the body out the colon along with the toxins. At the same time some of the toxins stay attached to the nutrients and pass through the receptors into our bloodstream. When this happens, our immune system begins working overtime trying to separate the toxins from the real food in our digestive system and, at the same time, trying to prevent toxins that have passed into our bloodstream from entering our cells and making us ill.

The FDA's Testing Is Not Always Accurate

The FDA tests and approves every additive that is processed into our food. The problem is that it does its testing in isolation. The laboratory mice, rats, and primates used for testing live under ideal, controlled conditions. The only toxic chemical compounds entering the test animal's

160

body are the food additive chemicals being tested. It is my opinion that, since every animal, including humans, has some limited ability to filter out and remove toxic substances, most tests conducted by the FDA are not really accurate and usually result in additive approvals for human consumption that are not necessarily safe.

To make their tests accurate, it would be necessary for seventy-eight percent of the test animals to have eight little dental amalgams implanted in their teeth so that, as they chewed, toxic mercury would be mixed with their food as it happens each day with seventy-eight percent of us humans. In addition, the FDA would have to hang the test animal cages out along a busy street two to three hours each day to replicate the amount of toxic vehicle exhaust fumes we humans breathe into our body each day. To be really accurate, some test animal cages should be placed at floor level in large industrial manufacturing plants eight hours-a-day breathing toxic workplace air like I did for ten years. To be even more realistic, diet soft drinks should be served daily to the test animals.

My Point Is...

Almost any toxic substance can be tested in small amounts in the human body over relatively short periods of time and be declared safe. This is because a healthy human body has some ability to reject, filter out, and purge toxic substances that can cause harm. But, when large volumes of other toxins are already present in our bodies and the immune system is overworked, the tiny flyspeck amounts of chemical food additives are not expelled from our bodies as shown in the FDA approval tests. Instead, because of our overworked immune systems, the chemical food additives accumulate in the tissues of our bodies at levels high enough to be detected and classified as a toxic substance capable of damaging our delicate cells. We must also remember that, when our immune systems are maxed-out creating antibodies to fight toxins, they cannot detect or combat bacteria, viruses, and fungi entering our bodies.

Other Toxins That Accumulate in Our Bodies

The most common processed food ingredient that has proven to be very dangerous to the human body is hydrogenated vegetable oils or partially hydrogenated vegetable oils. Corn oil, soy oil, safflower oil, and most other vegetable oils quickly become very rancid at room temperatures. To improve the liquid vegetable oil's short shelf life, the factory processor heats the liquid oil and bubbles hydrogen through it to convert it from a liquid to a solid state at room temperature. Vegetable oils converted to a solid have a very long shelf life before going rancid. For a semisolid, like margarine, the liquid vegetable oil is *partially hydrogenated.* The problem with this process is that twenty-five to forty-five percent of the vegetable oil changes to a very dangerous **trans-fatty acid**, a type never found in nature.

Our immune system accepts these man-modified fats as vegetables, but after they enter our bloodstream our immune system realizes that nearly half of the fat is as poisonous as arsenic or cyanide. Realizing its mistake, our immune system begins forming antibodies to fight this outlaw fat and ends up storing some of the toxic trans-fatty acids in various places in our body like our heart and brain cells.

I began eating exclusively margarines made from corn oil at age thirty-eight and continued to age sixty-one when it was then discovered that I had developed over those years severely blocked coronary arteries. I developed severe blockage while my cholesterol stayed around 150, never testing above 200. Free-radical damage to my heart created by *partially hydrogenated* low-fat spread made from corn oil is the most likely cause.

If you want to stay healthy, please don't eat any processed food containing a *hydrogenated* or *partially hydrogenated oil/fat.* I stopped in 1995, and I returned to good health. It's never too late to make improvements in your health.

MSG (monosodium glutamate)

MSG, a food "flavor enhancer," has proven to be the second-most dangerous food additive to my body. If my heart began beating fast and irregularly while eating a restaurant meal, the cause was MSG. Every restaurant manager handling my complaint always insisted they did not use MSG. I thought the managers were lying to me until one day I read that the FDA had approved MSG with disguised names to help cut down the complaints concerning MSG. Approved substituted names like sodium caseinate, hydrolyzed yeast, hydrolyzed vegetable protein, calcium caseinate, autolyzed yeast, textured protein, yeast food, yeast extract, and sometimes MSG are labeled natural flavoring. They all can cause headaches, numbness, depression, anxiety, heart palpitations, and weakness, according to Dr. Joe M. Elrod on page 56 of his latest 2003 book *Reversing Degenerative Disease.*

Aspartame, the Chemical Name for a Dangerous Can-of-Worms

NutraSweet® (aspartame) is a manmade artificial sweetener found in most food and beverage products labeled "sugar-free." Aspartame is responsible for about fifty percent of all adverse reactions to food additives reported to the FDA. Opponents of aspartame insist that NutraSweet®, when digested, yields ten percent methanol (wood alcohol). This is about 56mg of methanol generated by a 12oz aluminum can of most diet soft drinks. The Center for Behavioral Medicine Chairman, Ralph Walton, M.D., says that the methanol from aspartame becomes widely distributed throughout the body, including our brain, muscle, fat, and nerve tissue. Once absorbed by our body tissues, the methanol metabolizes to formaldehyde, which enters cells and damages the DNA, resulting in cellular mutations. Cellular mutations and the presence of formaldehyde are associated with cancer production in humans. Dr. Walton's research showed that **the only studies that didn't find problems with aspartame were those funded by the manufacturer (Monsanto)**. Although the FDA has had many requests that it retest the safety of aspartame, FDA always refuses. However, Europe, in 2004-05, is conducting new safety testing because of its accumulation of medical problems involving NutraSweet® and Splenda® which is the marketing name for sucralose.

Sucralose is produced by **chlorinating** sugar (sucrose). This involves changing the structure of the sugar molecules chemically by substituting three chlorine atoms for three hydroxyl groups. According to Dr. Joseph Mercola, author of *Total Health Program*, Johnson & Johnson emphasized that sucralose passes through the body unabsorbed.

I personally cannot use Splenda® because my immune system judges it to be a toxin that causes my heart to beat irregularly.

Genetically Modified (GM) Foods

Farmers who grow our food have, since 1995, rushed to planting GM seeds for one reason. They can harvest a crop at a much higher profit. Nutrition is not higher in GM foods, and in some GM foods, it is less. Genetically modified has no direct relationship with century-old processes of cross-pollinating, grafting, or selective breeding over many years to create a higher quality crop, resistant to plant destroying diseases. These century-old processes are limited by the natural controls of nature. GM processes are man-controlled. Using a high-velocity "gene gun," scientists can instantly insert specific genes into a plant or animal without having to go through the trial-and-error process of selective breeding. Plants in nature were created to resist the DNA from other plants, animals, fish, insects, bacteria, viruses, fungi, or any other living organism with genes. Using genetic engineering, companies developing genetically modified foods insert insect genes into potatoes, bacterial genes into corn, human genes into animals, and, if they so choose, animal genes into humans. There is no limit. The mix and match potential is endless. Natural law doesn't allow this. It's like trying to put a big pill down your dog's throat; the dog spits it out and rejects it every time. The rejection problem is why, in modern gene-modification engineering, man has decided to use a gun to force the union.

In the 1980s, John Sanford and Theodore Klein, two Cornell University plant scientists, developed the gene gun. Almost everyone agrees with them that "the gene gun revolutionized the emerging technology of genetic engineering by giving scientists a formidable way to shoot foreign genes into organisms," as quoted on page 93 of *Eating in the Dark, America's Experiment with Genetically Engineered Food* by Kathleen Hart. On pages 96-98 of the same book, the author tells of a demonstration that Sam Wise, a research scientist with Pioneer Hi-Bred, the largest seed company in the United States, performed for her. Describing the gene gun, she said, "The device is a square box about the size of a large microwave oven." Wise set up a dry-run experiment to demonstrate to Kathleen how forced gene-insertion is accomplished. On the floor of the box, Wise placed a Petri dish on which the corn embryos would be placed if this were real and not a demo.

At the other end of the box was the gene gun chambered with DNA-coated, tiny tungsten particles aimed at the Petri dish. The gene gun was then loaded with a standard twenty-two blank rifle cartridge to propel the tungsten particles coated with the selected DNA from, say, another plant, animal, or any other organism they want inserted into the corn plant. Once inserted, the corn is genetically modified and will continue to grow the inserted foreign genes along with its own genes year after year.

Before firing, the entire box was pumped down to a very strong vacuum to increase the impact speed. When researcher Wise depressed the firing button, Kathleen said, "I heard a faint pop and saw a tiny flash of orange light." Wise told Kathleen, "There are about thirty-nine patents involved in that shot." Wise then slowly let air into the box where he had placed a soft plastic disc in the Petri dish to simulate the expensive corn embryos. He then pointed to some gray specks in the Petri dish where the corn embryos would have been in a real experiment and said to Kathleen, "Those big holes would kill the cells, but those little bitty holes are what you're looking for."

Kathleen learned that genetic engineering is a hit-or-miss affair. They never know for sure how this newly created plant is going to react in our environment. Even with their newer, compressed helium gene guns that shoot DNA-coated gold beads into the corn embryos, it may be necessary to repeat this gene-gun procedure a hundred or more times to be awarded with a lucky shot. Forcing a gene that nature has taught a plant to reject into the plant's complicated genetic code is termed risky business. The changes this plant will make over time to compensate for this forced marriage, many scientists say, cannot be predicted.

Doris J. Rapp, M.D., board certified in environmental medicine, on pages 368-369 of her new book *Our Toxic World, A Wake Up Call*, lists examples of "specific combinations" that have already been used to create "at least 50 GE foods grown on over 70 million acres of land and sold in the United States." This is her list:

- The silkworm gene can be found in apples and apple juice.
- The petunia gene can be in some soybeans and carrots.
- The barley gene can be in walnuts.
- Potatoes can have a chicken gene.
- Tomatoes can have a flounder gene.
- A cancer chicken virus is used as a carrier so that a growth hormone gene can be introduced or implanted into farm fish so they grow faster.
- The leukemia virus is used in chicken to carry genes into developing poultry.
- Scorpion poison genes are used in cabbage to control caterpillars.
- Antibiotic-resistant genes are being used in foods as markers to indicate that successful gene-to-gene engineering has occurred.

Most of the ways in which genes are mixed in the genetically modified foods we eat today are considered secret by the FDA and are not available to the general public.

Making Big-Time, Record Profits from Genetically Modified Foods

When Monsanto wanted to increase sales of its weed killer Roundup®, it devised the following scheme: First, it created a new soybean with its gene gun that when sprayed with Roundup® would not die, but would instead absorb the Roundup® weed killer. This made it likely that remnants of the weed killer would travel throughout the plant to include the little developing soybeans themselves. Next, Monsanto demonstrated to the farmer a new lower-cost planting method:

1. spraying an unplowed field, using large 100ft booms on special big-tire trucks with Roundup® and liquid fertilizers
2. waiting a few days, and then planting the field without any soil preparation with Monsanto's Roundup® Ready special soybean seed
3. when the weeds start growing again, spraying the entire field with Roundup® and fertilizer again; this kills the weeds, but the Roundup® Ready soybean plants survive by repelling or absorbing the weed killer Roundup®

By spraying the soybean field with Roundup® and fertilizer three to five times in a growing season, the yield per acre becomes very high, and the high cost of soil preparation along with normally needed cultivation is eliminated. This method of growing soybeans results in less work for the farmer and more money in the bank at harvest time, despite their high cost for Roundup®. As a result of introducing Roundup® Ready soybeans, sales of Roundup® have soared. Most market analysts believe this to be Monsanto's most profitable product. Its marketing scheme worked well.

Problems Are Created

Presently there are major problems. First, the FDA did not require any testing to ensure that Roundup® sprayed on the soybean plant several times during the growing season is safe for long-term human consumption. Other countries have tested and don't like what they have learned. Nearly all have outlawed genetically modified seed for planting. In addition, most countries require all food products containing genetically modified ingredients to be labeled as such. As a result, the vast majority of homemakers in other countries do not serve their families with untested, genetically modified foods. They often call them "Frankenfoods," and refuse to buy them.

In Japan, where labeling of GM foods is required, mothers always select natural soymilk to feed their babies. Their attitude is: Let the American mothers offer their children as test animals for GM foods, if they so choose, but not our children. We value them too much.

Genetically Modified Corn

Genetically modified corn in the United States is even more disturbing. With a gene gun, several seed companies have produced GM corn seeds by forcing a long list of foreign organisms into the corn embryo. While the corn plant is forming the kernels we eat, it also is producing the genes of an assortment of bacteria, viruses, insects, or animals that act as poisons inside the corn plant designed to kill the corn borer and any other insect that might attack or any disease or fungus that might kill the corn plant or damage the corn ear. Traces of these powerful foreign organisms and poisons are often later found throughout the plant and the harvested kernels. True, the toxic remnants of these powerful GM pest-and-disease killers are usually found in micro amounts, but please remember, nobody knows the potential health problems for humans eating products made from GM corn. Long-term tests have not been conducted. The FDA is eliminating a lot of hard work for itself by using the American people for its long-term safety studies. The FDA accepted Monsanto's word that its GM foods were safe and called for no additional safety test for human consumption. Some of Monsanto's tests were as simple as feeding GM corn to rats for six months and then reporting that none of the rats observed became ill or died.

On page 381 of the above-mentioned book *Our Toxic World* by Doris J. Rapp, M.D., she writes, "A Dutch student, Hinze Hogendoorn, did a simple study. He put two piles of corn (maize) in a barn full of mice. The genetically engineered (GE) corn was untouched while the regular corn was all eaten. Do the mice know something we do not know?"

My comment is "Do the mice know something our FDA does not know?" The answer is an astounding Yes! Call your U.S. Senator. Ask him or her to have this simple test repeated in a cleaned-out room in the Senate Office Building so everyone can observe the results. Maybe this will convince our elected officials to take action and pass a "Citizen's Right to Know" labeling law for genetically modified foods.

It is my opinion that presently our elected officials are being awarded reelection campaign money for looking the other way concerning labeling rules just to protect the profits of the large international corporations that produce genetically engineered modified food. I believe that the U.S. Congress by its inaction has agreed that the FDA can use our little children, teenagers, and adults in the United States as test animals to monitor long-term health problems with genetically modified foods.

As hard as I try, I cannot think of a reason, except reelection money, why Congress has not established labeling standards for these new foods. I thought it has always been the American tradition to inform the consumer!

Why Not Buy Organic Foods Labeled "Not Genetically Modified" Now?

Organic farmers and their processors take great care that the genetically modified weed killers, pesticides, fish genes, cancer genes, and other strange organisms growing in and around GM crops in nearby fields do not contaminate their crop. They run tests on each harvest to make sure, so they can label their finished product "Not Genetically Modified." When labeling "No-GM" began, the consumer rushed to the health-food stores and supermarket health-food departments to buy foods they believed to be safer.

I believe the FDA complained to Congress that this violated its "no labeling rule" because, with a label, the consumer could tell the difference between GM foods and natural foods. Congress, I believe, reviewed the situation and encouraged a new labeling rule that prohibits labeling of any food in reference to being or not being genetically modified. Organic farmers and their food processors may now be subject to fines and jail time for labeling their products "Not Genetically Modified," or "No GMO." I have been told that some organic food companies are defying the no-label rule because they test each batch of their product and know for sure it is free of GM contamination. Organic food-grower organizations have plans to appeal in Federal courts, claiming that their First Amendment Constitutional rights to free speech are being violated. However, it appears to me that, with the present determined attitude of our lawmakers not to label, the Federal courts will rule against the will of the people and support our Federal government's position because our elected officials have not made it clear what is best for the people who elected them.

While we wait for our elected officials to pass GM labeling laws to protect our present and future health, we will be unknowingly eating about fifty or more foods that have undergone genetic modifications either in the United States or Canada. The FDA insists that GM foods are safe, and for the sake of our children and our grandchildren, I hope the FDA is correct. However, Europe, Japan, Russia, China, Korea, and many other countries have outlawed genetically modified foods or require strict labeling so their people are informed. Europe and Japan are conducting scientific, long-term studies to make sure GM foods are safe before accepting U.S. processed foods or grain.

What Can We Expect in the Future?

Many new companies are being formed. With their unregulated gene guns, they are cross firing at everything. They are shooting animal genes into plants to see what happens, trying to develop new and exciting Frankenfoods for kids, like breakfast cereal that glows in the dark, laced with the genes from fish that glow in the dark, or breakfast foods made from new grains that also produce "big muscle-" building additives so a child (even girls) can grow big muscles just by eating GM cereals for breakfast. By cross firing selected plant genes into other plant genes, they hope to force a single plant to grow an assortment of vegetables along with a daily allotment of vitamins and minerals. As they gain experience with even higher velocity and more accurate gene guns, they are sure a plant can be forced to produce human insulin, too. Some companies are trying to take over the drug industry by shooting drug formulas into plants and letting the plant create the medicine at a much lower price. In fact, some of these new companies believe that farmers of the future will grow the chemicals needed to make most of the chemical products available on the market today, including solvents, laundry detergents, motor oils, and diesel fuels.

Some of our scientists are worried about what this gene mixing will do to our environment. They fear we could easily lose control and contaminate many of the natural plants in the world that have for centuries provided us with delicious, healthy food. They already note that, when the GM cornstalks, which produced their own organisms that act like pesticides, biocides, and fungicides, decay and become part of the soil, the valuable, natural bacteria and microorganisms in the soil are sometimes killed. If our natural soil organisms die, the soil becomes worthless for supporting the production of food.

Want to Learn More about Genetically Modified Foods?

To know more about the genetically modified foods you are eating right now, read Kathleen Hart's above-mentioned book *Eating in the Dark, America's Experiment with Genetically Engineered Food*. Kathy traveled the world and labored about three years collecting the facts for this well-documented book.

Toxins in Our Meat

Farm animals breathe the same toxic air we do and often drink unprocessed water not safe for humans. Some of these toxins end up in the meat tissue we eat, but that is only the beginning. Chickens and turkeys are raised in confined spaces and typically are fed growth hormones to make them grow faster. They are usually fed antibiotics to hold down the death rate and steroids to increase the size of the valuable white breast meat.

Beef cattle raised in crowded feedlots are fed special rapid weight-gaining formulas containing GM grains, chemical growth hormones, antibiotics, and sometimes steroids to increase the yield of premium cuts of steak.

Pork production is even more alarming. Pigs being fed for market are housed in a sealed-up building with no natural sunlight. Pigs are often in indoor pens so small they cannot, as they reach market size, lie down. A flow of air to keep the fast-growing pigs cool constantly travels the 500-ft length of each windowless building. On a timer, overhead water sprinklers usually cool the confined pigs on a predetermined schedule because swine have no sweat glands and would die from heat exhaustion if not kept cool. Below the numerous rows of indoor pigpens is a series of constantly moving conveyer belts carrying hog manure and hog urine to large holding pond lagoons to be stored for sewage disposal sanitary processing. The feeder pigs are provided a constant supply of water and a special food mixture normally containing GM grains, growth hormones, antibiotics, and steroids.

The problem with this beautiful-looking meat is that it may have micro-traces of unwanted GM grain residues, growth hormones, antibiotics, and steroids. In addition, the hams and bacon are fast-cured with chemical injections and toxic nitrates.

As you might suspect, by adding up the chemicals fed to pigs as they are prepared for market and then recognizing the harsh chemicals used to fast-cure the meat, pork can contribute significantly to our body's unhealthy burden of toxins.

Your New House and Your New Office Building Can Make You Toxic, Too

Old houses and office buildings tend to be compatible with good health. New homes and new office buildings can make you sick. Most old homes and office buildings are not well insulated and constantly leak heated or cooled air to the outside. As a result, fresh air is constantly entering the cracks in the building, providing fresh outside air to the occupants. Most of these old buildings were not air-conditioned. Instead, they required opening the windows for warm-weather cooling. However, homes and office buildings built in the past thirty years, because of high energy costs, are built airtight and crammed with insulation. As a result, these buildings not only require a heating system, but also an air-cooling system. Some of the same inside air often recycles for days. There is minimal fresh air entering the building.

If you work in a modern, airtight office building, the air you are breathing today has the possibility of being the same air you breathed three days ago. The only difference is that the air contains less oxygen and more carbon dioxide, bacteria, viruses, fungi, and airborne toxic chemical compounds. The toxic chemicals come from a variety of sources. Toxic compounds are emitted from an array of office equipment like copy machines, laser printers, and ink-jet printers. The office workers often track in toxins from the street and from their homes. Office workers also exhale toxic carbon dioxide all day long at their desks.

Modern buildings are constructed from materials containing toxic chemicals that give off gases and odors for years. This is called building "out-gassing." Common toxic chemicals emitted from materials used to construct modern buildings are benzene, styrene, carbon tetrachloride, and other compounds along with the chemicals toluene and formaldehyde constantly being released from the paint. Formaldehyde, which is closely associated with cancer, is also released from carpet, carpet glue, particleboard furniture, wood paneling, fabric, couches, and curtains. In addition, these airtight buildings often become breeding grounds for fungus, germs, bacteria, and combinations of chemical toxins that become trapped and re-circulated throughout the heating and air-conditioning systems.

Building owners are aware of this problem because doctors have named the illnesses it causes "sick-building syndrome." These health problems can be greatly improved by providing filtered, fresh air into the building and replacing all the air about three or four times each twenty-four hours. This, however, would greatly increase the cost of energy to operate the building because all the incoming air would need to be adjusted for temperature by heating or cooling about four times each day.

Most airtight buildings are engineered to change only twenty percent of the air each twenty-four hours to keep utility costs down. Lack of fresh outside air is why these buildings are so toxic. The owners of these toxic buildings depend on the office workers to remove the toxins from their building. Each office worker inhales the toxins from the office air into his or her bloodstream for eight hours each day and, if healthy, removes ninety percent of the toxins from his or her bloodstream each night. Your liver will filter out some of the office toxins and deposit them in your fecal discharge; the kidneys will place some of the toxins in your urine, and your daily workout at the gym will remove some of these office toxins with your sweat.

Please note, however, that, even under the best conditions, about ten percent of the office toxins will be deposited in the fat cells of your body and will slowly set up the conditions to make you chronically ill. But, please remember, according to Federal law, your office working conditions are not allowed to be toxic.

Modern engineering can make available to your building owner air/heat exchanger/filters that can be retrofitted into the walls of your office building. The exchangers simultaneously exhaust the toxic room-temperature air and bring in fresh outside air. As the air passes through the exchanger, the temperature of the out-going air is transferred to the incoming fresh air. As a result, toxic air can be exhausted, and fresh air can be provided, without increasing utility bills.

I feel that, in this modern age, there is no reason for any of us in the workplace to breathe stale, toxic air that can contribute to illness over time.

I believe it is your responsibility to protect your own body from toxins that can eventually cause illness. Ask your building owner or your supervisor for certification that your workplace meets Federal Clean Air Standards. If you do not get satisfaction from the building owner or your boss, have a consultation with OSHA or the EPA. Tell them you want to make sure the place you spend one-third of your time has air that is clean, so you can avoid possible future illness. Ask that the air in your workplace building be tested and certified.

Please remember that, if you wait until you and your fellow office workers start getting ill, like most people do, it may be too late; you may be too sick to ever recover and go back to work again.

Heavy Metals Your Immune System Considers Toxic

Heavy metals come from deposits in the earth. Some, like aluminum, are scattered near the surface, and others like lead and mercury, are located very deep below the earth's surface. Twelve are considered toxic and should never enter our body and stay for any length of time. They are foreign to our body and serve no useful purpose while inside it. Accumulations in our cells with these toxic metals are likely to result in cell mutations, cell damage leading to organ malfunction, and chronic illness.

The Toxic Twelve are:

aluminum (Al)	antimony (Sb)
arsenic (As)	barium (Ba)
beryllium (Be)	cadmium (Cd)
lead (Pb)	mercury (Hg)
nickel (Ni)	thallium (Ti)
tin (Sn)	uranium (U)

Most of the Toxic Twelve are actively involved in our industrial and chemical manufacturing processes, resulting in these toxins entering our body daily as part of the toxic air we breathe. In addition, rather small amounts are absorbed by plants and ingested with our food. Once industry mines these heavy metals from deep in the earth and brings them to the surface for an industrial purpose, some of the metals continue to recycle and accumulate all around us forever. At the same time as these toxic metals are circulating in the polluted air around us, we continue to mine more of them and each year increase the amounts in our environment. For example, lead is involved in a large array of manufacturing/chemical processes and new products. In 2003, an estimated 500,000 tons of lead presently on the surface was recycled. In addition, we mined and brought to the surface 1.3 million additional tons. In 2004, we expect to recycle about 600,000 tons of lead and mine an additional 1.5 million tons. Lead in our environment has increased each year for many years.

Thallium May Soon Be a Major Threat to Our Health

Presently, thallium is developing into what may be the biggest threat of the Toxic Twelve heavy metals. Our human body cannot tolerate much thallium because it interacts with and modifies the actions of active enzymes in our body. This creates strange illness symptoms that doctors have difficulty diagnosing and treating. Medical science knew in the mid-1800s when thallium was discovered that it was potentially very dangerous to the human body. The scary thing about thallium is that both the metal and its salts are readily absorbed through our skin directly into our bloodstream. We don't have to swallow it or breathe it into our bodies to become seriously ill. The only reason thallium has not been a problem in the past is that there are very low concentrations in the earth's crust (only 0.7 parts per million), and industry in the past has found very little use for this toxic metal. As a result, the EPA has given thallium very little attention. However, this may soon change.

On January 14, 2004, our U.S. Department of Interior circulated the following alert, without comment, concerning possible health risks. The alert said:

Thallium metal and its compounds are consumed in a wide variety of applications; for example, thallium is used in semiconductor material for selenium rectifiers, in gamma radiation detection equipment, in infrared radiation detection and transmission equipment, in crystalline filters for light diffraction for acousto-optical measuring devices, in mercury-thallium alloy for low-temperature measurements, in glass to increase its refractive index and density, in the synthesis of organic compounds, and in a high-density liquid for sink-float separation of minerals. In addition, research activity with thallium is ongoing to develop high-temperature superconducting materials for such applications as magnetic resonance imaging, storage of magnetic energy, magnetic propulsion, and electric power generation and transmission. Also, the use of radioactive thallium compounds for medical purposes in cardiovascular imaging to detect heart disease is increasing.

As you can see, use of thallium is rapidly increasing because it is involved in "leading edge," state-of-the-art development of both future and present space-age applications. Increased use of thallium means new challenges to our health. We should expect the EPA to step up and meet these new challenges to our health before we get ill. To date, the EPA seems to be asleep concerning thallium, waiting, I suppose, for "tragic news" to wake it up.

The Essential Nine

The good news is that there are also nine basic non-toxic metallic elements found in the earth that are essential to our bodies' good health. Each element has an exclusive assignment in your body to keep you healthy. In addition, when your body is attacked by an outside toxin or organism, all of the Essential Nine join together in a synergistic fashion to form a platform on which your immune system is supported to help attack the toxic twelve.

The Essential Nine are:

calcium (Ca)	copper (Cu)	iron (Fe)
magnesium (Mg)	manganese (Mn)	molybdenum (Mo)
selenium (Se)	sulfur (S)	zinc (Zn)

My Closing Statement

Because we now know the many ways in which toxins enter our body, we should not be discouraged. Please remember, eleven years ago I was so ill that both my family and my doctor believed I had only a short time to live. Fortunately, I met Jesus who arranged for a Counselor called the Holy

Spirit to take up residence within me. We spent a lot of time talking about my health problems. From those many hours spent with the Counselor, combined with the many hours of reading medical books, I adopted and began following The Four Basic Principles for "Getting Well." Principle #1 in Chapter 12 of this book states, "All toxins and toxic heavy metals must be removed from your body before healing can take place." This is what I did:

1. I selected a new-type medical doctor, and because of his advanced training, he knew how to test for and remove the accumulation of toxins and toxic heavy metals from my body that was making me seriously ill.

2. As my new-type medical doctor removed the toxins from my body, he and his staff helped me select a more healthy diet prepared from fresh organic fruits, vegetables, dairy products, and safe meats. To complete my nutritional needs, my doctor prescribed an assortment of vitamins and minerals, determined by laboratory testing of my body's needs.

3. I admitted to myself I did not have the inner-strength needed to accept the responsibility to make the medical decisions necessary to proceed along this new path of "Getting Well." By joining Bible Study Fellowship, a well-organized weekly Bible study class that required reading and meditating on scriptures each day, and during five years of study, I gained that inner-strength needed to get completely well.

4. As I continued daily exercise, I found that exercise not only participated in the removal of toxins from my body, but also released a high level of energy and a relaxed feeling of confidence that accompanied me throughout each day.

As a result, "Getting Well" became one of the most exciting and rewarding events of my life!

Now that you are aware of and understand toxins, in the next chapter, "Why Food Supplements Are Necessary," you will learn how, after detoxification, I used vitamin and mineral food supplements as a tool to build my body back to a wonderful state of wellness.

Doctor's Commentary

Wayne makes an important observation—that toxins accumulated in the body over time do lead to myriad medical complications. Seemingly unrelated clinical diagnoses, such as in Wayne's history of atrial fibrillation and abnormal heart rhythm, are common examples. I remember several years ago attending a medical lecture by a cardiologist, who was a board-certified electrophysiologist—a specialist in diagnosing and treating heart electrical/rhythm abnormalities. He stated that, in all of his years of experience, atrial fibrillation and abnormal heart rhythms were always related to some type of toxin until proven otherwise. I have certainly found this true. In treating patients with atrial fibrillation and abnormal heart rhythm, 100 percent of the time they will have evidence, on provocation testing, of elevated levels of toxic heavy metals, including lead, mercury, cadmium, aluminum, and arsenic. Sometimes, the patients will have several different types of toxic heavy metals that they have accumulated. In addition, not surprisingly, they all tend to feel tired and exhausted with a litany of additional vague, seemingly unrelated complaints.

In my opinion, toxins that accumulate in our bodies gradually poison every aspect of normal function, resulting in the body deviating dramatically from its health potential. However, it is rare to find physicians experienced in addressing the toxin issue. Many healthcare providers, such as dentists, will scoff at the idea that toxins, such as heavy metals in the body, would pose such significant complications. Ideally, our bodies should be capable of excreting and eliminating micro-amounts of biological toxins. Our internal biochemistry on an ongoing basis throughout the day should constantly destroy accumulated and self-generated toxins and remove them from the body. Some individuals are less efficient at this process than others. Additionally, the United States and other parts of the world face greater challenges with environmental exposures to toxins from our water, air, and foods. We do not have the same scope of governmental regulations that citizens of other countries enjoy. Therefore, we have much higher inclusions of food additives.

I had heard the statement that, if we really had a government of, by, and for the people, then we would have clean air to breathe, clean water to drink, and an unadulterated food supply. However, as is well known and frequently the case, politics and big business, i.e., profit margin, generally are the main forces for maintaining the status quo. Other countries, such as France, have much fewer chemical additives in their food supplies. I have seen a number of patients, including my wife, who have a tendency to develop allergy symptoms by consuming grain-derived products in our country, experience absolutely no complications or symptoms when consuming products made in other countries that are not using genetically modified grains. As most people will argue, organic, chemical-free food products frankly taste better. Remember Wayne's quote, "If you do not recognize the name of the ingredient on a label, it is likely that your immune system will not either." As pointed out, testing, if done, is generally minimal and tends to be limited to laboratory rodents, bacteria, or different mammals to test, under controlled conditions. It is often difficult with simplistic testing to really predict with any degree of accuracy what the long-term human health complications may be after years of consumption. And testing is usually done in an unrealistic manner. As Wayne cleverly pointed out, lab animals do not have potentially toxic, metal dental fillings, and they are not generally fed the standard American diet of high sugar and a nutrient-depleted food supply.

As a matter of fact, many "veterinary grade animal chows" are actually much more nutrient-dense in trace minerals and other health-providing compounds than our prepared supermarket food. Even compounds, such as trans-fatty acids and many others, have been found in recent years to increase risk of heart disease and other abnormalities. Unfortunately, the symptoms of this toxic accumulation tend to be rather vague and often seemingly unrelated to each other, as described by any standard medical textbook. For that reason, patients are often tossed into a medical experience and unable to acquire a definitive diagnosis or clinical understanding through conventional testing. More often than not—especially in our HMO-adopted medical delivery system—the patient is likely to be handed a prescription for an antidepressant, since the doctor often feels that the real problem is "all in their head." The patient who lives in his or her body every day knows with much greater precision than any healthcare provider precisely what is going on, and that they do not feel well.

Unfortunately, finding an open-minded, comprehensive, and holistically focused healthcare provider can be a challenge. It takes the initiative and research of an exceptional patient, such as Wayne, to steadfastly search out and find a medical advocate who can help to gradually unravel complex symptoms. Using advanced medical testing to ascertain what types of biochemical anomalies may be present and what types of toxic compounds may be present is paramount. Besides toxic air, water, and food products, one must also consider the environment. The so-called sick building syndrome is, in my experience, a relatively common one and generally occurs in two variations: new buildings that have a plethora of potentially toxic chemical compounds used in adhesives, carpeting, framing, wallboard, and so on that gradually leeches into the air and is inhaled by the inhabitants. Second, older buildings, many of which accumulate problem areas of moisture retention, tend to develop molds and hence numerous mycotoxins that can poison healthy bodies. In addition, building compounds that may have been used in the past, such as asbestos, are toxic. Common office equipment, such as copiers, printers, and computers, are also pervasive. Stray electromagnetic radiations that emanate from computers and other electrical systems, including fluorescent lights, can aggravate symptoms. I have seen many patients who become symptomatic upon exposure to the radiation from computer systems and ultraviolet lights. In essence, after consulting with several thousand patients, I have come to the humble conclusion that most people at some point in their lives would do themselves a great service by undergoing a detailed analysis of toxin accumulation and metabolic capacity, and then having them removed through a medically supervised detoxification process. I think that, if every person underwent this procedure, it would dramatically diminish the likelihood of acquiring chronic illness in the future.

—Dale Guyer, M.D.

Chapter Seventeen
Why Food Supplements Are Necessary

In 1954, age twenty-two, at Gary Air Force Base in San Marcos, Texas, while taking pilot training, I told the flight surgeon that my twenty-year-old wife Betty was supplementing her and our one-year-old daughter's diet with vitamins and minerals. I asked if I should be taking them, too. He not only forbade me taking any, but also suggested that Cindy, our daughter, might be damaged from what he thought was a harmful overdose of nourishment for her age.

In 1970, at age thirty-eight, when I was diagnosed with high blood pressure, I informed my doctor that I had four healthy kids whom my wife insisted take, along with her, a daily assortment of vitamins and minerals. Since all were very healthy, and I was ill and the only one on drugs, I asked, "Should I be taking food supplements, too?" I will never forget how he laughed about how unwise it was to use a tight family budget like we had for such foolishness.

I didn't know whom to believe, my wife Betty who gleaned her information mainly from women's magazines and mail-order books on health or several medical doctors I met who each insisted that the only vitamins and minerals the human body needed were provided from well-balanced meals. Confused, I borrowed a 1,500-page doctor's handbook on nutrition from Dr. Walter Able, a partner of mine in our truck service business whom I mentioned in Chapter 8.

This doctor's nutritional handbook was set up so that a physician could reference by illness the foods to avoid and the foods to eat to help the patient get well from the ailment the doctor diagnosed. Over the next three months, I read the 1,500 pages. I was amazed how smart medical doctors seemed to be about the proper nutrition needed by the human body, that is, until I returned the book to Dr. Able. He asked, "How much of the book did you read?" I replied, "All 1,500 pages." My answer caused Dr. Able to say, "Congratulations, you now know about ten times more about nutrition than the average family-practice medical doctor." I was both shocked and disappointed and said so. Dr. Able admitted he had not read the nutritional manual all the way through like I had and then outlined in about five minutes the small amount of nutritional training he had received in medical school. A year went by, and I still did not get in the habit of taking vitamins and minerals like Betty and our four kids were doing.

On a Saturday morning in March 1970, I received a call from a Texaco station owner I knew. He said that a medical doctor driving a late-model Chrysler New Yorker had pulled off Interstate 465 with an overheated engine. Since my friend knew we were always open on Saturday, he wanted to know if we could fix the overheating problem. I said, "Sure, send the doctor by, and we will take care of his problem."

During the four hours it took two of my mechanics to repair the New Yorker, the doctor introduced himself as Dr. Brady, a research medical doctor with the American Tobacco Institute. He spent about half his time heading up a medical research group in Washington, D.C., looking for ways to solve health problems created by smoking. His remaining time was spent testifying before Congress or holding lectures around the country sharing with health organizations what his research group was learning.

While we waited, I began asking Dr. Brady a lot of questions. I soon learned that his approach to protecting a smoker's health was the liberal use of vitamins and minerals, especially very large doses of vitamin C. I told him about my wife's decision, over our family doctor's objections, to serve daily vitamins and minerals to herself and our four children, but explained that I was following my doctor's advice and not taking them.

Dr. Brady suggested I get on Betty's plan, too, just like the rest of the family. On our shop's coffeepot table, the doctor spotted an empty two-pound coffee can, which he filled with ascorbic acid (vitamin C) powder from what I would judge to be a 50-lb bag that came from the trunk of his Chrysler. "Here," he said, "take this home to your wife and ask her to put a big teaspoon-full on everybody's cereal every morning. Have everyone take a good multivitamin, and with the other vitamins and minerals your wife is using, you will be on your way toward raising a healthy family." Betty was glad to receive all that free vitamin C, and I started taking it every morning, as well. I didn't take the multivitamin because I was on high blood pressure medicine and mild nerve medicines; my doctor feared drug interaction. Because I continued on high-blood-pressure and other medicines for the next twenty-three years, I did not take vitamins and minerals for fear of an interaction with the various medicines I was taking.

Twenty-Three Years Later, in 1993

I was sixty-one years old, had sold my share of the truck service and parts business, and was retired, but felt weak and ill. About one year later, I was rushed to emergency and came very close to dying. After one year of conventional medical treatment, I was in many ways worse off. I certainly was not getting better.

Then, while continuing to receive conventional medical treatment every week at the hospital, I began additional treatments by paying from my own pocket a medical doctor with the training to remove the toxins and heavy metals from my toxic body along with prescribing vitamins and minerals he tested to determine what my body needed to get well. This doctor also said that the warning I had received that vitamins and minerals would react in a harmful way with drugs was false information provided by an incompetent M.D. There are a few exceptions, he admitted, that will interact, but the drug manufacturer does a good job informing doctors in those rare cases when its drugs interact with certain food supplements, and it is the medical doctor's responsibility to warn the patient at the time the drug is prescribed.

Eighteen months after starting to use vitamins and minerals, my illness symptoms were gone, I felt great, and I declared my health greatly improved. Although I continued to take prescription drugs along with a long list of vitamins and minerals, not once did I have any form of a drug interaction. After eighteen more months of nutritional therapy, I was completely well, and I no longer needed any drugs, including high-blood-pressure medicine I had taken for twenty-six years. The date was January 1997.

I wrote a letter to my family and friends telling them about being well again. Since 1997, I have a checkup with Dr. Guyer each six months, and he adjusts my nutritional plan if needed. Today at age seventy-two, I am without aches or pains, produce a perfect EKG, exercise every day, and can pass all blood profile tests, except for glucose, which we continue to work on and improve. Actually, all I do to maintain good health is follow The Four Basic Principles for "Getting Well" presented in Chapter 12.

What Are Food Supplements All About?

This is the same question I asked myself in January 1995, at age sixty-three, when for the first time in my life I began taking mega-doses of certain vitamins and minerals. They were prescribed by my new-type medical doctor whom I selected as I grasped for a flimsy straw representing my last hope of "Getting Well."

Within ninety days of beginning chelation detoxification and nutritional therapy, my body notified my logical mind that I was on my way to "Getting Well." My logical mind, filled with over forty years of medical doctors' advice proclaiming that vitamin and mineral supplements were not recommended for good health, became terribly confused, so I headed back to the library and bookstores to gain some more knowledge.

In the Year 1900, Medical Scientists Were Very Confident about Their Knowledge

Medical science many centuries ago began to understand and record the relationship between minerals and good health. It could identify the same minerals in the earth with those found in plants, animals, and humans. This scientific understanding seemed correct in 1900 and complete because it coincided with God's Word that He had created man "from the dust of the ground." With this mineral knowledge, doctors were confident they knew the basic ingredients of life needed to cure most illnesses.

Over the years, however, the lists have grown, and we now know that our body needs eighty-four minerals for good health, of which twenty-two are deemed essential. If there is a shortage of one or more, the balance of the body's systems can be thrown off. Some scientists view minerals like dominoes standing on-end. If one falls down, it often knocks down the effectiveness of several other minerals around it, causing a greater health problem than normally expected.

Year 1912: The Announcement of Vitamins Shakes Up Medical Scientists

In addition to minerals, scientists always observed other substances, but until 1912 didn't have a clue what they were. A Polish biochemist named Casimir Funk coined the word *vitamine*. Funk believed there was only one substance that supported life in addition to minerals. He named the substance by combining the Latin word *vita* meaning *life* with *amine* because he thought the substance contained nitrogen.

Our American scientists, who believed they were the world's leading life-science researchers, were caught off-guard and embarrassed that a foreign scientist had scooped them. Quickly they expanded their mineral research to include the substance the Polish biochemist called *vitamine*.

Almost immediately, the U.S. scientists informed the Polish biochemist that he was wrong. The substance he named *vitamine* was not a single substance as he said, but was a collection of many different substances, and the fact that the substance contained nitrogen was not important, and therefore the "e" was being dropped from the name. As a result, these *life*-supporting substances were renamed *vitamins*.

The American scientists laid out an aggressive program of research to identify the various life-supporting substances. They decided to use the alphabet letters to name each vitamin as they made positive identification. It wasn't long until the hardworking scientists located at various colleges, medical schools, and university research laboratories announced names for the life substances all the way from vitamin A to vitamin K. "We see it differently," voiced the scientists in the rest of the world who also were working as hard as the American scientists. Vitamins F, G, H, I, and J, they said, are not separate substances; instead they are different forms of vitamin B. The U.S. scientists agreed, and that is how B-1, B-2, B-3, B-5, and B-6 vitamins were created, leaving room for future discoveries all the way to vitamin B-12. At that time, some U.S. scientists wanted to move vitamin K back and rename it vitamin G or H, but the Dutch in Europe objected because vitamin K is necessary for blood coagulation, and the Dutch spell coagulation beginning with a "K."

First Fifty Years of Vitamin Research

Over the next fifty years ending in 1962, medical research scientists throughout the world conducted studies to learn the involvement and importance of each vitamin concerning our health. While doing this, they began to discover additional important trace minerals, various acids, amino acids, enzymes, co-enzymes, free-radical actions, natural chemicals, and electrical actions that caused reactions so complex that it seemed impossible for even the smartest group of scientists to understand how all this worked together to keep the human body healthy. Medical schools didn't attempt to teach these complex sciences to medical students. Their attitude was that vitamins and minerals are associated with what people eat, and practicing medicine has to do with the treatment of diseases, bacteria, viruses, infections, and surgery to repair damage from disease or accidents. Instead, most medical schools and medical doctors seemed to have spent their time during this first fifty years working with drug companies developing new drugs that produced immediate fast relief of illness symptoms. By 1962, both doctors and patients were growing fond of these immediate-relief drugs, and demanded more.

World War II: A Big Boost to Drug Company Growth

Prior to World War II, many prescriptions for medicines written by our medical doctors were compounded and prepared for the patient from a long list of basic natural and chemical ingredients made available to local pharmacists. Drug companies in the U.S. were special small operations supplying some patent medicines but also the basic ingredients to local pharmacists for making drugs. In fact, after the war began in

1941, frontline U.S. Army doctors could not obtain penicillin although Alexander Fleming had discovered it in 1928 while working at St. Mary's Hospital in London.

Small amounts were being made in England, but the British Army was consuming all being produced. While U.S. soldiers were dying unnecessarily with out-of-control infections during their first year in combat, the United States Congress had to ask the Rockefeller Foundation to build a penicillin factory to stop the unnecessary dying of our young men. Rockefeller quickly conscripted a brewery into penicillin production. However, by the end of the war, Glaxo, located in England, was the largest manufacturer of penicillin.

Drug companies expanded quickly to serve the needs of combat soldiers in Europe and the tropical islands of the war with Japan. Many of the medicines drug companies began producing were medicines formally made by local druggists. By the end of World War II in 1945, drug companies had productized existing medicines, created many new drugs, and patented most of them. After the war, these small drug companies found themselves much larger and in complete control of most prescription drug compounds, but the FDA did not allow patenting of either vitamins or minerals.

After the war, both consumers and the doctors were enthusiastic about all the new medicines developed during the war and made available with a simple prescription.

As a result, drug companies began developing closer relationships with large universities that had medical schools by offering cash research grants in exchange for their participation in drug research. This close relationship caused most medical schools to allocate more classroom time for teaching medical students to treat illness symptoms with drugs. It appears that medical schools chose to teach the use of drugs and stayed basically away from preventive medicine, probably because they knew that it would involve the complexities of nutrition and the use of vitamins and minerals to prevent illness. The task of teaching nutrition properly would add an additional two years to a student doctor's curriculum.

My studies of medical history caused me to conclude the AMA, the trade union for doctors, supported the medical schools' position not to teach the prescribing of vitamins and minerals because it believed that the consumer would pay more money to a doctor who got quick results calming illness symptoms with fast-acting drugs, compared with the slow pace of curing a patient by addressing the cause of the illness and then treating with slow-acting vitamins and minerals combined with patient lifestyle changes.

I Know Their Thinking, Because I Have Experienced It

Why medical doctors do not prescribe vitamins and minerals was verified by a face-to-face conversation I had with my cardiologist in 1994. I told my cardiologist that I read in the newspaper that sixty-five percent of all cardiologists surveyed take vitamin E every day and that I wanted to know if he took vitamin E. He said he took it every day. I replied that I had been his patient for almost a year and wanted to know why he hadn't prescribed vitamin E to help me.

He folded his arms, sat down beside me, and said, in a friendly voice, that there were several reasons:

#1 He did not have training in the use of vitamins and minerals for treating heart disease.

#2 He had agreed with his insurance company to prescribe only heart treatments recommended by the AMA, which authorizes treatments approved by the FDA, and the FDA had not accepted any long-term scientific studies of vitamin E as a valid treatment for heart disease that he was aware of.

#3 He then gave me an example by saying that, if he scheduled me for an angioplasty balloon treatment, it would take maybe two hours, and then he could bill my insurance company about $10,000-15,000, and they would pay it quickly. If he scheduled me for open-heart coronary bypass surgery, taking five hours, he could bill my insurance company around $50,000 on up, and they would pay that quickly, too. But, if he spent two hours teaching me how to use vitamins and minerals to treat my heart disease, he could bill my insurance company at the very most $150.

"If you were my business advisor," he asked, "where would you recommend I spend most of my time?" I told him that I understood. I then asked him to refer me to a medical doctor who had learned at medical school how to treat heart disease with vitamins and minerals, and he replied that he did not know of a doctor who had that type of training in medical school.

Later, I told this story confidentially to another medical doctor who smiled and said, "If you want to know what medical treatments will be recommended by the AMA in the future, **just follow the money trail**." I interpreted that to mean that treatments that pay the most money for the time spent by the doctor will be the recommended treatments we will receive.

The lesson I have learned over the past thirty-eight years while being treated by a variety of medical doctors is that the primary reason most medical schools do not teach the prescription of vitamins and minerals as a way to prevent or cure disease is that there is no money in it for the medical doctor. Insurance companies will not pay for preventive medicine, and as a result doctors cannot bill services involving nutritional advice prescribing vitamins and minerals. Another reason is that large drug companies cannot file for patents on vitamins and minerals, so, again, there is no big money in it for drug companies either.

Years 1960 to 1970 Were Big Decision Years for Vitamins and Minerals

The NIH announced that heart disease was the number-one killer of men and asked for a national effort to determine why. Quickly, two opposing viewpoints developed as to the cause.

The American Heart Association (AHA), along with most cardiologists, believed that high-fat diets along with high cholesterol levels in the blood were causing plaque buildup in the arteries leading to heart disease and, often, instant death. When the FDA asked them to prove that cholesterol was the cause, they could not prove it scientifically. However, the open-heart bypass surgeries Dr. Michael E. DeBakey was doing indicated to him that cholesterol and other animal fats were the primary cause of the plaque blockage leading to serious heart disease and unexpected fatal heart attacks.

The large majority of the scientific world studying nutrition opposed the support of cholesterol as the cause for heart disease. Some of their proof was the fact that, prior to year 1900, heart disease was not a health problem. It barely existed, and the traditional diet was animal fat and meat as the centerpiece of the family's three daily meals. Nutritional researchers insisted that lack of daily exercise and the eating of processed foods with low nutritional values caused the increase in heart disease. Also, they offered the fact that fifty percent of the people who drop dead from a heart attack had cholesterol levels above 200 and fifty percent had cholesterol levels below 200, proving that your cholesterol level is not the controlling factor.

Dr. Weston A. Price had for thirty years traveled the world and studied the healthiest people. He found that disease of any type was almost nonexistent in some societies because they got plenty of exercise, digested a lot of products made from milk, and ate a traditional diet of homegrown fruits and vegetables seasoned with animal fats along with a variety of meat served three times each day. These healthy people had cholesterol levels at 240 to 350, but had very low inflammation levels and almost no heart disease or cancer. Dr. Price recorded the findings of his studies in his book *Nutrition & Physical Degeneration*, published in 1970.

During approximately this same period, Dr. Linus Pauling, a world-renowned chemist, genius, and double-Nobel Prize winner, made the following health claim: "Heart disease can be successfully treated without surgery or prescription medications leading to its quick reversal." He was talking about addressing heart disease with nutrition with a traditional diet, supplemented with high levels of vitamins and minerals. He was known as a specialist prescribing mega-doses of vitamin C. When Dr. Pauling became famous for his nutritional research, immediately the large drug companies along with the AMA, the union for medical doctors, launched personal attacks concerning his credibility. Some die-hard, closed-minded "old fogy" M.D.s continue these attacks even today, but Dr. Pauling won the final debate. He had the privilege of outliving most of the medical doctors and drug company executives opposing him those many years. While still taking his recommended daily dosage of 12,000mg of vitamin C, he died at age ninety-four.

Another medical doctor, Dr. Kilmer McCully, also insisted that heart disease was not caused by high cholesterol. Dr. McCully graduated from the Harvard Medical School with a reputation for distinguished scientific and clinical abilities that won him a Harvard Medical School professorship spanning fourteen years. In 1969, Dr. McCully shocked the medical world when he questioned the cholesterol theory of heart disease. His research at Harvard Medical School and Massachusetts General Hospital concluded that a high *homocystine* level would damage cells and tissues of the arteries, and that cholesterol would collect over the damaged areas in an attempt to heal the artery damage. If the patient's homocystine level remained high over time, the artery would experience new damage causing the buildup of cholesterol to grow and eventually block the coronary artery, resulting in a heart attack. A high homocystine level, he said, "was created by a deficiency in folic acid, vitamin B-6, and vitamin B-12." Dr. McCully challenged the widespread belief that risk for atherosclerosis and heart attack is caused by diets high in fat and cholesterol. He compiled his work in a book, *The Heart Revolution*.

Immediately, Dr. McCully's announcement received great praise from much of the world, but not from the United States. Drug companies teamed up with the AHA and, with the support of the AMA, the trade union for medical doctors, launched a series of personal attacks on Dr. McCully and his work. These attacks were so effective that eventually Federal research funds supporting Dr. McCully's work at Harvard were cut off, and as a result the Harvard Board of Directors immediately fired Dr. McCully.

For about two years, Dr. McCully could not find work because he had been labeled by the medical industry as an outlaw scientist who wasted good Federal research dollars doing frivolous, unimportant work. Eventually, Dr. McCully landed a job paying far less money at the Veterans Administration Hospital in Providence, Rhode Island, where he continues his research today.

I met Dr. McCully and spoke to him for a moment in May 2003. I told him that, just a month before in April, I had had my annual vascular system checkup, and that my cardiologist mentioned that he now tests for homocystine levels because, as he said, "It has been recently discovered that high homocystine levels play an important role in heart disease." My cardiologist continued by saying, "I am surprised yours are nice and low."

"They are low," I told Dr. McCully, "because my advanced medical doctor, Dr. Guyer, prescribes the vitamins and minerals needed to keep them low." I asked Dr. McCully if he was surprised that my cardiologist, for the first time, tested my homocystine level.

He said, "No, they are beginning to recognize my work."

You would have expected Dr. McCully to be bitter about the shabby way in which the drug companies, the medical doctors' AMA union, the FDA, our NIH, and Harvard Medical School have treated him all these years, but he wasn't. He was very gracious and seemed pleased that heart patients could now at last benefit from his dedicated work. However, that same night as I sat in my Washington, D.C., hotel room alone, I grew somewhat saddened thinking about all the millions of heart patients over the years whose lives were shortened because their medical doctors refused to test their homocystine levels and treat them with vitamins and minerals like Dr. McCully had recommended for the past thirty-plus years.

Why Drug Companies and the Medical Industry Attack Vitamins and Minerals

It is my opinion that the reason all these drug companies and medical people were so opposed to what Drs. Weston Price, Linus Pauling, and Kilmer McCully had to say about curing heart disease was because drugs were not involved. These three research doctors showed that most heart disease could be cured simply with a good traditional diet supplemented with vitamins and minerals combined with moderate exercise. By the mid-1970s, drug companies had bet their future by investing billions of dollars into new heart drugs, including cholesterol-lowering drugs, and if the general public believed that good nutrition supported by vitamins and minerals could treat and prevent heart disease then the expected big profits of the future for drug companies would not happen. Medical schools and the union for medical doctors, the AMA, were worried because the fast-anticipated dollars to be made by medical doctors seeing a high volume of patients and writing drug prescriptions would not develop either. The medical doctors themselves were really worried because they knew that if proper nutrition supported by prescribing vitamins and minerals was the treatment of the future then they would have to go back to medical school for two additional years of training.

Procter & Gamble and Other Big Food-Processing Companies Got Involved

While the medical industry was debating whether cholesterol along with other animal fats was the cause of heart disease and fatal heart attacks, the giant food-processing companies spotted a great opportunity to increase sales and make a lot of money. They began to saturate TV commercials with ads announcing that the NIH reports that heart disease and unexpected fatal heart attacks is now the number-one killer of men. These long ads would then explain that the AHA believed that the cause for heart disease is high cholesterol and other animal fats forming plaque resulting in blocked blood flow to the heart. (The ads did not reveal that the FDA had no accepted studies showing this to be true.) These TV ads stated that the AHA recommended we take drastic and immediate action by switching to low- or zero-cholesterol food products.

In just a few months, housewives wanting to protect and save their husbands began switching away from animal fats to vegetable oils. Men like me started paying attention to these TV ads and without consulting anyone began planning major changes to our diet. Sales of butter and other dairy products nose-dived. Beef and pork sales plummeted. Poultry and seafood sales increased while anything labeled sugar-free, fat-free, or cholesterol-free quickly became the product of choice. There was little concern about the lack of nutritional content in these new foods.

In less than two years, these food company ads along with numerous magazine articles convinced most Americans, including me, that cholesterol and animal fat were the cause of heart disease resulting in sudden fatal heart attacks. The ads were not based on FDA-approved research; however, during the 1960s when these food company ads began, we were not informed by the FDA or the NIH that ongoing scientific studies had not shown cholesterol to be the cause of heart disease and that the ads were based on "a theory," not good medical science.

Once the American people were convinced their high cholesterol level was causing heart disease, other research showing that poor diet, lacking in vitamins and minerals, was the cause, fell on deaf ears. This produced a perfect answer for medical doctors who were groping for the cause of heart disease. When confronted with explaining why a patient had developed heart disease, the doctor could now point his or her finger at the patient and say, "It's your high cholesterol that is causing the problem." The patient, thinking it was his or her own fault, submitted to any treatment the doctor recommended. Expensive drugs, expensive tests, and expensive surgical procedures became the order of normal treatment. Doctors found themselves in control of their patients' billfolds and health insurance funds. To support this new opportunity of exploiting cholesterol as the cause for heart disease, most hospitals expanded by announcing a new larger cardiac department every few years.

Even without scientific evidence that cholesterol caused heart disease, drug companies began developing a long list of new expensive drugs to treat heart disease including new statin drugs like Lipitor® to lower our blood cholesterol level. No one informed us that cholesterol was our friend and performed forty-eight essential functions in our body to keep us healthy. However, there were warnings about the bad health effects of lowering cholesterol from normal levels. Uffe Ravnskov, M.D., Ph.D., warns in his book *The Cholesterol Myth* that, when your normal healthy cholesterol level of 240 is forced down to 160, your inflammation level in the blood increases six times, and your risk for developing cancer increases five-fold. This doctor/researcher also reports that high homocystine levels plus the lack of a proper level of vitamins and minerals in our diet sets the stage for heart disease, not high cholesterol levels.

How Did Most People React to the News That Cholesterol Is the Cause of Heart Disease?

Most people reacted like me. I greatly reduced my intake of red meat and dairy products, increased my intake of vegetables and fruit, switched from butter to margarine made from corn oil, and started consuming processed foods labeled "no sugar," "low fat," and "zero cholesterol." Beginning in 1967, I remained on this diet for twenty-eight years and did not supplement it with vitamins and minerals. My first cholesterol test was 144. My young doctor said I was safe from heart disease if I could maintain levels below 200 all my life. I ate this high-carbohydrate, low-fat diet for twenty-eight years. I had my blood cholesterol checked regularly over those years. At no time did it reach 180. I felt very safe from heart disease.

You can image my surprise when twenty-five years later in 1993, at 3:30 A.M. on September the 10th, I entered the hospital emergency room with great stress in my chest on the verge of having a heart attack. My cholesterol level that morning in emergency tested 160. Three weeks later at my first follow-up office visit, my cardiologist insisted I lower my cholesterol even more, so I went on a vegetarian diet and a month later it was 130. I stayed below 130 for the next two years. You can also image my surprise when they told me I had a large amount of calcified plaque in my coronary arteries. Two years later, tests showed that the calcification in my arteries was continuing to grow and weaken my heart even more although I had maintained my cholesterol levels below 130. I thought I had done everything right over the years, but, obviously, following my doctor's advice turned out to be the wrong thing to do.

How I Recovered

Fortunately in 1995 I became a patient of a complementary medicine doctor who quickly recognized that the high-carbohydrate, low-fat diet I had been eating for the past twenty-eight years was not supplying my body with all the vitamins and minerals needed to stay healthy. I developed heart disease due to a high homocystine level and inflammation that combined with it to create free-radical damage. My high homocystines, my new doctor said, were caused by insufficient levels of the B-vitamins, and maintaining a too-low cholesterol level over time caused the inflammation. This doctor tested my body's nutritional needs, changed my diet to a balanced protein traditional diet with meat, and then added certain vitamins and minerals, and today my heart is healthy again.

What Should You Do?

The answer is, I don't know. You must make that decision yourself. Probably your typical conventional family practice medical doctor cannot help you, because most medical schools do not teach improved nutrition using vitamins and minerals as a treatment for "Getting Well." If I were sick today like some of you, I would go back and read Chapter 15, "Selecting a New-Type Medical Doctor," and then make a selection and follow my new doctor's advice for "Getting Well."

If, instead, you are healthy and want to learn how to prevent disease from happening in your body, then you must reprogram your mind to a new way of thinking by changing your belief system that you, not your doctor, are responsible for your own health. When you recognize that "practicing medicine" is what doctors do while waiting for the patient's body to "heal itself," then you are on your way.

If I could roll back the clock thirty-five years and with what I know now, it is certain I could have prevented my heart disease from developing by following The Four Basic Principles for "Getting Well," presented in Chapter 12. Today, if I were thirty-five years younger, completely healthy, but with a preventive medicine goal of avoiding disease, here is what I would do:

1. I would buy the book *Toxic Relief*, written by a Florida doctor, Don Colbert, M.D. Doctor Colbert graduated from the Oral Roberts School of Medicine in Tulsa and completed his internship and residency with Florida Hospital in Orlando. He is board-certified for family practice and has extensive training in nutritional medicine. He believes like me that toxins must be removed from our body before nutrition can be properly absorbed. His book *Toxic Relief* teaches why toxins need to be removed from our body and how to remove them yourself at home. Also, his book teaches how toxins get in our body and how to recognize when action should be taken to remove them. Dr. Colbert's clinic is located in Longwood, Florida. His telephone number is 407-331-7007, and his Web site is www.drcolbert.com. This book should help accomplish The First Basic Principle for "Getting Well."

2. I would buy the book *Prescriptions for Nutritional Healing*, written by Phyllis A. Balch, CNC, a certified nutritionist, and James F. Balch, M.D., a medical doctor. The book states, "This is a comprehensive in-home guide that will help you achieve and maintain the highest level of health and fitness through careful dietary planning and nutritional supplementation. Even if you are free from so-called disorders, you will benefit from this book because it gives advice on how to achieve optimum health, build up your immune system, and increase your energy level." Having this book at your fingertips will help you achieve The Second Basic Principle for "Getting Well."

3. I would read Dr. Bernie S. Siegel's famous book *Love, Medicine & Miracles* and would then counsel with my local church pastor and ask advice for nurturing the spiritual side of healing strength that lives within us. Most churches maintain a reference library supporting the pastor's guidance program. In my case, I joined

Bible Study Fellowship, a group of 400 men who met weekly and discussed our Bible lesson we studied and prepared on our own during the week. With God's strength within me, I developed into an "exceptional patient" capable of carrying out The Four Basic Principles for "Getting Well."

4. I would join a local fitness club that supplies to its members personal trainers who can teach the proper way to exercise. Most people stop exercising because they never learned to exercise properly and end up abusing their body. Proper exercise caresses your body and is joyful. Exercise helps remove toxins from our body and acts as a catalyst to create the maximum benefit from our nutrition and food supplements. Before starting any exercise program, discuss it with your primary-care physician and obtain the okay for you to carry out this Fourth Basic Principle for "Getting Well."

Why You Must Supplement Your Diet with Vitamins and Minerals

When your great-great-grandparents cleared the trees from their land and planted their first garden, the soil was virgin and contained most of the eighty-four minerals they needed for good health. The only fertilizer they had available was the composted manure from their cattle and horses. They were, from the very beginning, organic farmers. The food they ate was the most nutritious possible and provided all the vitamins and minerals they needed. After planting the land each year for forty years, they passed the land to the next generation, your great-grandparents. After forty years of planting and harvesting, the food grown by your great-grandparents no longer contained all of the eighty-four minerals needed for good health. Some minerals were depleted in the soil, and as a result their food contained less vitamins and minerals. By the time your grandparents began growing food from the same land, the topsoil had been planted over eighty consecutive years. The vitamins and minerals available to you or your parents were reduced even more. Fortunately, most of our parents or us grew up healthy because vitamins and minerals are available from many sources. If, as children, you grew up drinking untreated well water or fresh spring water, ate fresh fruits and vegetables from your garden, and ate grass-fed beef, pork, and poultry, your nutritional requirements were most likely marginally adequate.

But, today and for the past forty years, nutrition available to us from the food we eat has been greatly reduced. Minerals that are absorbed into the plants we eat come from the topsoil. Originally when our great-great-grandparents cleared the land and planted their first crops in the virgin topsoil, nearly all eighty-four minerals were available from the soil. Today, after planting more than 100 years of consecutive crops, most of our farmland is barren and contains only a few of the eighty-four minerals we need for good health.

True, the fruits and vegetables we buy from the supermarket look nutritious, but that is not necessarily true. Modern agriculture has developed ways to grow food with chemicals that make them appear to be loaded with vitamins and minerals. However, laboratory testing does not confirm that the expected nutrition level is present. There are only three minerals fed into a plant by chemical fertilizers, and the remainder of the minerals in the fruits and vegetables must be absorbed from the farm-field topsoil. The big problem is we have never learned to man-make enough new topsoil to allow for the loss experienced each year.

If the required vitamins and minerals are not at the required level in our food, then we are eating "hollow calories" high in carbohydrates that give us high glucose levels that produce short-term energy, but lack the vitamins and minerals needed to keep our vital organs healthy on the long term. I have found that to stay healthy we have no choice but to supplement our diet with vitamins and minerals.

A Test That Proves That All Food Is Not Nutritious

In 1996, our NIH selected 400 R.N.s who did not like broccoli and asked them not to eat broccoli for the next five years. At the same time, they selected 400 additional R.N.s who liked broccoli and asked them to eat broccoli at least twice-per-week for the next five years. At the end of the five-year test period, the NIH announced that the group that included broccoli in its diet cut its risk for breast cancer by a full twenty percent. The natural chemical found in broccoli that will fight cancer is *sulforaphane*, discovered by Johns Hopkins researchers. Newspapers from around the world carried this NIH announcement.

Six months later, the NIH was forced to modify its claim that eating broccoli could cut the risk of cancer in women. It seems that an experienced nutritional researcher, after reading the broccoli/cancer story, visited his local market and purchased a fresh head of broccoli at ten different supermarkets and then tested each head for the level of sulforaphane. All ten heads appeared equally fresh and nutritious. However, two of the heads of broccoli tested at a normal, expected high level of sulforaphane, and two of the heads had zero detectable sulforaphane. The other six heads of broccoli tested with varying amounts below the standards expected of sulforaphane.

Of course the reason the sulforaphane varied so much was because each of the ten heads of broccoli grew in different topsoil containing a varying amount of minerals. If a plant cannot absorb the needed minerals, it cannot produce a healthy level of sulforaphane, and unfortunately you cannot determine the nutritional level by just looking at the broccoli head. So in my opinion it is wise to play it safe and supplement one's diet with vitamins and minerals.

Other Reasons Why We Must Supplement Our Diet with Vitamins and Minerals

Today, we tend to buy food at the supermarket that is processed and packaged conveniently for fast meal preparation. Whether it is a can of baked beans, vegetable or chicken noodle soup, frozen vegetables or frozen TV dinners, cake mixes, or a box of crackers, the giant international food companies that process and prepare this type of food we eat have three concerns in mind before they consider nutritional value. Their first concern is that they buy their basic ingredients from the lowest-cost source so they can sell at a competitive price while maintaining maximum profits. As a result, the ingredients are often shipped from a great distance. Overseas suppliers are common today, which often accounts for great loss of nutritional value during shipment, before the ingredients arrive for actual processing.

Second, the food processors are concerned about their packaged food looking and tasting good. This is the reason that an assortment of chemical artificial flavoring is added during processing, along with synthetic food coloring, taste enhancers, and other chemical additives.

The food processors' third concern is delayed spoilage and extended shelf life. To accomplish this, they usually add a long list of chemicals with names that you cannot pronounce or identify. Some of our highly processed food today have so many chemicals added it could actually be termed "embalmed." Because of these powerful preservatives, food manufacturers do not have to be concerned about food poisoning or shelf-life dates anymore.

Food manufacturers give little attention to nutrition. Don't take my word for it—read the labels and add up the nutrition listed. You will soon learn that it is impossible to gain enough nutrition from processed foods to absorb the minimum vitamins and minerals needed to stay healthy. In my opinion, we must reinforce our food with supplements to prevent disease.

One of My Favorite Stories

A few years ago a Russian medical student bought several boxes of breakfast cereal made by a U.S. manufacturer that listed several vitamins and minerals added to make the cereal more nutritious. For his class project, he set up three isolated pens with thirty-five laboratory rats in each pen. He fed to the first group a standard mixture of fresh grains he called "rat chow," and his rats lived an average of twelve months. He fed to the second group of thirty-five rats the highly processed "breakfast cereal," and that group lived an average of only three months. He then ground up the cereal boxes, added the amounts of vitamins and minerals listed on the box, and fed this mixture to the third group of rats, which lived an average of six months.

Since laboratory rats are used to forecast reactions in humans, we can make two quick observations: 1) we will live longer if we eat a lot of fresh unprocessed foods free of chemical additives; 2) if you are going to supplement your diet, make sure to buy high-quality vitamins and minerals because it is obvious, based on the results, that the U.S. cereal manufacturer used lower-quality food supplements than the Russian medical student.

How Much Do Medical Doctors Know about Vitamins and Minerals?

Most advice books I have read about nutrition recommend that you ask your family doctor questions you might have about taking vitamins and minerals. There must be legal reasons for everybody to recommend we talk to our family doctor about nutrition, because it certainly, in my opinion, is not based on the average medical doctor's level of nutritional knowledge. In fact, I consider it dangerous to my health to follow nutritional advice from a person with such lack of nutritional training.

Based on my personal experience, it is my opinion that most doctors have very little training in nutrition. To be safe always ask your doctor to show you his or her nutritional certification of training qualifying him or her to give professional nutritional advice before accepting his or her advice. The certified training should total a two-year course of study.

Medical schools are probably aware that their graduates have insufficient nutritional training to give complete nutritional advice. A story I heard makes us aware of the level of nutritional training that most doctors receive. I am not sure of the source, but this is the story: The board of directors of a large East-Coast medical school wondered how much nutritional knowledge its average medical student learned and retained.

To answer its concerns, it sent a computer-generated questionnaire to each doctor who had graduated during the previous five years. Apparently, about half of the doctors receiving the questionnaire gave it to their receptionists to fill out, and about half of the doctors filled out the questionnaire themselves. The computer, after analyzing the results, reported to the board that most medical doctors know a little bit more about nutrition than their receptionists. However, if the receptionist was a member of WeightWatchers, then he or she knew a little bit more about nutrition than the doctor.

I believe that many (male) medical doctors take vitamins and minerals every day because their wives demand they do so, but these same doctors do not recommend them to patients because of doctor peer pressure. After a friend of mine received his third coronary artery angioplasty treatment in six months, his cardiologist asked if there was anything my friend had not told him. My friend said, "Yes, there is one thing. My wife makes me take a large assortment of vitamins and minerals every day. Do you think these supplements might be interfering with my treatments?"

His cardiologist replied, "No, I don't think they are interfering with your treatment, because I have a lot of experience with vitamins and minerals. You see, my wife makes me take a large dose of vitamins and minerals every day, too."

Up-Close and Personal

I hope you are convinced by now that you are not going to get completely well unless you rid your body of toxins, establish a good organic natural food diet, supplement your diet with the exact correct amounts of vitamins and minerals, and then begin a good exercise program. This takes a lot of effort and determination, but I can tell you from personal experience that it is worth it. It is wonderful for me at age seventy-two to be completely free of aches and pains with daily energy matching some men half my age. Working hard each day to restore your health is the second-most gratifying work you will ever do. After you are well, like me, then you will find that the most gratifying work you will ever accomplish is to help others get well! Just like you.

The best way to accomplish "Getting Well" is to have an advanced medicine doctor, like Dr. Guyer, guiding and teaching you about all the complexities that take place in your body during the natural healing process while you are pursuing The Four Basic Principles for "Getting Well," like I did. However, I also studied hard and learned a lot about "Getting Well" on my own.

After you begin your journey in this new world for "Getting Well," you will meet others on the same journey. You will learn a lot from these ill patients, especially their personal stories as to how they grew their faith and became *exceptional patients*.

There are pitfalls too. Believing the advertising claims made by companies and doctors that sell and promote vitamins/minerals and herbs can be a big mistake. I estimate that their advertising claims are at least ninety percent false or self-serving. If all claims for healing were true, cancer, diabetes, and heart disease would have been wiped out years ago. We are so accustomed to major drug company's TV commercials telling us about all the wonderful things their latest fast-acting new and in-vogue "miracle drugs" will do for us that we may get the idea that vitamins and minerals should also have us back ice skating by the weekend too. Some men I know believe that Viagra® gives them so much control that they could actually drive in a NASCAR race just like the TV commercials suggest. But, vitamins and minerals don't work that way.

Vitamins and minerals are not fast-reacting "miracle drugs" acting as standalone treatments. Instead, they are a combination of thirteen vitamins and eighty-four minerals supporting each other and working within our body in harmony with a complex array of natural acids, amino acids, enzymes, co-enzymes, friendly bacteria, and chemical compounds so complex that the world's best medical scientists cannot duplicate or completely understand them.

The fact that we as patients do not understand this process is no reason to believe that each and every nutritional ingredient is not individually very important to our maintaining optimum health. Remove just a few of the eighty-four minerals from our body and some of the remaining minerals become ineffective because of their dependence on each other. Staying healthy depends on never running low on a single vitamin or mineral. The amount of any individual vitamin or mineral that our body requires varies from day to day, so the best policy is to make sure that we have available at all times at least the *Recommended Dietary Allowance* (*RDA*) set by the Food and Nutrition Board of our Federal government. Please remember that the very moment a single vitamin or mineral is depleted, unnecessary illness begins to develop in our body.

When I was ill, I took many times the RDA of most vitamins and minerals. But, you must remember that I had a medical doctor testing my body's needs and prescribing these high dosages. For example, when my body was very toxic, my doctor prescribed 14,000mg of vitamin C daily. I maintained this level for two years. Today, now that my body is relative free of toxins, Dr. Guyer prescribes only 2,000mg of vitamin C daily, just enough to help fight off the new toxins trying to enter my body.

If you don't have a medical doctor like I have to teach and guide your nutritional program, then you must become a serious student and study nutrition yourself. It may not be as difficult as you think. Please don't forget that, by reading a 1,500-page doctor's handbook on nutrition, I learned about ten times more about nutrition than the average family-practice doctor knows. You, too, could quickly pass your family doctor's level of knowledge. But, please be cautious, as it is possible to become toxic on vitamins and minerals.

There are four "fat-soluble" vitamins, and there is a limit to the maximum safe dose you can take. It may vary from person to person. The four fat-soluble vitamins are A, D, E, and K. Being a natural fat-soluble vitamin means that excessive amounts must process out of our body through the blood, and primarily the load on our liver limits this. If our liver is overloaded, then a fat-soluble vitamin may get trapped and become toxic. The remaining nine vitamins, B-1, B-2, B-3, B-5, B-6, B-12, biotin, folic acid, and C, are water soluble, and excessive amounts are usually quickly diluted, and reasonable amounts are normally washed out of our body very easily.

The important thing to remember is to take it easy at first and let your body get comfortable with small doses of vitamins and minerals before going to a higher level. It may be best for you not to go to a higher level unless you have established a nutritional or therapeutic need to do so.

My Final Comment

During the first two years of my illness recovery, I began using therapeutic doses of vitamins and minerals, and it became obvious that supplements were a major factor in my "Getting Well." I found it difficult to accept how truly powerful and effective they were. I began to expand my understanding by asking myself, "Why do some people live beyond 100 years? Is it their superior genes? Is it their diet? Is it their lifestyle? Or, is it just plain-old good luck?" In the next chapter, "Understanding Longevity," you will learn the lifestyle changes to make, so you, too, will have a good shot at 100 years.

Doctor's Commentary

Wayne hits upon an often-debated phenomenon, at least within medical circles. Are food supplements—vitamin supplements, minerals, herbs, and so on—really necessary to ensure health? Most ill-informed physicians will claim an emphatic no, as Wayne's physician at Gary Air Force Base did in 1954, based on an assumption that the practice may be harmful because one could get all necessary bodily nutrients from the diet. The misinformation presented to Wayne in 1954 is still prevalent in medicine today. Although volumes of clinical research support nutritional supplementation, enhancing biological antioxidant status has been falsely associated with decrease risk of chronic illness.

In the diminution of chronic illnesses of human aging, ranging from arthritis to cancer to heart disease, the ongoing conception, at least on a day-to-day clinical basis in primary care, is less supportive. It has been suggested that new, relevant clinical information in medicine can take one to three decades to trickle down into everyday medical practice. I believe that is the case, as it relates to doctors gaining confidence in nutritional consultation with patients. From past to present, a negative domino effect ensues. Consider Wayne's case in 1970 at the age of 38 when diagnosed with high blood pressure. Instead of relying on CoQ-10, magnesium, and other more natural approaches to help with stabilization of blood pressure, Wayne was started on pharmaceutical interventions that would invariably make the situation worse and further deplete his body of essential minerals, such as potassium and magnesium.

This is also a commentary on the reductionistic ideas of modern medicine. If someone has high blood pressure, the standard practice is assumed to be to include quality medicine that merely treats symptoms rather than a deeper look into why this patient might have had the problem in the beginning. Examples of this paradigm are common throughout medicine. As Wayne commented, the information on the increased risk of heart disease or atherosclerosis with elevated body levels of homocystine was known since the late 1950s, yet largely ignored, and colleagues ostracized its discoverer.

Had that screening been initiated early for afflicted individuals who then could have been started on a few pennies a day of multivitamins, significant heart disease could have been prevented. However, as we all know, had a new pharmaceutical drug been developed that was as effective at improving heart disease outcomes as simply supplementing the diet with vitamins B-6 and B-12, the promotion and the marketing efforts on the part of the pharmaceutical company would have been tremendous, sparing no expense, and practically everybody in the country would have been placed on this powerful new medication. However, such is not the case with vitamins, as they are relatively non-profitable.

Doctors are not totally to blame for their ignorance about nutrition. Our training, as Wayne pointed out, is very limited in medical schools. Dr. Able, Wayne's friend, at least had a rather voluminous handbook on nutrition that he lent to Wayne. Apparently, he had not read much of the book himself. Nonetheless, his exposure is probably ten times better than the average physician.

Therefore, most of the researchers and physicians investigating vitamin therapies and conducting studies in this realm have become mavericks or labeled "radicals." However, knowledge of the important potential role of nutritional compounds dates back many years. Even knowledge that vitamin C diminishes the toxic affects of smoking is fairly old information. However, I would suspect that it is rare for family doctors or internists to know this. When consulting with patients, it is unlikely that they would go so far as to recommend antioxidants supplementation for patients who use tobacco products or consume alcohol—although counseling should be suggested to enable them to completely discontinue use.

Wayne was given a free sample of vitamin C powder. High doses of vitamin C to many people could cause diarrhea or loose stools, thus dissuading them from further trial. However, it apparently worked out well for Wayne and started him on a path to healing. Unfortunately for Wayne, it was an example of "too little too late." By 1993 at 61, he had sold his business and still existed in the class of the walking wounded and was even rushed to the emergency room on more than one occasion near death. Finally, Wayne was successful in linking with a nutritionally directed physician who correctly pointed out that much of the nutritional information promoted by the medical establishment was misleading, inaccurate, and generally incompetent advice. But often these assumptions are taught to physicians in medical schools. The statement that "vitamin C causes kidney stones" is an example of one belief system taught to me in medical school. Most doctors seldom have the time to check original references and material to ascertain that information is correct. As a matter of fact, recent studies have demonstrated that this is an inaccurate assumption even though it is promoted and included in many common medical textbooks. Actually, vitamin C supplementation in males may actually decrease the occurrence of kidney stones.

All this information can be overwhelming to the average consumer, especially when starting to incorporate complementary approaches to improve overall sense of wellness. I have seen a number of patients who have been through the medical gauntlet, diagnosed and treated at ten to twelve other facilities with no success, then advised that the slowly deteriorating condition is one they would have to learn to live with. When they improve, they are, in one sense, overjoyed, but in another apprehensive. Their logical mind often reverts back to the belief system encouraged by their medical doctors that they cannot get better. It can be an evolutionary process for individual patients to be comfortable with changing their paradigm.

One must also keep in mind that this is part of our subjective training as medical consumers. We are continuously barraged with television commercials, radio ads, and medical information with commentary on the latest "magic bullet," promising better moods, better erections, hair growth, increased energy, and improved sex. Often, these products fall far short of expectations. Nutritional and supportive therapies, however, tend to be slower in restoring the body to overall wellness.

Sometimes, patients can be discouraged by the sluggishness of improvements in their overall health. They have often forgotten that it may have taken ten to twenty years to get where they are, and that their subjective changes will generally not occur overnight. Even for Wayne's ongoing clinical regimen, it took several years to restore his health. I do not see that the immediate future of medical practice is going to be more considerate of holistic medicine. The status quo is not going to be easily discarded, which gets back to "following the money trail." There is an enormous profit built into the current system of high-volume HMO-style medicine, as well as the focused use of high-cost surgical procedures and prescription drugs. It will probably be a long time before less expensive, less invasive approaches are commonplace, especially since in reality they will make a lot less money.

—Dale Guyer, M.D.

Chapter Eighteen
Understanding Longevity

During my six-month checkup in June 2000, Dr. Guyer, after looking over my latest lab reports, announced, "Wayne, I don't see any reason why you should not live to ninety or perhaps beyond." This was great news, but it caught me off-guard because Betty and I had, in 1999, sold our 4,000-square foot dream home, thinking that my life, because of my illness, could be shortened. I didn't want Betty saddled with the house maintenance and grounds keeping of the large landscaped lot and the one-acre, spring-fed pond at our back door.

Dr. Guyer's comments created a spark in my life I had not expected. My wife and I relocated to Florida in October 2000 to begin our annual snowbird season. The next week, I headed to the student library of the University of South Florida in Sarasota to see what I could learn about longevity. At first, I began reading computerized research papers on longevity to discover that scientists have never made up their minds about the "good gene effect" versus the "environmental lifestyle effect," concerning longevity.

After a full day of boring reading, I stumbled onto a January 1973 *National Geographic* magazine feature article, "Every Day Is a Gift When You Are Over 100, Search for the Oldest People." The article's headline is "A Scientist Visits Some of the World's Oldest People." This long but very informative article was written by Alexander Leaf, M.D. Dr. Leaf had also become bored and confused reading research papers trying to find the common fiber connecting people who live so much longer than average. Accompanied by photographer John Launois, he traveled the world and learned first-hand the secrets to living beyond 100 years

Nearly all of these people who lived beyond 100 were physically active their entire lives and were absent of any type of illness. Dr. Leaf interviewed 130-year-old Khfaf Lasuria living in the former Soviet Union's Abkhazia who had retired as a "tea leaf picker" at age 128. "I still enjoy a little vodka before breakfast," she said. Out in the tea fields where Khfaf had worked, Dr. Leaf visited with ninety-eight-year-old Duripshi Gunba while he was picking tea leaves. His at-rest blood pressure was recorded as 104/72. Mr. Gunba admitted he had "a fondness for red wine." "He has a lot of mileage left," said Dr. Leaf. Duripshi Gunba's father had picked tea leaves to age 125.

Reading Dr. Leaf's article led me to other articles on societies with life expectancies above 100 years. From these articles, I selected nine societies and began looking for a common theme contributing to the reason why they lived so long.

Why You Should Read This Chapter

Hopefully this chapter will prepare your mind for the changes that can easily be made to move your expected lifespan in the United States from seventy-seven years to ninety years and perhaps beyond.

While reading this chapter, please look for ways in which these nine societies have applied The Four Basic Principles for "Getting Well," introduced in Chapter 12, which if followed, I believe, will guide you back to good health and longevity greater than you might normally expect.

The Societies I Chose That Shared a Common Theme for Living 100 Years and Beyond

Abkhazians of Georgia (former Soviet Union)—lived high up in the mountains

Hunzas of Pakistan—lived high up in the mountains

Vilcabambas of Ecuador—lived high up in the mountains

Bamas of Mainland China—lived high up in the mountains

Azerbaijanis (former Soviet Union)—lived high up in the mountains

Armenians (former Soviet Union)—lived high up in the mountains

Tibetans—lived high up in the mountains

Titicacas of Peru—lived high up in the mountains

Okinawans of Japan—lived at sea level

The Effects of Pollution on Longevity

Eight of these cultures lived in the sheltered mountain valleys they carefully selected on the "inside slope" of the mountain at elevations between 8,500 and 14,000 feet. These elevated plateaus provided luscious grazing meadows for their animals and rich farmlands for their crops. In addition, the air that surrounded them and their animals was always fresh without toxins and pollution.

Most of the air that circulates around the world that we breathe is polluted with smoke particles, volcanic ash, and industrial waste. But, when the prevailing winds containing the worldwide pollution make contact with the outward slopes of the mountains, the air and the pollution is forced up and away from the mountain peaks, resulting in no polluted air entering the valleys where the people lived. In fact, the passing of upward wind currents over the peaks of the mountains actually created a vacuum on the inside mountain slopes, drawing into their environment fresh clean air filtered by the network of stream vapors in the valleys below.

Rain washes pollution out of the air, but where these mountain people live, the rain, much like the polluted air, is also swept up over the mountain peaks, resulting in less than two inches of rainfall annually to the inside mountain slopes, and therefore rain does not wash much pollution onto their mountain plateaus.

These mountain people have no automobiles or heavy industry to pollute their air, water, or food. Therefore, their local areas were found to be relatively free of any form of toxins or pollution.

Compare this to the United States where relatively flat country permits pollution to actually intensify as the worldwide polluted air flows from west to east. Our own industrial waste and automobile exhaust fumes gather in the air currents as the air travels. About half of the U.S. population lives west of Indianapolis and about half lives east. West of the Mississippi River, in general, you'll find the best air, except for areas along the far west coast of California that at times develop toxic smog. On most days, people living on our east coast breathe our most toxic air.

Remember how the pollution-free mountain people of the world lived on the inside slopes of the mountain; the far west-coast population of California live just the opposite. The people live on the outer slope of the mountains. This means that, when the worldwide polluted air currents strike the various California mountain ranges, some of the air flows up over the mountain peaks, but also some of the polluted air curls back over the coastal population combining with the local industrial waste and massive automobile exhaust fumes, making the west coast of California, when weather conditions are just right (or just wrong), more toxic than our east coast.

Colorado Springs is often cited as having the closest to pollution-free air in the United States. Its being located on the inside slope of the mountain, like the eight healthy mountain societies we just learned about, is no doubt the reason.

Because of their environment, the people in these eight mountain societies were found to be free of toxins in their bodies, which is The First Basic Principle for "Getting Well" stated in Chapter 12.

The Effects of Nutrition on Longevity

The water source in these mountain communities for drinking and irrigating their crops comes from the glacial melting on the inner slope of the mountains where pollution has not been deposited by wind or rain. They call this glacial melt "Glacial Milk" because the highly mineralized water is opaque and whitish in color like milk. Glacial Milk is a mixed liquid containing a solution of over seventy of the eighty-four mineral elements essential to the health of the human body. Glacial Milk is created by friction between the living parent rock of the mountain and the giant ice fields as the ice slides down the mountains and melts. The average particle size of these Glacial Milk minerals is so small that a single mineral particle can be visualized only under an electron microscope. This small size makes the mineral element very easy for the human body to absorb.

Glacial Milk also grows the most nutritious fruits, vegetables, and animals known to mankind, compared to the United States where our croplands have been reported years ago to be void of many essential mineral elements. With these essential elements missing from our diet, our lifespan will be greatly shortened from the 90 to 120 years dictated by our genes.

These mountain people's diet includes chicken, mutton, beef, goat's and cow's milk, cheese, yogurt, butter, bread, tomatoes, cucumbers, lettuce, green onions, garlic, beans, fruit, red peppers, tea, and wine, plus salt. Because their food and water is so nutritious, the average person need consume only 1,200 to 1,900 calories each day to absorb the amount of vitamins and minerals needed to maintain his or her lean and healthy strong body.

Compare this to the United States where we eat the same type of foods they eat, but our food is not at a high-enough nutritional level to keep us healthy. Instead, I discovered we must consume a lot more calories to absorb sufficient vitamins and minerals to overcome our food cravings. As a result, our body gains weight trying to meet our nutritional needs with food alone. I learned to overcome the low levels of nutrition found in our supermarket foods by supplementing my diet with vitamins and minerals. I discovered that incomplete nutrition was the cause of my weight gain, not lack of willpower.

Among these mountain people, researchers found almost no dental cavities, cancer, heart disease, diabetes, Alzheimer's, or arthritis. These people were basically disease-free their entire lives. It is estimated that the diet they eat contains vitamins and minerals twenty to forty times the RDA established by our FDA as sufficient for good health.

In the United States, most people's diet today is made up of approximately seventy-five percent highly processed foods resulting in a very low *nutrition/calorie* ratio. This is referred to as "hollow calories," which are high in carbohydrates, that if not burned as energy each day, converts to fat around our waist at night while we sleep. These highly processed foods also are very low in vitamins and minerals needed to keep us healthy.

The Friendly People of Okinawa

Natives of Okinawa live on a beautiful island and, like the people living high up in the mountains, are surrounded by little or no pollution. The trade winds that flow gently over their peaceful island have been doing so for hundreds of miles, passing through the mist created by the waves of the open ocean. This natural flow of air currents has washed the worldwide pollution from the air before reaching Okinawa.

Because of the gentle ocean currents surrounding Okinawa, live coral grows in abundance, forming reefs everywhere. In fact, the sand that sheds as the live coral grows formed the entire island over time. Should there have been strong ocean currents, the coral sand shedding from the growing coral would have been swept out to sea, and the island would never have been formed. But, it is there, for us to study and learn from. Growing coral is a composite of approximately seventy-four minerals and trace minerals found in the mountain people's "Glacial Milk," plus other life-supporting nutrients from the sea we haven't discussed.

Actually, the entire island is made up of a giant pile of essential minerals. The fresh water they pump from the ground is loaded with these minerals. Their fruit trees produce high levels of natural vitamins, not to mention the cache of vitamins and succulent nutrition created in a wide variety of vegetables grown on the island.

Thirty years ago, the life expectancy in Okinawa was 100 years. Today it stands alone as the only society in the world that has increased its life expectancy to 105 years. Today, the Japanese claim a life expectancy of eighty-two years. However, on the mainland of Japan, where there are large amounts of automobile exhaust fumes, industrial contamination, and airborne volcanic ash particles, the life expectancy is just seventy-seven years, the same as the United States. It is only after it *averages-in* the 105-year-old people living on Okinawa that Japan can brag about a life expectancy of eighty-two years.

Chapter Eighteen

What Have We Learned about Longevity?

First we know that our life will end when a vital organ in our body becomes undernourished, followed by disease, and then fails to function. We also know that most people born in the United States have a time clock passed on in their genes for 90 to 120 years of life here on earth. Our review of the oldest living people in our world confirms that living this long is possible. We learned from these centenarians (100-year-old people) that we must keep our bodies free of chemical toxins, toxic heavy metals, and substances foreign to our body, like food additives, because our blood must stay pure if our organs are to remain healthy.

Second, we have confirmed, by studying the mountain societies and the people of Okinawa, that our immune system must have an overabundance of vitamins of minerals available in our digestive system, in our blood, and at cell-level, every moment of the day, if we want to remain disease-free throughout our life. The very instant when our body runs out of just a single vitamin or mineral, cell damage begins and, if continued, disease follows.

Believing that we can get all the nutrition our body needs from the food we eat is a dangerous and false assumption, not supported by scientific evidence. In fact, scientists report just the opposite. That is why a Federal directive added folic acid to our baked goods recently.

What Should We Do Now?

It is my opinion that the solution to our problem of living a long, healthy, enjoyable life is to take charge of our own health and incorporate into our lives The Four Basic Principles for "Getting Well" as presented in Chapter 12.

What Is the Life Expectancy of the Nine Societies Today?

The good news I have already shared with you. The life expectancy in Okinawa has increased to 105 for those people who continue to live on the island and follow traditional lifestyles of their ancestors. Natives who have relocated to the mainland of Japan or to the United States in about five years develop reduced life expectancies of seventy-seven years, the same as the normal population. This, to me, proves that genes are not the controlling factor for how long we live; instead, the cleanliness of our environment and the completeness of our nutrition is the most important.

The worst news comes from the Republic of Armenia where life expectancies of 100 years have now dropped to sixty-seven. About twenty years ago, Russia began storing nuclear waste in the outward slopes of the Armenian mountains. Now the mountain streams have a high level of radiation that flows throughout their mountain villages.

The Azerbaijan Republic has drilled for oil, and now its mountain streams are hopelessly polluted, but it has used its new wealth to build a large hospital to care for the increasing number of sick mountain people.

The Hunzas of Pakistan have commercialized their unique mountain valley by developing the "Valley of Eternal Youth" where they operate elaborate spas for cleansing the body and teaching visitors a new healthy lifestyle to support longevity.

The people of Vilcabambas of Ecuador have also cashed in their reputation for long and healthy lives by creating the Vilcabambas Ecological Center. Visitors come from around the world to study longevity.

The Tibetans continue to claim to be the oldest living people in the world. However, I just recently read that their most famous citizen, the Dalai Lama, was seriously ill.

The Abkhazians of Georgia continue consistently to live to ages above 100 while they carry on their tradition of picking premium mountain-grown tea leaves and selling them to the world markets.

The Titicacas of Peru have capitalized on their reputation of living a long healthy life by developing a flourishing tourist business where you stay in rustic homes with the Titicaca Indians, which allows you to see how little their lives have changed over the years.

The Bamas in China have commercialized their healthy lifestyle reputation by developing and manufacturing a long list of products they claim will help you live a long, healthy life. Their product lists include rice wine and snake wine bottled with real snakes preserved in the alcohol. Cannabis soup and houmayou soup, made from hemp seeds, are popular export items, too. Bama country, where 300,000 people now live at 4,500 feet elevation, is so cut-off by the surrounding hills that the automobile has yet to become part of their culture. However, of the 300,000 residents, only seventy-three in year 2002 were above age 100.

Final Comment

During our discussion about these nine societies in this chapter, we failed to mention the effect exercise has played in their ability to live consistently beyond 100. You should be pleased to know that this will be addressed in the very next chapter, "Exercise, the Miracle Drug!"

Chapter Eighteen

Doctor's Commentary

Once again, Wayne correctly observes that doctors often contribute to a patient's "unbelief" system rather than to a belief system in his or her own wellness. First, Wayne mentions receiving great news, which caught him off-guard, that his laboratory tests were shaping up well enough that one would expect him to be able to embrace a solid and highly functional state of health, to which he had not been accustomed in decades. As is often the case, many patients are ill-advised by their physicians in matters of longevity. What is possible is significantly more than what is often stated. Our genes are, in most cases, programmed to give us a quality 90 to 120 years of life. However, the environment that we bathe those genes in, either by our choice or by circumstances outside of our control, is not always optimal. While it may be so for some, such as the tribes that Wayne described, the rest of us live in the modern industrial age and are not so lucky. In this arena, I have observed significant challenges; one is that our environment is significantly less than pristine. As discussed previously, there is so much toxicity and garbage in the world that I am surprised that our bodies' function as well as they do. Creating a lifestyle that enables the body to detoxify and that enhances its ability through medical treatments, such as chelation therapy, is probably a very good idea for almost everyone in North America and industrialized countries. The other limitation is that if you go into the grocery store and take a cursory inventory of options available on any aisle, you will see that almost 90 percent of those potential choices are unhealthy. They are loaded with chemical contaminants and synthetic food additives that have questionable health merit. The calorie-dense but nutrition-poor consumables ensure the maintenance of the status quo, or so-called Standard American Diet (SAD). We have little control over the environmental and food chains, because of big government, big business, and big profits.

There are items over which we do have control. It is our own choice what we consume, even though, for most citizens, the typical diet falls far short of what might be an optimal healthy diet; certainly, it is far short of the nine different cultures Wayne mentions. Therefore, it is important in the larger sense that an ideal patient or self-advocate take it upon himself or herself to detoxify the body and choose a more optimal diet.

People who have been consuming SAD for many years through no fault of their own have not been bathed in "Glacial Milk." They become so nutrient-deprived and exhibit such a host of symptoms that it takes a more significant effort nutritionally to rebuild them. While changing the diet is one favorable contribution, I have found that most people, even those whom we label categorically as healthy, will feel significantly improved by undergoing intravenous vitamin therapy or self-administering their own injections of trace minerals, vitamin B-12, and other nutrients. The injectable route offers a way rapidly to rebuild nutrients depleted for years, often at the intracellular level. In rebuilding the body's reserves, almost every cellular function works better. Also, I find that dietary selection tends to be easier. Poor dietary habits—such as the inclusion of excess alcohol and caffeine, tobacco usage, carbohydrate craving, and broad-scale consumption of junk food—tend to diminish significantly as the person's nutritional status is rebuilt and repaired. Even cultures eating healthier foods, such as those Wayne mentioned, often consume levels of vitamins and minerals that are many times higher than the recommended daily allowance established by the FDA. While we may not be fortunate enough to live in the pristine environments of world regions such as Okinawa, I believe that we can still enjoy comparable longevity and quality of life, if we make a concerted effort to become self-advocates and ensure our overall health.

—Dale Guyer, M.D.

Chapter Nineteen
Exercise, the Miracle Drug!

In the waiting room of a major city hospital stood the oldest son of seventy-three-year-old Fred. Fred's cancer surgeon was saying, "Removing the cancer from your father's stomach did not go as planned this morning. As soon as I opened up the abdominal cavity, I realized the cancer had spread from the stomach throughout the entire digestive system. I removed the diseased areas of his digestive system along with all of the cancer possible, but I am sorry to inform you that we had no choice but to sew your father up with a lot of cancer remaining inside him. Some of the cancer was entwined with other organs. Your father is terminal, so I am not going to recommend he be put through the trauma of radiation or chemo. The cancer is just too far advanced and too widespread. These treatments won't help him. What I do recommend is that you explain as gently as you can that we did everything we could for him, and I am very sorry to say this, but our surgical team believes your father has less than three months to live."

Fred's son invited his father to move in with him and his wife to recuperate from the surgery. Fred accepted cheerfully. Two weeks went by, and Fred began feeling better. The son had not yet worked up enough nerve to tell his father that he was terminal and would be dead before Christmas.

Fred, unaware he was scheduled to die within ninety days, began taking daily walks downtown, because "this makes me feel better," he explained. One of Fred's favorite resting areas during his walks was the park bench located along the sidewalk in front of a large plate glass window to a fitness center. He enjoyed watching people exercise.

One day a "personal trainer" approached Fred and invited him inside, "out of the heat and in to where it is air-conditioned." Once inside, the trainer began showing Fred how to use the exercise equipment. By the end of the week, Fred, to his son's surprise, announced he was now a member of the local fitness club and would be exercising every day, "rain or shine," as Fred put it.

As Fred progressed, the trainer recommended he start taking a powdered food supplement to be mixed with raw vegetable or fruit juice. "It contains lots of vitamins and minerals, to help put some meat on those skinny bones of yours," explained the trainer.

As the calendar reached the one day before Fred's three-month appointment with death, the son, noticing that his father was looking better and was gaining weight, decided to not tell anyone what the cancer surgeon had said in the hospital waiting room eighty-nine days earlier about his dad being terminal.

Four months later, Fred celebrated Christmas with his son's family who came home for the holidays. Everyone was telling Fred how good he looked. But, this is only the beginning of Fred's story.

Can you imagine the surprised look on the cancer surgeon's face when Fred, five months after Christmas, made an appointment for his one-year checkup, and the surgeon could find no cancer in Fred's entire body?

Six years passed, and the cancer surgeon was again surprised when Fred's son sent the doctor an invitation to Fred's eightieth birthday party. Ten years slipped by, and the doctor again received another letter from Fred's son. The main part of the letter read, "We had planned on having another birthday party to celebrate dad's ninetieth birthday, but he remarried five years ago, and he and his bride now live full time in the Bahaman Islands. As they told us, 'We are too busy with our friends on the island. We won't have time this year to come home for a party.'"

Is Fred's Story a Miracle?

Yes, I would say, Fred's story is a miracle, but it is not an unusual happening. Is Fred's story difficult to believe? To some people, this is not a believable story, but you will find that most medical doctors would say, "Yes, I believe Fred's story." Surveys indicated that ninety-five percent of all medical doctors say they believe in the miracle of unexplained healing of a serious or terminal illness. It is not because they can explain how it happens, but rather because they have witnessed it happening so many times during their professional careers.

To me, Fred's healing is simply the way it is supposed to happen. Our body was designed during the creation process to heal itself, not just of minor illnesses, but of major diseases of organs, with the rejuvenation of complete systems, too. Most of us underestimate the sophisticated workings of our own immune system.

Our human brain can outperform the most powerful computer man has ever made. Our brain has recorded every detail of our fetal development and all changes taking place in our body from birth to our present age.

Our immune system is delicately connected to our brain, and on request from our immune system, our brain can download the secrets of creation and the details of a complete record of all actions and reactions that have taken place in our entire body since day one. Knowing this, we can begin to piece together what took place during Fred's miracle healing.

1. Fred's complete digestive system was relatively free of toxins that interfere with healing. His surgeon had surgically removed the toxic diseased tissue and flushed the remaining toxins from the organs that remained. In other words, The First Basic Principle for "Getting Well" was accomplished.

2. Fred was providing an overabundance of vitamins and minerals to his body from the food supplement package he purchased from his fitness center. We must remember that vitamins and minerals are the tools our immune system must have to create new cells and actual healing. The Second Basic Principle for "Getting Well" was also accomplished.

3. Fred's mind was projecting, "I am 'Getting Well'!" He had taken charge of his illness and was doing what all *exceptional patients* do, taking action by following their own instincts created by their Inner Focus of Control, supported by faith in their God's divine power. This met the requirements of The Third Basic Principle for "Getting Well."

4. Fred exercised every day, The Fourth Basic Principle for "Getting Well." Exercise is absolutely essential to "Getting Well." Exercise is the master catalyst that energizes and challenges every cell of our body by motivating the healing process. During exercise, *endorphins* are released from our brain, and they circulate throughout our body. After release, endorphins tend to return a physical body function to normal, while regulating the release of growth hormone (GH). High endorphin levels in our body are associated with better empowerment to the immune system. Also, during exercise as discovered just ten years ago, thirty-one different *beta-endorphin* amino acids are released from the pituitary gland and circulate to all parts of our body. Research scientists are busy studying them, but have not yet defined what each of these beta-endorphins does. Dr. Haruyama, a medical doctor from Tokyo University, recently wrote a book, *A Great Revolution in the Brain World*. In his studies, Dr. Haruyama suggests that beta-endorphins "boost the immune system against diseases and cancer cells" and that "nerve fibers are in fact physically linked both to the human immune system as well as the nerve system...." His work also suggests that this may be one of

215

the ways in which our immune system receives guidance for using vitamins and minerals to create new cells that repair our body.

The great thing is that we do not need a written prescription from our doctor or approval from the FDA to take these powerful miracle drugs like endorphins that heal our body naturally. Nature has already prescribed them, and all we need to do to receive them is to exercise.

Some of you may have doubts concerning your body's ability to heal itself, but I don't. I have experienced it. Following is my personal story about exercise.

How I Grew My Own Coronary Artery Bypass

After narrowly avoiding a heart attack on September 10, 1993, a Cardiolite Stress Test and other tests revealed that my left-anterior descending coronary artery was seventy-percent blocked. Because of a surgery cancellation, I was scheduled as the first patient early the next morning for an 8:00 catheterization and then on to bypass surgery at 9:00 A.M.

The cardiologist who performed the catheterization and my own cardiologist were shocked to discover that my entire left artery was not seventy-percent blocked, but instead was 100-percent blocked. With no blood flowing down this left coronary artery, they were puzzled as to how I was still alive.

Immediate additional testing revealed that my body had formed a new small artery as a natural bypass around the actual blockage. This small trickle of blood supplied by the new small bypass artery, along with that allowed by some new very small horizontal collateral arteries transferring blood from my right coronary artery to the left muscle of my heart, was enough blood flow to keep me alive. Because the surgeons were not sure where these new arteries supplying blood to my heart were located, they canceled the open-heart bypass surgery fearing they might do more harm than good.

Instead of surgery, I was prescribed exercise, in the hope of enlarging these small new collateral arteries and increasing the blood flow to my heart muscles. I was enrolled in a monitored heart rehab program at a local hospital heart rehab center. I reported at 6:45 A.M. each Monday, Wednesday, and Friday and, while wearing an electronic monitor, exercised twenty minutes on the treadmill and twenty minutes on an Airdyne bicycle, followed by twenty minutes of light weights and floor exercises

At first the exercise was very painful as these new small arteries began to stretch. At the end of the first year, the pain was lessened, and my circulation had increased about thirty percent. My risk for a heart attack was greatly reduced.

But my real break came when Dr. Walter Able, my business partner, sent me an article from *USA Today* telling about how medical scientists were learning to grow new coronary arteries in large German Shepherd and St. Bernard dogs. First, they placed a small donut-like device around each coronary artery, which over six months slowly squeezed and restricted the blood flow to the dog's heart. Next, they fed each dog a high-quality diet complete with abundant vitamins and minerals. Each night before bedtime, they injected human growth hormone (HGH) into the large muscle of the dog's rear leg. While the dogs slept for nine hours, the HGH was absorbed throughout the leg muscle. The next morning, each dog was placed on a treadmill and exercised for one hour, distributing the HGH throughout its body. Within six months, the dogs' original coronary arteries became totally blocked, but a new set of coronary arteries grew and bypassed the blocked arteries. The dogs continued to be healthy and lived a normal life without physical restrictions.

I began to investigate and found that, in Europe, medical science was about five years ahead of the U.S. and was experimenting successfully by growing new coronary arteries in selected human beings following the same protocol used on the dogs. By talking to pharmacists, I learned that the only medical doctors who were authorized to prescribe HGH were those registered as specialists working with children's growth problems. The pharmacists also warned that, if I could obtain a legal prescription for HGH, the prescription would cost about $1,200-1,500 a month and that insurance companies would not normally pay.

Not giving up, I discussed my desire to use HGH with Dr. Guyer. About one year later, he informed me that Upjohn had bought the Pharmacia AB, located in Stockholm, the manufacturer of the Genotropin®-brand HGH, the drug used in the experimental program in Europe on humans, growing new coronary arteries. After Upjohn bought Pharmacia, it was announced that it would extend its European program to carefully selected adult patients in the United States.

Dr. Guyer submitted my name along with reasons why I wanted to use HGH. To be authorized to write prescriptions for HGH, it was necessary for Dr. Guyer to take additional medical training in its proper use and to become legally registered to do so.

Pharmacia named its research effort in the United States "The Bridge Program." But, to qualify, it was necessary for Dr. Guyer to conduct extensive tests on me for about one year. Pharmacia wanted to be sure my body was completely compatible with Genotropin®. Some adults cannot take HGH shots because they cause leg and arm pain along with swelling in various parts of the body.

During the one year of testing, it was determined that 0.4mg of Genotropin® was the correct amount for me to inject into my large thigh muscle, five nights a week, just before going to bed. As with the dogs, it took about nine hours for the hormone to be absorbed into the thigh muscle, and the next morning thirty minutes of walking or treadmill distributed the hormone throughout my body.

As of March 2004, I have been injecting HGH on a continuous basis for six years. In 2003, Upjohn sold Pharmacia to Pfizer, which is continuing The Bridge Program.

My Results from Injecting Human Growth Hormone for Six Years, with Exercise

I have continued to accumulate increasing amounts of calcification in both my left and my right coronary arteries to the point that today both are totally blocked. Scans on the Ultra-fast CT screen show clearly, in black, a full three-inch-long area that is blocked solid in the left artery. However, a small healthy new artery has grown beside the old blocked artery and is presently about two and one-half inches long. Although a little undersized, it is doing a good job feeding blood to my left-front heart muscle.

The right coronary artery is blocked solid intermittently, with several new collateral arteries entering the old artery at different locations and feeding blood horizontally from an unknown source.

The circumflex coronary artery that supplies blood to the rear of my heart has remained clear of calcification and has responded to my heart muscle's plea for more blood by developing longer branches extending to the lower muscles with new collateral arteries supplying blood up the lower front of my heart.

In January 2002, my Cardiolite Stress Test images showed both the left and right coronary arteries very dark, indicating severe blockage, but they also showed that all areas of my heart muscles were receiving adequate blood from the new and collateral arteries. Because there is such a large amount of blood flowing throughout my heart muscles, some doctors speculate that there may be a spider-web-like network of small arteries not detected by imaging equipment. This is only a guess, but one thing we do know is that I can produce a perfect EKG without any indication I have any type of heart disease, and my blood pressure is normal without using drugs.

Questions I Am Most Frequently Asked about Growing My Own Bypass

- *Is the process of growing your own coronary bypass painful?*
  Yes, however there were several different types of pain involved. First, I had to learn to recognize what each pain meant and, second, how to control it. The nurses during my three years of heart rehab taught me how to interpret the different pains and how to deal with them. I experienced really sharp vertical pains when the exercise was forcing the creation of new arteries. I would feel pressure with light pain when the arteries were trying to expand and become larger. Sometime a dull ache on the left side of my heart meant the heart was tired and wanted to rest. This dull pain translated into "don't exercise today." Occasionally, while exercising I would feel a pleasant streak of internal warmness in my heart. I was told that this was new nerves developing in the muscles. I was constantly on the alert for the slightest pressure or pain in the center of my chest. If this happened, I was instructed to lie down and request immediate medical attention. This seldom happened because I was taught always to stay on the safe side while exercising. I never exceeded a heart rate of 130 bpm, and my exercise nurses convinced me that my body would get ninety percent of the exercise benefits at a 110 heart rate as it would at a 130-heartbeat rate. But, I want you to know that, during the other twenty-three hours of the day when I was not exercising at rehab, my body was very calm, and I experienced zero stress in my chest or pain in the heart, even when I mowed the lawn or took long walks.
- *How long does it take to grow new coronary arteries?*
  We know with dogs it takes six-months. I understand that in Europe they take about three years to produce success with an outpatient on a plan of injecting human growth hormones, special diet, and exercise. Here in the United States, I feel sure that others on the Pharmacia Bridge Program have had success like me, but I have never seen anything in writing or shared any personal experience with others. I have been doing heart rehab exercises for over ten years with nearly seven years' use of HGH. No one in the U.S. medical field whom I know of talks about

the possibilities of heart patients growing their own bypasses. I suspect the primary reason is that there is no money in it for a cardiologist. Writing prescriptions for HGH, dictating a special diet, and coaching patient exercises would not sound very exciting or profitable to most cardiologists I know.

- *Can I grow my own coronary artery bypass?*

Perhaps you can, but more than likely the practical answer is no! First of all, I do not know of a single cardiologist or hospital that offers a program for growing your own coronary arteries using HGH, special diet, and exercise. I also suspect that the FDA has no sincere intentions of approving such a program. Don't forget that I was rejected for angioplasty or bypass surgery in 1993. I was placed on an exercise program, and I really had no choice but to fight to survive. The way it turned out, it was the best thing that could have happened to me. Today, as my coronary arteries collect more blockages, my heart responds by building new arteries. Although my heart has massive blockage, I believe that my risk of a sudden heart attack is very low.

—————Warning—————

To the best of my knowledge, there have been no studies recognized by the FDA showing the injection of HGH to be beneficial or safe for use in adults. Pharmacia's literature lists only a few benefits for the 172 adults involved in its approval testing. Growing new coronary arteries is not listed. The literature warns to discontinue the use of the product immediately if a tumor is discovered anywhere in the patient's body, because growth hormones may cause rapid growth of the tumor. I strongly recommend that you not use HGH unless a medical doctor, trained in its use, identifies a good health reason for you to use it.

Why Did I Want You to Know about My Growing My Own Heart Bypass?

I have taken the time to share my experience, not to promote a new type of bypass, but instead to demonstrate how powerfully exercise can contribute to the natural healing power of a human body. HGH by itself did not grow new arteries in my heart. My heart was responding to daily exercise for three years before I began injecting HGH, and my body was slowly growing new coronary arteries on its own. The growth hormone speeded up and guaranteed that the new arteries would grow faster than the blockage. Because of my age, my body's production of growth hormone was very low. A simple laboratory blood test determined the level of my growth hormone and justification to augment it.

Had I not exercised five days every week for the past ten years, releasing powerful natural drugs from my brain—endorphins and beta-endorphins—my new replacement coronary arteries would not have developed, and without the new arteries, I would have not survived.

My real reason for presenting exercise in this manner is to motivate you to start a daily exercise program of your very own. As the result of my own experience, I have come to believe strongly that every person, regardless of age or physical condition, can greatly improve his or her health by releasing the natural healing power available within his or her own body with exercise. I believe that, with medical supervision, even a person confined to a bed can do daily arm-movement and leg-lift exercises that will release some of the natural healing power from within his or her body.

Many of the people who must spend most of their day in a wheelchair have already proven that an exciting array of daily exercises is possible and beneficial. Anyone who can stand erect and take just tiny, slow baby steps, in my opinion, has no excuse not to exercise. Walking is an excellent exercise. Will there be some pain? Yes, you can expect some mild pain at first, but it will vanish as you progress. With professional instruction, you will learn to be in control of the pain. Your personal trainer will teach you how to turn it off and on. If your doctor approves of you learning to exercise, you will find, like I did, the effort to be well worth it.

What Should You Do Now?

First, regardless of your age, make an appointment with your primary-care physician. Tell your doctor that you have made the decision to begin a daily exercise program. Ask for your doctor's recommended physical restrictions. Request that he or she write a brief note that you can give to your personal exercise instructor.

Next, remember that most people do not continue to exercise because they did not learn at the beginning, from a professional, how to exercise properly. Once you learn a routine, designed just for your lifestyle, you will find that daily exercise is great fun and so rewarding that you will insist on adjusting your schedule to allow for this healthy illness-reversing experience.

Finally, select a local fitness center ($30-50 monthly) that provides a certified personal trainer who can provide professional guidance in designing a program that blends with your lifestyle. This fitness center may be privately owned or part of your local hospital.

If you decide not to use a fitness center and want to exercise at home, may I suggest you purchase the 2003 paperback *Reversing Degenerative Disease, Six Natural Steps to Healing*, written by Joe M. Elrod, Ed.D.

Dr. Elrod holds multiple degrees in exercise physiology and has completed postdoctoral research in the areas of nutrition, exercise physiology, heart disease, cancer, and arthritis. A man of God and a former university professor, he is now a health consultant who has worked with diverse groups, including AT&T, McDonald's, NASA, and various universities, hospitals, and medical schools.

Dr. Elrod's book is directed toward using exercise as an important medicine to help cure disease. When you have finished reading this 230-page book, you will know what changes exercise can create in your body, what foods to eat, and what food supplements to take, and the book also has detailed pictures showing how to exercise properly.

My Final Thought

We all know that regular aerobic exercise keeps our heart and lungs strong, builds our muscles, and develops a strong flow of blood throughout our body. But, we should also know that every organ in our body is linked energetically to a muscle. Therefore, an organ can be no stronger than the corresponding muscle. Always remember that an aerobic exercise (like walking) alone will not exercise all these important organ muscles. Your exercise program must include a balance of aerobic exercises, strength training with light weights, and stretching exercises to keep all your organs healthy. This is important, because, when just one organ fails to function, all our remaining healthy organs cannot save us. Instead, we quietly die.

Doctor's Commentary

I have often told patients that, if I could get everyone to be compliant with two therapies, my clinical schedule would be much less hectic. The two therapies are diet and exercise. Exercise is, without a doubt, one of the few remaining non-FDA-regulated therapies widely available and free-of-charge. In an age when pharmaceutical companies gouge consumers with enormous profiteering, exercise is the one proven, successful therapy treating weight loss, controlling blood pressure, enhancing mood, reducing anxiety and pain, and improving overall functional status. Exercise far and away helps ameliorate damage resulting from pharmaceuticals. It is surprising that most patients will not take the initiative to include exercise in their overall wellness program. In addition, the immunologic changes associated with exercise, as outlined in Fred's case, can even prove a worthy complement in the treatment of chronic, even terminal, disease.

The paradox I have found in medicine about so-called miracle stories is that often no one cares about miracles. They are rarely studied. If one were to pick up any medical journal, most of the commentary apart from advertisements and pharmaceutical companies is related to pathology or the abnormal function of the body. Virtually no articles discuss the normal function of the human body and the associated modalities that may be added to a treatment plan to help improve a person's opportunity to live a highly functional, normal life experience. Even studies showing prayer to be effective are often not labeled as such. Different descriptors, such as "non-local healing," are used in academic and intellectual circles apparently to add greater philosophical comfort to scientists engaging in this dialogue. Exercise also releases many biochemicals, which are associated with the body's incredible repair systems, in addition to mood enhancers, such as endorphins, and metabolism regulators. In Wayne's case, exercise supported with hormone replacement therapy, human growth hormone in particular, contributed in a dramatic way to improving Wayne's capacity to grow an entirely new circulatory system for his heart.

It is unfortunate that very promising therapies, such as growth hormone, often sit idle, while other therapies, perhaps significantly less helpful, are the commonly prescribed status quo remedies. While there are well over 100 studies published on the use of human growth hormone and an impressive safety track record, very few doctors know much about the use of the growth hormone apart from what they have read about its overuse in athletic circles. Even most endocrinologists do not routinely order a laboratory assessment of growth hormone levels and tend to be reluctant to prescribe growth hormone to patients who might benefit.

In my clinical experience, one of the great challenges is creating a patient-centered exercise program that an individual can enjoy and will respond to in an optimal manner. I see many patients who have worked out, often numerous hours, every day in a gym with only marginal results because they lack a well-designed program. Patients can spend hours on a treadmill making little progress in any arena. When asked about their training style, they relate that they were on the treadmill for two hours or more, perhaps reading the most recent Stephen King novel. My response would be that if their intensity was at such a low ebb that they could read, then their intensity level was not going to provide ongoing clinical benefit.

In my experience, most patients do best through the integration of different activities that emphasize the various facets of the human structure, particularly strength and flexibility. To achieve this, one needs a balanced program of weight training and aerobic conditioning, as well as stretching exercise to maintain flexibility. Combining these elements requires a well-versed personal trainer. Adding exercise to an ongoing treatment program only amplifies the effectiveness of all other inclusions.

—Dale Guyer, M.D.

Chapter Twenty
Treatments That Made Me Well

My thesaurus lists synonyms for treatments that apply to medical care as doctoring, nursing, prescribing, remedying, medicating, curing, therapy, therapeutics, and regimens. My medical dictionary defines treatment as "the action or manner of treating a patient medically or surgically." My *Webster's New World Dictionary* does not mince words. Treatment is stated as meaning "act, manner, method, etc., of treating medical or surgical care." To most medical doctors, however, before a treatment can be used, it must be on a list approved by the FDA and the AMA that most insurance companies agree to pay. To me, a good and proper medical treatment is any action or therapy that restores our body's own self-healing ability.

Because I have no formal medical training, I will limit this chapter to those medical treatments I have received and for which I can accurately report to you the result each of them had on my health.

My Surgery Record

At age five, my tonsils and adenoids were removed. At age sixteen, my appendix was removed. At age forty-eight, a large five-inch by seven-inch black birthmark was removed from my lower-left back. At age fifty, my gallbladder was removed. At age sixty-seven, a large colony of live nanobacteria was surgically removed from my lower-left jawbone. At age sixty-eight, a large colony of live nanobacteria was removed from my upper-right jawbone. At age seventy, calcification blockage was removed surgically from my left carotid artery.

Based on my present knowledge, I believe the removal of my tonsils and adenoids was a mistake. I had not been ill. The removal of my appendix and gallbladder is highly questionable because I had had only two short flair-ups of illness with each, I had missed no school or work, and I had completely recovered at the time of the operations. The removal of my pre-cancerous birthmark, I believe, was an excellent judgment-call by my family doctor. The removal of the two jawbone cavitations of nanobacteria was mandatory to stop a fast irregular heartbeat and to stop a two-year-long pressure buildup on the right side of my brain. Of course my carotid artery surgery could be termed as life-saving.

Often surgery is wise and necessary. Sometimes it must be done on an emergency basis, but usually we have time to get a second or even a third opinion that confirms that it is absolutely necessary or that we will be healthier without the surgery. Medical history reeks with reports of unnecessary surgery recommended by overzealous surgeons. Second and third opinions, however, will usually intercede and protect us from unnecessary surgery. But, I have found that, to be useful, second and third opinions must come from physicians who do not know the first-opinion doctor and who do not practice medicine at the same hospital. In 1994 when I was seeking second opinions for treating my irregular heartbeat, a senior doctor advised me that I needed to travel to California or New York for a good second opinion. "All of us doctors in the Midwest," he said, "went to the same medical schools, practice medicine together, and think alike, so you will get the same opinion from all of us."

My Drug-Treatment Record

In 1970 at age thirty-eight, I was prescribed my first medicine, a diuretic pill named HydroDIURIL®, to control my high blood pressure. This medicine reduced my energy level, but my doctor did not respond to my complaint with a mineral replacement program. He said, "I know diuretics are removing minerals from your body, but the only mineral you need to be concerned about is potassium," so he prescribed a blue potassium pill. This had little effect on my reduced energy level. Ten years later at age forty-eight, my doctor announced that he had the perfect medicine for my blood pressure problem, 25mg of Tenormin®, a beta-blocker. I agreed that it was a better medicine and that some of my energy came back. One year later, he raised the dosage to 50mg each morning, and everything slowed down again, including my energy level, blood pressure, heart rate, breathing rate, ability to think, and the amount of insulin being produced by my pancreas. I was diagnosed as having a lazy pancreas and was prescribed another drug to control my high blood-sugar level. I took these medicines during the next twelve years, during which I also developed panic attacks and was given a forever-changing assortment of nerve pills like Valium®.

Two years later, at age sixty-one, I was diagnosed with heart disease including a severely irregular heartbeat. My cardiologist replaced Tenormin®, a beta-blocker, with Verapamil®, a calcium channel-blocker. In addition, I was prescribed Lanoxin®, a heart muscle drug, Coumadin®, a blood thinner, and ISMO, a nitrate drug, and then we experimented with other drugs trying to control my irregular heartbeat.

I believe that all of these medicines helped me survive during my health-challenging years of ages forty-eight to sixty-three. But, I discovered chelation therapy and nutritional therapy in 1995 along with exercise therapy. Two years later, at age sixty-five, I had returned to good health and did not need any of the above drugs, including high-blood-pressure medicine I had taken for the twenty-six previous years.

My Use of Chelation Therapy

I received my first EDTA chelation treatment at age sixty-three in 1995. The purpose of this first IV treatment was to challenge my body by breaking loose and removing, through my kidneys, some of the toxic heavy metals that accumulated over many years in my body. By collecting my urine for the twenty-four hours following the chelation treatment, lab testing gave my new-type medical doctor a reasonable idea of the severity of toxins in my body and how those toxins related to my illnesses.

After thirty EDTA chelation treatments that removed large volumes of toxic heavy metals from my body, I began to settle down and could feel the natural self-healing process of my body beginning to develop from within.

After two years of chelation treatments, my heavy metals and toxin levels were greatly reduced, after which all my twenty illness symptoms, including my irregular heartbeat, vanished.

Conventional AMA doctors constantly and often aggressively proclaimed that chelation therapy would not cure any disease, especially heart disease as many doctors who use chelation in their practices claim. Technically, these AMA doctors are correct. In my opinion, medical doctors using chelation are wrong to tell a patient that chelation therapy will heal their disease. We must always remember that the only thing chelation therapy will do is remove heavy metals and toxins from our body. The only diseases that will be healed are those caused by the heavy metals or toxins. The actual healing process is generated by our immune system. After our body becomes free of toxic substances, our immune system can then become strong and free enough to direct the natural process of our body healing itself. Chelation therapy does not produce healing. Instead it removes the obstacles that prevent our immune system from doing its normal job of healing.

The way I see it, complementary/alternative medicine doctors are degrading and misrepresenting chelation therapy when they present it as a treatment that will cure a disease. After the heavy burden of heavy metals and toxins was removed from my body with chelation therapy, my immune system was then free to direct healing of my twenty disease symptoms. I believe that the only thing chelation therapy treatments did for me was to remove the toxins that were preventing my own immune system from keeping me well.

I also find, in my opinion, modern conventional medicine doctors as shirking their responsibilities to chronically ill patients by refusing to become involved in removing the toxins from their bodies that are causing serious illnesses. EPA scientific studies have warned us for years that toxins from our polluted air and toxic chemicals from many sources enter our body, accumulate, and cause serious illnesses. Modern-day conventional, politically correct medical doctors have chosen to ignore this scientific evidence and have replaced it with their own belief that the amount of toxins stored in the human body is small, and therefore harmless, so they see no reason to run tests and remove them.

This is what Hippocrates (460—377 B.C.) had to say about what medical doctors "believe." "To really know is science; to merely believe you know is ignorance."

When I first began chelation therapy treatments in 1995, my cardiologist and other medical doctors insisted they give me their opinion about my using chelation therapy. Their opinions of chelation therapy created in my mind a medical-treatment horror story of the worst kind. This is what Hippocrates had to say about doctor's "opinions." "There are in fact two things, science and opinion; the former begets knowledge, the latter ignorance."

Other Things I Learned from Hippocrates, the "Father of Medicine"

Hippocrates was a Greek physician born in 460 B.C. He became known as the founder of medicine and was regarded as the greatest physician of his time. He was the first to teach that the body must be treated as a whole and not just a series of parts.

For forty years, he traveled throughout Greece and healed the sick. Hippocrates believed in the natural healing process of rest, a good diet, fresh air, and cleanliness. When he diagnosed a person with a degenerative disease, such as cancer or tuberculosis, his first step in the treatment process was to detoxify the patient's body. To accomplish detoxification, he directed the patient to fast for a prescribed number of days while eating a special "Hippocrates Soup" along with daily enemas containing prescribed herbs and essential oils.

After detoxification, Hippocrates prescribed special food recipes that were scientifically recorded as a treatment for a specific disease and were administered along with his prescription for rest, fresh air, and cleanliness. When Hippocrates died, he passed on over 700 food recipes, each prescribed for a different illness.

Hippocrates lived eighty-three years. During his last twenty-five years of practicing medicine, he founded a medical school on the island of Cos, Greece, and began teaching his ideas. He soon developed an "Oath of Medical Ethics" for physicians to follow. Our physicians take this oath today as they begin their medical practice. "As to disease," Hippocrates advises doctors, "make a habit of two things—to help, or at least, to do no harm."

Hippocrates gave additional advice to doctors and also patients. Here are a few:

- "Walking is man's best medicine."
- "Opposites are cures for opposites."
- "Many admire, few know."
- "To do nothing is sometimes a good remedy."
- "Things that are holy are revealed only to men who are holy."
- "Healing is a matter of time, but it is sometimes also a matter of opportunity."
- "Prayer indeed is good, but while calling on the gods a man should himself lend a hand."
- "A wise man should consider that health is the greatest of human blessings, and learn how by his own thought to derive benefit from his illnesses."

Nutritional Therapy

Nutritional counselor Shawn Yakimovich reminds us (at www.sigma-logic.com/nutritional_therapy.htm) of the scientific reality concerning nutrition:

Every cell in our bodies is made from the food we eat. Plants capture the energy of the sun and absorb minerals from the earth to make the fats, proteins, carbohydrates and vitamins and minerals essential for the sustenance of all other forms of life. The food we consume is the product of amazing natural transformations involving earth, air, sun and water. When we eat this food, it imparts the energy of these elements to us, building healthy, robust bodies full of vitality, energy and creativity.

This is only true, however, if the food we eat is whole, pure and unprocessed. In this day and age, much of what we consider "food" doesn't resemble anything living at all! Degraded foods are leading to compromised health, which shows up as diabetes, heart disease, digestive problems, certain cancers, food allergies, skin disorders and other degenerative, chronic diseases with malnutrition at their root.

The body has an enormous capacity to heal itself. The foundation of this power is good nutrition. We literally are what we eat, digest and absorb. Therefore, what we eat can heal us or harm us.

If you eat three nutritious meals each day, prepared only from whole, pure, unprocessed, organically grown fruits and vegetables along with "range-fresh eggs" and "grass-fed" red meat certified free of antibiotics, steroids, and growth hormones, then you probably have little need to know about nutritional therapy. But, if you are like me, trying very hard to eat the required seven to nine servings of organically grown fruits and vegetables each day but sometimes falling short of the mark, then you need to learn about a wonderful medical treatment called nutritional therapy. I like to think of nutritional therapy as an act of instantly releasing nutritional power that supports our body's ability to heal itself. First, let's review conventional medicine's approach to treatment of our disease symptoms.

Conventional medical treatment: Based on my experience, I believe that, when most of us have an ailment and go to our typical family practice medical doctor, he or she listens carefully as we describe our illness symptoms. After asking a few questions, he or she usually prescribes one or more drugs created by the drug companies, manufactured especially to make our particular disease symptom go away. Most drugs are unnatural to the human body and usually accomplish nothing more than destroying diseased cells, blocking a body action, modifying a normal function, or creating a new chemical reaction within our body. If actual healing takes place while we are taking the medicine, it is our body's own immune system that has caused it to happen by building new cells. Prescription drugs do not grow new cells. If our body does not respond to healing, then we have a chronic illness and most likely will be taking prescription drugs the remainder of our life.

Advanced medicine treatment: When I develop an ailment, I usually see my conventional family practice medical doctor first, who invariably prescribes drugs to address my medical problems. If I begin to realize that he does not know the cause of my ailment, I know from experience that it will be pure luck if I get well. So, I make an appointment with my advanced medicine doctor, Dr. Guyer, who concentrates on treatments like nutritional therapy that make possible my body's ability to heal itself.

To better understand how nutritional therapy is used as medicine, I will share an experience that happened to me.

During the spring of 2003, I began to have low blood pressure. I could exercise and get it up to near normal, but within an hour it would be back down to a typical 80/50, which made me feel like going back to bed. I saw my family doctor who prescribed thirty days of a drug that raised my blood pressure back to normal. When I ran out of medicine, my blood pressure immediately returned to 80/50. My doctor gave me several possibilities as to what was causing my low blood pressure and offered to refer me to an endocrinologist. I declined, because it had been my experience that specialists usually prescribe an even-longer list of drugs than family doctors. Instead, I made an appointment with Dr. Guyer.

Dr. Guyer called for blood, saliva, and urine lab work on Monday and by Friday informed me, "Weakness in your adrenal glands is causing your low blood pressure."

"How will you correct these defective glands?" I asked.

"I won't," Dr. Guyer said. "Instead, we will encourage your body to grow its own new adrenal cells. Hopefully within two months or so, your adrenals should be like-new again."

My treatment consisted of, each Friday morning for six weeks, injecting myself with live adrenal cells, then immediately receiving a nutritional IV made up of a specially prescribed formula of pharmaceutical-grade vitamins and minerals selected to support the growth of my new adrenal cells.

After four weeks of treatment, I no longer needed a prescription drug to raise my blood pressure. At the end of six weeks, my treatment was completed. It is now one year later, and my blood pressure has remained normal.

For those who doubt that a sick organ can be stimulated to repair itself by growing new healthy cells, consider how our healthy body can use nutrition to stay in top working order. AlexSandra Rehlinger, a nutritional therapist certified by the British Association of Nutritional Therapy, reminds us of the following:

- Every few days, nutrients are used to replace much of the lining of your gut with new cells.
- Your skin is replaced every month or so using nutrients from the food you eat.
- In three-four months, your whole blood supply is completely replaced.

- In six months, almost all the proteins in your heart, kidneys, liver, and muscles are replaced.
- The DNA of your genes is also completely new within six months.
- In a year or so, all your bones and even some enamel of your teeth are made from new cells.

And, in seven years, you have a virtually completely new body, all constructed entirely out of the nutrients you eat.

Some people do not accept Rehlinger's statements as being completely valid. I agree that the body will not repair or regenerate new cells for everyone this fast, because an abundance of vitamins and minerals is required to grow new cells. The average person in the United States is nutritionally deficient, so his or her cells may actually be slowly dying off, and cell replacement may not be happening very fast or at all.

But, we cannot overlook the fact that, to grow new cells, our DNA, the cell's unique blueprint, must be present to guide the creation of new cells, and our present-day scientists only understand how five percent of the DNA in our body functions. Ninety-five percent of our DNA continues on its own to direct cell design and growth, and even the best scientists do not understand exactly what is happening. So, Rehlinger's statements could well prove to be highly accurate in the future as medical science continues to accumulate more knowledge about what ninety-five percent of our DNA does to affect cell growth in our body.

Closing comment: As we age, our body's ability to absorb nutrients declines, which accelerates aging and invites disease. By supplying our body with an abundance of good nutrition, the effects of aging can be reduced, and disease can be avoided because our immune system can then use these nutritional tools to grow new cells. A fast and effective way to treat an illness is with a nutritional IV of a special prescription of powerful nutrients that a nutritional doctor carefully prepares, after testing our body's needs. He or she then feeds these pharmaceutical-grade nutrients directly into our bloodstream. This is nutritional therapy at its most effective level, which effectively grows new cells and cures most diseases within a reasonable length of time.

Please remember that ten years ago my mental condition was such that I struggled to remember the names of my two grandsons. For the past eight years, I have supplied my body with an overabundance of good nutrition. Seven years have passed and, as we know, have been enough time for most of my old brain cells to be completely replaced with new cells. My old brain, ten years ago, would have found it impossible to write this book, but my new brain is really enjoying it!

Hormone Replacement Therapy

After my very first complete medical evaluation in 1997 by Dr. Guyer, he said, "Some of your hormones test low, and this is contributing to your low energy and your body not yet being 100-percent well. We need to bring all your hormones into balance. Hormones," he said, "must work together and complement each other to be totally effective."

I was surprised to hear Dr. Guyer saying that I had hormone problems. I thought hormone problems were reserved for females. I quickly learned, however, that I, too, had nine hormone glands. I tried to study and understand what these hormones did and how they worked together. I found that the diagrams in medical books explaining the process looked to me like a Rube Goldberg design. There is good reason why most medical doctors don't understand how hormones work in our body—they are very complicated.

I did learn, however, that we have about 100-trillion cells in our body that must function in harmony together, and it is the combination of hormones that directs the actions of our cells. Without the presence of the exactly correct amount of hormones at the exactly correct place, our cells would just sit there, and our body could not grow, move, or function properly.

I also learned that toxins are usually classed as carcinogenic when measured in the parts per million. However, the reference book *Radical Healing*, by Rudolph Ballentine, M.D., states on page 274 that hormones are affected by toxins at minuscule levels of parts per trillion. The book quotes Theo Colborn, Dianne Dumanoski, and John Peterson Myers, a medical research team, who offer the following comment on parts per trillion as it relates to hormones: "While they may not cause cancer, toxins at levels we thought insignificant can play havoc with our hormones."

For the past seven years my hormone replacement program directed by Dr. Guyer has consisted of:

- growth hormones injected by me five days each week
- testosterone injected by me every other week
- four different hormones I apply daily that are prescribed by Dr. Guyer in amounts just for my needs and mixed into a cream by a compound pharmacy
- insulin injected by me daily

I have an appointment with Dr. Guyer each six months, and he adjusts the amounts I inject and makes adjustments in my hormone-cream formula based on laboratory testing. The results have been excellent. At age seventy-two, I have no aches or pains, have no medical restrictions, maintain mental sharpness, exercise every day, and enjoy high energy levels.

Massage Therapy

Back in 1995, I was trying to get the toxic heavy metals out of my body. After fifty EDTA chelation therapy treatments, the heavy metal tin still tested at a high toxic level. My chelation doctor said, "We have to do something else to get rid of this tin. I want you, from now on, to get a deep-muscle, complete body massage the night before you come in for a chelation treatment." Lab testing showed that before I started massage treatments, each chelation treatment was removing 300 parts per million of tin. With a body massage the night before, the parts per million of tin removed jumped to 900 parts per million. From that day on, each time I am scheduled for a chelation therapy treatment, I get a one-hour deep-muscle body massage first.

In 1999, I began to develop a pain in the front shin-muscle of my right leg when I elevated the treadmill during daily exercise. I asked my family doctor about the problem, and he wrote a prescription to relax my muscles. The medicine didn't work, so I asked Chris Mattern, my massage therapist, what he thought. Chris carefully examined my leg (something my medical doctor did not do) and said that the muscle was tense and needed to be stretched. He then taught me how to do a toe-pointing exercise in bed each night before I went to sleep and then to repeat the exercise each morning before I got up. This instruction fixed my problem within three weeks, and now when I feel that leg muscle a little tense, I just do the simple toe-point exercise Chris taught me five years ago.

Neural Therapy

Surrounding each muscle group and dividing certain muscle groups in our body is a thin membrane sac called a "fascia." Because these sacs are interconnected and breathe through our lymph nodes, the complete fascia is called an organ. The fascia plays an important role in processing toxins from our body. If the passageway between two or more fascial sacs gets plugged, toxins can build up, resulting in swelling, pain, or the creation of a disease.

Your surgeon cuts through the fascia during major surgery. Sometimes, when it heals, the fascial sac gets tucked into the incision, and when scar tissue healing takes place, several long stress wrinkles or folds can be created out over the working surface of the sac. These wrinkles can interfere with the smooth flow of the lymph fluids that are processing toxins out of our body. The blocking of the lymph fluids can cause swelling, pain, or actual disease.

In October 2001, I began to have intermittent swelling in my feet and lower legs. My cardiologist in Indianapolis said that my circulation was okay and that the circulation to my feet was fine. My second-opinion cardiologist in Florida also said that the swelling was not caused by lack of blood circulation. Next, I had a foot-bone surgeon check my feet. He said that my foot bones were okay and that he did not know what was causing the swelling. Next, I contacted another foot doctor who specialized in treating the feet of diabetics. He gave the same answer, "You have a good pulse in both feet, and I don't know why your feet are swelling." All four doctors recommended diuretic drugs. I finally gave in and took them for three months. At times, I thought that the water pills were working but then swelling would come back even when I doubled-up on the drug. After consulting with my family doctor, who also admitted he did not know the cause of the swelling, I didn't know what to do.

Finally I gave up and made an appointment with Dr. Guyer. Because I had a three-inch appendix-removal scar, a nine-inch gallbladder-removal scar, and a ten-inch birthmark-removal scar on my back at the waistline, Dr. Guyer recommended that my old hard scars be treated with needle injections of neural therapy to soften them up. By softening the scars and making them more flexible, hopefully they would release the wrinkles and stress in my abdominal fascia sac that were created during my various surgeries. This would permit my lymph fluids to flow freely again and remove the toxins that were causing the swelling.

With weekly massage therapy to my legs, back, and abdominal area, followed by about 100 to 200 neural therapy injections into my abdominal scars each week for six weeks, the swelling in my lower legs and feet stopped being a problem.

Mesotherapy

Mesotherapy is a treatment that stimulates the mesoderm, the middle layer of our skin. The connective tissue of our body, called collagen, which makes up most of our bone, ligaments, tendons, and muscles, is derived from the mesoderm.

Actual meso treatment consists of a trained doctor injecting, with very short multi-needles, medicines or concentrated nutrients into the mesoderm in the area of the inflamed or damaged bone, ligament, tendon, or muscle. As a result, rapid healing in an isolated area of an inflamed or damaged body part can take place.

In my case, when I had swollen inflamed ankles and lower legs, Dr. Guyer injected anti-inflammatory medicines into the mesoderm of my lower legs at the same time he injected neural therapy into the scars of my abdominal area. I estimate that he made 100 separate injections of mesotherapy into each leg. The next morning, all the swelling was gone, and the color of my skin was normal again. Two additional mesotherapy treatments were required to cause a complete cure. Mesotherapy was used on me to get immediate results as a short-term treatment, and neural therapy was used for a complete long-term cure.

This medical treatment was developed in France, and presently about 15,000 physicians in Europe are trained to use mesotherapy. Dr. Guyer represents just a handful of advanced medicine doctors who have traveled to France, taken the required training, and become certified. A larger group of plastic surgeons on the west coast of the U.S. has taken the training, but uses it for "body sculpturing." By injecting the correct amount of fat-dissolving medicines into just the right areas of the mesoderm, your waist reduces to teenage size, and your body can be shaped any way you want. All you need is a small picture showing what you want your body to look like accompanied by a large bag of money.

Ozone Injections

During the winter of 2001, the live colonies of nanobacteria that had been surgically removed from my lower-left jawbone in 1999 and from my upper-right jawbone in 2000 returned with a vengeance. I was in Florida, but the dull ache in my jawbones was so annoying that I flew overnight back to Indianapolis and saw Dr. Guyer early the next morning. He numbed both my upper and lower jaws, waited a few minutes, and then injected several large syringes of freshly generated ozonated water throughout both my upper and lower jawbones. Within six hours the aching stopped. The next morning Dr. Guyer repeated another round of ozone injections; I boarded ATA Airlines in the early afternoon the same day and flew back to Sarasota.

I continued to be free of jaw ache, and two months later when Betty and I returned to Indianapolis for the summer, Dr. Guyer began to run tests to determine what was going on in my jawbones. An MRI of my head revealed that the nanobacteria colonies had spread into the bone surrounding my right eye, out near my right ear, and into my right face bones. A specialist surgeon refused to remove the bone particles containing nanobacteria from my face because he feared spreading the bone infection into other nearby bones. Dr. Guyer began injecting ozone around my ear bones, directly into my eye bone, and then into my face bones as well as my jawbones. He repeated the ozone injection three times during the summer and again in October just before Betty and I returned in November to Sarasota for the winter. Since I have had this series of low-cost ozone injection treatments, my ear, jaws, face, and eye bones have remained calm and without ache. Follow-up nuclear bone scans of my head in October 2003 did not detect hot spots of possible active nanobacteria colonies.

Medical Doctor Follow-Up to All Treatments Is Necessary

Before we departed for Florida in November 2001 and because I was approaching seventy years of age, I asked Dr. Guyer to run tests looking for the presence of cancer cells. Dr. Guyer decided on three blood tests. Two were standard cancer blood tests, and one was a DNA by Qualitative PCR test.

During the first week of January 2002, while in Florida, I received a telephone call from Dr. Guyer. "I have good news and bad news," he said. "The good news is that the blood tests indicate your body is free of cancer cells. The bad news is the DNA test discovered the presence of 'mycoplasma' in your blood, and this is serious." He said, "I think there might be a connection between the nanobacteria we have been treating in your jawbone and this mycoplasma. I want to start you on 500mg daily of an antibiotic called tetracycline right away, and it would be good if you could fly back to Indianapolis and stay a week for more intensive treatments and more tests."

In March 2002, I returned to Indianapolis and was treated for five days with large doses of liquid antibiotics fed by IV directly into my bloodstream. After one week, I returned to Florida and remained on tetracycline and other forms of antibiotics for about a year. Dr. Guyer had to prescribe several nutritional therapy IVs during that year when I was on antibiotics to help keep my immune system functioning at a high level.

In the spring of 2003, DNA tests showed that the number of mycoplasma "hits" found in my blood had dropped from 500 to only 50. This was good news, but Dr. Guyer also knew that we needed to find a way to make my body free of this dangerous disease agent, and antibiotics were not getting the job done.

Because we had been successful treating the nanobacteria in my jawbone with freshly generated ozonated water, Dr. Guyer recommended we try a treatment commonly used in Europe called "blood-ozone" therapy.

Blood-Ozone Therapy

Dr. Guyer assigned one of his assistants, Amgad Ghattas, M.D., who has received extensive training in the medical use of ozone, to treat me.

1. With me lying on a comfortable bed, clothed in a surgical gown and covered with a warm blanket, Dr. Amgad sterilized my arm, and then inserted a large needle into a large vein and drained 250cc of my blood into a 500cc plastic IV bag.
2. Immediately, he turned on the ozone generator and converted pure medical oxygen (O_2) into ozone (O_3), which was then infused into medical-grade water, 250cc of which was injected into the 500cc bag and mixed with my blood.
3. Next he treated the 500cc mixture of blood and ozone with heparin that prolongs the clotting time of blood. He continually observed the blood/ozone mixture as it flowed back into my bloodstream. Periodically, Dr. Amgad made a judgment to add more heparin.
4. After all the blood/ozone mixture was back in my body, Dr. Amgad immediately connected a 250cc bag of a hydrogen peroxide (H_2O_2) mixed with other supporting ingredients and very slowly drip-fed it into my bloodstream.
5. After the hydrogen peroxide drip was finished, Dr. Amgad started a fast nutritional IV drip of vitamins/minerals that were carefully selected special nutrients designed to rev-up my immune system so that it, too, could help kill the mycoplasma disease agents. This entire series of treatments took five hours.

After six treatment periods, my blood tested free of the mycoplasma disease agent, and with follow-up testing we know that I have remained completely free of mycoplasma.

Special notes: The type of mycoplasma I had is the disease agent the U.S. Army uses to create "germ warfare." I was exposed to it in the Army, and we now believe that this type mycoplasma is the same disease agent that caused sixty-five percent of the 300,000 Gulf War veterans to become so ill. Medical researchers now believe that several million non-military people in the United States also have an inactive form of mycoplasma hidden in their body that could activate at any moment and create a disease.

For additional information, enter "mycoplasma" on Google, and for medical information select any article written by Dr. Garth L. Nicolson. Dr. Nicolson works for the National Institutes of Health and is the medical authority to the U.S. Military concerning mycoplasma. If you want to know the details of mycoplasma and how our military used and dispersed it, read articles written by Donald W. Scott.

Intravenous Hydrogen Peroxide Therapy

Our body has two general types of bacteria within. One type is "aerobic bacteria," which use oxygen for fuel and leave carbon dioxide as a by-product. The best example is the friendly bacteria found in our intestines that aid digestion. These bacteria thrive in the presence of hydrogen peroxide. The other type is "anaerobic bacteria" that use carbon dioxide for fuel and leave oxygen as a by-product. Anaerobic bacteria are pathogens, the organisms that cause disease. All viruses also are anaerobic and cause diseases in one or another species, too. None are friendly. Hydrogen peroxide *kills, or severely inhibits the growth of, anaerobic bacteria and viruses.*

Now, get set for a big surprise. Your own "white blood cells" manufacture pure hydrogen peroxide and excrete small amounts of it into your bloodstream as the first line of defense against anaerobic bacteria and viruses that are trying to develop into various diseases. It is only after this natural flow of hydrogen peroxide is depleted that our immune system forms antibodies and asks our white blood cells to sacrifice themselves in an all-out war against a developing disease.

The second important assignment that hydrogen peroxide has in our body is to make chemical contact with biological waste products and industrial toxins and make them into inert substances by oxidizing them. Again, if all the hydrogen peroxide is used up because of the high level of toxins in our body, then our immune system is forced to spend its time analyzing, designing, and constructing antibodies that serve no other purpose than to fight these toxic foreign substances. It is worth noting that, while our immune system is busy fighting toxins, disease-causing bacteria and viruses can slip into our body unnoticed and unchallenged. Now you can understand why it is so very important to remove all toxins from our body before we can expect to get well.

Intravenous hydrogen peroxide therapy is a simple, safe medical procedure of diluting medical-grade hydrogen peroxide to a composition level normally found in our body and slowly feeding it into our bloodstream. This provides our immune system with its preferred first line of defense, hydrogen peroxide, which kills disease-causing bacteria and viruses along with a secondary mission of destroying toxins.

Colon Hydrotherapy

Back in 1995 when Dr. Zimmer, my first complementary medicine doctor, began the process using chelation therapy to remove the toxic heavy metals and other toxins from my body, he also addressed the toxin buildup that had accumulated over the years in my colon. At first he prescribed colon cleansing formulas and special enemas. Both gave some relief, but he wanted to make sure there were no serious problems in my colon because I had been passing some raw blood at times in my stool.

Dr. Zimmer recommended I see a "colonic therapist" who specializes in removing 100 percent of all old fecal matter, plaque, and toxins from the colon. She made a record of what came out of my colon and reported the results to my doctor.

Ellen's small clinic was pristinely clean and sanitary. Ellen is a second-generation full-time professional. Her mother was a certified colonic therapist before Ellen. I was instructed to remove all my clothing in a private dressing area within an arm's length of the special treatment table. After putting on a standard, open-down-the-back hospital gown, I was instructed to lie down on the table and cover myself with a sheet.

I signaled with a small bell that I was ready and then Ellen came into the room. She first elevated my feet by placing a twelve-inch-high stand under them. Next, with a pair of scissors, she cut open a factory-sealed clear plastic bag and removed a new sterilized adaptor with a special plastic hose attached. After placing lubricant on the adaptor, she asked me to take a deep breath while she reached, with her gloved hand, under the sheet and inserted the special adaptor into my anus and then plugged the hose into her hospital-quality stainless steel colonic machine.

Ellen had prepared the machine for my appointment with fresh, body-temperature water. The machine continued to maintain any temperature she dialed. On the front of the machine was a series of gauges and control-valve handles. In addition, there was a brightly lighted six-inch by eighteen-inch sealed box. Running the full length of the lighted box was a one-inch diameter clear glass tube.

The treatment began when Ellen slowly turned on the warm water, and it gently began entering my colon. The machine's gauges informed her when the water encountered a restricted area. She would then reverse the direction of the water and out through the glass eighteen-inch tube, for both Ellen and me to observe, flowed the fecal matter. The fecal matter is caught inside the machine in a bag for lab testing or disposal.

Ellen repeated this process several times until the warm water had entered the full length of my five-foot-long colon. She then filled my colon with water again and taught me how to do a gentle one-hand massage around over my abdominal areas where the colon is located. After reversing the water flow, more fecal matter could be observed flowing out through the long glass tube. The actual first treatment took about forty-five minutes and cost sixty-five dollars.

The first treatment cleaned out what looked like normal fecal matter. Three days later, the second treatment began removing old, very dark, hard fecal matter that had been lodged in the muscle folds for months or even years. "It's that old, dark toxic fecal debris," Ellen said, "that gets lodged and restricts the normal actions of the colon's muscles, and this is where trouble begins." The next week, the third and fourth treatment began removing mucus and strings of blood that had developed in the muscle folds under the old, dark, hard fecal debris that can, over time, create colon disease. During the fifth treatment, a paper-thin, very dark, what looked like a tobacco leaf-like, material began peeling from my colon wall. Ellen said this was plaque on the thin membrane colon wall that had taken years to form and was blocking the normal nutritional absorption action of the colon. On the sixth and last treatment, Ellen did a final flush check and added a new colony of friendly digestive bacteria that a colon must have to stay healthy.

At the end of the six treatments, Ellen's records showed that over thirty feet of old, dark, hard, toxic fecal debris had been removed from my colon along with about seven feet of mucus, stringy blood, and yellow yeast, measured as it passed through the glass tube.

The treatments gave me a new sense of wellbeing, and for the first time in years I began to have a healthy bowel movement three times a day, on schedule within two hours after each meal.

The healing effect of a colonic treatment is long lasting. Three months after my treatment, I had a colonoscopy. The doctor treated the one small area where raw blood was seeping through the colon wall. In 2001, five years after my colonic, I had a follow-up colonoscopy. The doctor reported no polyps, and the colon was a nice healthy pink like he would expect in a much younger man. The doctor said that there was no need to schedule another colonoscopy for ten years. I will be eighty-years old then.

Chiropractic Therapy

Twice in my life, I have had two different problems treated by a chiropractor. Both experiences were positive. In the summer of 1995, when I first started chelation therapy treatments, I developed inflammation in my right hip joint. When I moved my hip forward and backwards, like when I walked, my hip felt fine, but if I tried to rotate the hip, there was pain. Dr. Zimmer, my chelation doctor, had examined it and determined I needed some cortisone shots directly into the hip socket to cure the inflammation. He had given me a prescription to have an x-ray of the hip, and then I was to return the same day and he would administer the shots.

As I walked out of Dr. Zimmer's office, I met Dr. Bland, an out-of-town chiropractor. Dr. Bland had an appointment with Dr. Zimmer for a chelation therapy treatment. Dr. Bland was fifty-five years old but looked thirty-five. Dr. Bland had previously explained to me that he was convinced that he could slow down the aging process by keeping his body free of toxins, applying super nutrition, and having daily exercise. I would say, by looking and talking to him, that he was accomplishing it, too.

Dr. Bland asked me how I was doing. I told him about my hip problem and that Dr. Zimmer was going to shoot it with cortisone. Immediately Dr. Bland advised, "Don't ever have cortisone injected into a hip joint. There are other safer ways to handle the inflammation, and once you start cortisone injections you will be doing them the rest of your life."

Dr. Bland invited me back into Dr. Zimmer's office, borrowed one of the examining rooms with a long bench, and began working on my neck, back, legs, and hips. When he was finished, he said, "Tomorrow you will be sore in both hips, but as the soreness wears off, your inflamed hip should be okay. If not, here's my card, give me a call." He did this for free, and to this day, ten years later, that hip has continued to work without problems.

In 1997, after I completed my "Getting-Well" treatments with Dr. Zimmer, I had a routine annual x-ray to make sure that my heart was not enlarging. That same afternoon the radiologist called and asked that I return for more x-rays. He had discovered a growth of bone protruding from my spine at vertebra number ten and wanted to take more pictures. After a series of five more x-rays, my family doctor scheduled me to see a bone surgeon for possible corrective surgery.

Since my appointment with the surgeon was not for three weeks, I took my five new x-rays to a local Brownsburg chiropractor and asked him what he thought was going on at vertebra number ten. He mounted all five x-rays up on a big lighted glass wall viewer and immediately said, "Number ten vertebra disc is out of position, and what the radiologist believes is a bone spur is simply the edge of the slipped disc."

The chiropractor then with the aid of a machine snapped the disc back into proper position. He said, "You will have to come back four or five times because the disc will probably keep tying to slip out, but eventually it will stay in position." He then gave me instruction about what not to do to help keep the disc in place and gave me an exercise routine that would aid in strengthening the back muscles that hold the spine in place.

After five treatments by the chiropractor at $35 each, the disc stayed in place. I canceled my appointment with the bone surgeon and went back to the radiologist, told him what had happened, and asked for another x-ray to make sure it looked okay. He agreed that the vertebra looked fine, but predicted I would need back surgery someday anyway.

My spine was corrected by the chiropractor eight years ago, and there have been no problems with it since.

Enhanced External Counterpulsation (EECP) Treatment

Beginning about January 2002, I began to notice during exercise that my body was getting a little weaker, and I could no longer walk the treadmill at four mph for a full thirty minutes each day. By October, I was down to three mph and was beginning to feel stress pain in my legs, and angina was developing in my chest during exercise. Concerned, I had a Cardiolite Stress Test at the hospital and had the calcification measured in my heart at a private heart lab. The Cardiolite Test showed that a sag was developing in the muscle on the left front of my heart. The other test showed that the calcification in my coronaries had increased about thirty percent since my last test two years earlier in 2000. Combined, the two tests indicated that the blood supply to my heart muscles was growing weaker.

The question was how to stop the developing heart condition that was reducing blood flow to my heart, and how could I build the blood flow back to where it once was. A cardiologist recommended open-heart bypass surgery right away, but he was not aware I had been turned down for bypass surgery in 1993. I put the thought of surgery on hold and reviewed my heart problem with my family doctor and Dr. Guyer. Dr. Guyer recommended EECP. My family doctor didn't know what to recommend, because he knew that I was not a good candidate for bypass surgery, and he had never heard of EECP.

EECP stands for enhanced external counterpulsation and is a noninvasive means of creating additional blood flow to the heart for some selected patients. Oversize blood pressure cuffs are placed around the legs, thighs, and hips of the patient and connected by a complex set of one-inch hoses to a powerful air compressor.

The patient lies on a padded table with his or her chest wired to a special computer that receives his or her heartbeat. Between each heartbeat, there is a period when the heart is at rest before the next beat. Instantly at the beginning of the rest period, the computer controls inflation with air from the air compressor into the big cuffs, which very tightly and aggressively squeezes the legs, thighs, and hips of the patient and then quickly releases the pressure before the next heart beat. This creates an automatic treatment sequence such that, each time the patient's heart beats, his or her legs and lower body are so tightly squeezed, during the rest period, that some of the blood in the lower half of the body is forced into arteries going directly to the area of the heart. This excessive blood expands and contracts the walls of the arteries at the rate of each heartbeat. Over time, this exercise makes the arteries larger and more flexible, resulting in an increased blood flow to the heart. The initial standard program consists of thirty-five one-hour treatment periods for seven weeks.

Wanting to investigate EECP in October 2002, I was surprised to learn that my cardiologist was not knowledgeable of EECP and that none of the hospitals in the Indianapolis area offered this FDA-approved treatment. However, when Betty and I relocated in November to Florida for the winter, I learned that The Heart & Vascular Center at the Sarasota Memorial Hospital had offered EECP for the past seven years.

I was required to submit a detailed history of my heart problems that was reviewed by Randy B. Hartman, M.D., F.A.C.C., F.C.C.P., F.S.C.A., a cardiologist, to determine if I was a possible candidate for the treatment.

After Dr. Hartman determined that I was a possible candidate, copies of my medical history were sent from Indianapolis to Sarasota. I was then scheduled to be examined by Dr. Hartman. He called for a complete blood workup and for other vascular tests to be conducted with emphasis on the strength of my heart and the strength of my artery walls, blocked arteries, and hanging calcification out in the bloodstream that might break off from the pressures of EECP treatment. After the tests were completed, Dr. Hartman's final concern was whether I would benefit from the treatment. This approval process took three months, but I was eventually approved.

The EECP treatment room at The Heart & Vascular Center has two machines that provide about twenty treatments each day. The supervisor in-charge of the EECP treatment at The Heart & Vascular Center is Don Stuckey, R.R.T. Don greets us each day and takes our blood pressure and pulse rate, and then asks and records on his computer record system any angina being experienced in the chest, along with our exercise activities during the past twenty-four hours and our perceived energy level on a scale of one to ten.

I was required to wear standard women's pantyhose next to my skin to prevent chafing from the action of the large blood pressure-type cuffs rapidly inflating and deflating. Don furnished each patient with a pair of bright blue, full-length stretch-type bicycle pants, as an outer garment, with large lettering going down the right leg saying, "EECP Natural Bypass."

Each patient's heart beats differently, which requires Don to have the skills and experience to adjust the computer controlling the EECP machine, to match exactly the heartbeat characteristics of each patient. However, in my case Don had to find the locations of my new heart nerves that had grown and replaced my old damaged nerves. The standard lead-wire pattern on the chest normally used to send ECG information from the heart to the computer would not work for me because my new heart nerves were transmitting from near the center of my chest.

For the first week, Don supervised my treatment very closely watching for any adverse reactions to the treatment. He turned up the air-pressure a little each day to give my leg muscles time to adjust to this new-type exercise. By the time I had completed half of the thirty-five treatments, my body was so comfortable that I would fall asleep during the one-hour treatments.

I found EECP to be very effective for me. My heart, after treatment, has a nice steady beat, with a typical blood pressure of 120/70, my chest feels calm, and my heart reacts very quickly to my physical needs. There is little doubt in my mind that the little collateral bypass arteries that I continue to grow ahead of my heart's blockage growth are much larger arteries now, and are carrying a much increased blood flow to my heart.

Although Don never discussed other patients' medical conditions, I could tell he is very pleased with the number of patients he has helped over the years from their wheelchairs back to the golf course.

Prayer Therapy

On my first attempt writing Chapters 1 through 6 of this book, I decided not to talk about God's role in my "Getting Well." I began to justify in my own mind that the reader would prefer I devote one chapter, later on in the book, to the role God played in my "Getting Well," instead of including Him in the details as I wrote the story. I sent the first six chapters to my eight readers/advisors, and each indicated that what I had written was not very interesting.

While rewriting the six chapters, I decided to make my own separate comments about how my faith in God had helped me get well. My readers gave me higher marks this time, but I could tell they still were not too enthusiastic about my writing.

Knowing that the buyers of my book probably would not finish the book if the first six chapters were not interesting, I decided to pray and ask God for guidance before I rewrote the first six chapters for the third time. My message from God was very forcible and direct: "Tell your story," God said, "exactly the way it happened! Don't hold back on a single detail. Remember," He reminded me, "I directed everything that happened in the past, and I selected you to survive just so you could tell this story and give comfort and hope to others who are chronically ill, too. Now get on with it!"

After God's reprimanding message, I completely rewrote the first six chapters, but this time I tried to make clear to the reader exactly how it happened and that God had been in charge, not me nor the doctors, and that our actions were just part of His plan. After reading the first six chapters again, my readers/advisors gave me high marks by saying I had bonded with them. Some of them circled my interactions with God and wrote on the manuscript draft "Good," Excellent," or "Very Powerful."

After my experience doing it God's way, each time in the future when I began a new chapter I would pray and ask God what he wanted me to say in that new chapter. I would then clear my mind of all that was going on in this world and just lie down on the couch or take a walk to a secluded area alone and wait for the chapter to begin developing in my mind. I made no quick notes. Instead, I trusted my mind to completely organize and remember my thoughts by believing that God would guide the input. My meditation always lasted a full day, sometimes two. Once I spent nearly a week before I was organized well enough to start a new chapter.

During this initial period of starting a new chapter, I had very few conversations with God. I stayed in a listening mode. Eventually the outline of what the chapter was all about began to develop in my mind. When I felt that a workable plan for the chapter had developed, I would transfer my mental notes concerning the new chapter to a single sheet of paper using a pencil. There was no need to make many notes. I found that a few carefully selected words scribbled on paper that pinpointed my thinking could at any time in the future trigger paragraph after paragraph of detailed story information and actions that my conscious or unconscious mind had stored away over the years, and I now felt eager to write about it.

After completing the initial starting period of writing a new chapter, I could relax and truly enjoy writing at my own pace and schedule because I knew where I was headed with the chapter. If I was not sure at any moment of the flow of what I was supposed to be writing, I stopped and had a private conversation with God in humble prayer, and He usually, if my writing motives were on-track and honest, switched my brain back on, and the words would again begin to flow. I seemed to be always reminded that my job was to share information that would hopefully motivate and help the chronically ill to "Get Completely Well," and if I helped just one or two people, my effort would be worth it.

By using prayer therapy as my primary tool for writing *Getting Well*, I close this book with a warm satisfying feeling that I have done my very best to accomplish the assignment entrusted to me. May God Bless All of You By Making You Healthy Again, Just Like Me.

Doctor's Commentary

Most therapeutic approaches achieve only symptom management, whereas the best approaches tend to look at base causes or alteration of biochemical homogeneity, i.e., defining the core problem and working to restore the internal biochemical terrain, so that the body can heal itself. This was the case with Wayne's significant array of neurotoxic chemicals, especially heavy metals. Additionally, Wayne's medical fingerprint, or history of sorts, reads much like that of the typical patient who has found himself or herself in the category of "walking wounded," i.e., many things are out-of-balance or the patient feels terribly unwell and has a minimized functional capacity. While much of his or her standard laboratory testing is normal, most of the therapies prescribed by his or her well-meaning, conventionally trained physicians fall short of making significant improvements and perhaps make matters worse. Unfortunately, Wayne also experienced what was likely unnecessary treatment in having his tonsils, appendix, and gallbladder removed. The chronic nanobacteria infections of his jawbone are somewhat common. Therefore, it has always been my recommendation that patients confronted with a surgical or invasive procedure get second and third opinions if there is uncertainty about the proposed path.

I have often been amazed that patients, who have traveled across the country to receive multiple evaluations from multiple specialists and a certain therapeutic procedure, receive multiple opinions. You would think that there would be more consistency in assessment. I hate to say it, but certain surgeries and procedures are overused because of their profit-generating potential. Alternative medicine is not alien to this entrepreneurship. I have seen patients prescribed chelation therapy when they did not likely need that service or were not likely to benefit.

Second, well-intentioned medical doctors did not give Wayne sound advice early in his life when suggesting that he ignore the nutrient and multivitamin supplementation regimen that his wife and children were doing. In Wayne's family, he was the only individual not taking food supplements, yet he was also the only one to require pharmaceutical interventions and multiple medical procedures of various types over the years. This scenario began to unfold when he was prescribed a diuretic pill at 38. Certainly, these preparations can be helpful in controlling blood pressure; one might better ask what would be the reason that Wayne would have a problem with high blood pressure. Nutritional therapy, such as magnesium and CoQ-10 in supplemental form, has been shown in clinical studies as far back as the 1970s to have favorable effects on blood pressure. Additionally, similar nutrients have multiple uses at the cellular level in the body—in energy production, stabilization of the immune system, muscle contraction and function, regulation of heart rhythm, control of blood lipids, and so on. Therefore, if Wayne had taken a simple approach such as magnesium and CoQ-10, he probably could have achieved adequate blood pressure control and many other biochemical improvements. However, the prescription antihypertensive medicine served to treat only the symptom and probably went a long way to further depleting his body of essential minerals, somewhat adding to a long list of toxic interventions to his body that gradually eroded his sense of function. Many of the multiple drug regimens prescribed today make patients feel worse to the point that they often need more drugs to cover up the side effects of previous drugs.

Additionally, the commentary on EDTA chelation therapy deserves attention. It has been my assessment that at least nine out of ten people tested will show evidence of some type of heavy metal bioaccumulation, i.e., levels of known toxic metals such as lead, mercury, cadmium, aluminum and arsenic. Subsequent treatment with chelation therapy will, in most patients, dramatically improve their self-assessment of well-being, and additionally create measurable objective improvements, such as an enhanced regulation of blood pressure, heart rhythm, improvements in energy, improvement in vision, and, in some cases, hair growth. Still, chelation therapy remains one of those topics that seem to be hotly disputed in the minds of conventional medicine despite the fact that the FDA approves EDTA for treatment of lead toxicity.

In terms of the heavy metal toxicity, one must keep in mind that we are not required to have had a history of industrial exposure to toxins to lead us to develop this bioaccumulation. There are enormous variations on this factor. Some people are able to process toxins in their bodies more effectively than others. Others may have genetic or drug-induced metabolic anomalies that make it more difficult for the body to clear toxins acquired from our environment. Frankly, almost every citizen in our country is exposed to numerous types of toxins that will gradually accumulate.

The other component revolves around diet. It would be ideal if everybody were able to eat organically grown products and high-quality foods. I have seen it often stated by scientists that there is no difference between organic products and the general synthetic hothouse or mass production agricultural approaches to food delivery. I would argue that the same people who may foster that opinion have never sat down at the dinner table and tried the organic tomatoes that my grandmother raised for many years. Anyone who has ever had a chance to compare quality farm-raised products side-by-side with hothouse-prepared items will immediately attest to the obvious differences. Besides improved taste, however, one acquires a significant advantage of enhanced levels of antioxidants, polyphenols, and health-supporting biochemical compounds, many having still-unknown benefits.

Many of the therapies very helpful to Wayne in achieving his revitalized state of optimal health are therapies only more recently available in our country, but they are fairly old by European standards. However, only in the last few years have growth factor extracts and live cell therapy products become more routinely available for citizens of the United States. I remember one patient whose brother many years ago had visited a clinic in Europe and received injections of live-cell therapy. Prior to arriving at the clinic, his body had been very crippled with arthritis making it difficult for him to walk. Additionally, his mental condition and general overall physical condition were very sluggish. He reported to his sister that after a few days of live-cell injections, he was out on the court playing tennis with absolutely no joint pain. Such is the restorative potential of some of these overlooked therapies. Hormone replacement therapy, especially of the bio-identical type, should also be reviewed, as well as the importance of understanding the hormones in a symphonic balance.

An overall summary that remains unusual, at least for medical practice in our country, is that all of these therapies have been used for several decades throughout the world, primarily in Europe with significant success rates. Many therapies that I have found to be successful I did not learn in medical school, yet they have been done in Europe for 20 to 40 years. This therapeutic knowledge is not part of the medical training of most doctors and remains overlooked as a potentially valid inclusion in an individual patient's healing journey. It is my hope that introducing these healing therapies will provide additional information that is useful for you and your family. Improving your overall health and healing potential has been our primary goal while writing *Getting Well*.

—Dale Guyer, M.D.

Afterword

Wayne Cox and Dr. Dale Guyer are visionaries in the field of advanced medicine. They have teamed up to provide for you practical help and hope to invite you to begin your journey toward "Getting Well." Wayne has asked you to join him on the path of taking ownership of your health care, with commitment, vision, and courage. Dale is a guide on that path, and is a physician who knows how to remove the root causes of disease, infuse the body with nourishment, and help the naturally rejuvenated cells remember how to be in alignment with the true healing source, the Physician Within. The maxim "The doctor treats, but nature heals" is clearly demonstrated in this book.

Wayne's courageous journey begins and ends with faith and experience of the Physician Within. His journey reminds me of another pioneer in this work, Norman Cousins. As Norman pointed out, "The healing system is activated by the belief system." Dr. Cousins was able to document in his book *The Anatomy of an Illness* the profound healing power of laughter and good cheer through his own experience of healing from a degenerative, "hopeless," painful bone disease. He, too, teamed up with a physician who helped to nourish the spirit~mind~body to create its own powerful force of healing. The proverb "A cheerful heart is a good medicine, but a crushed spirit dries up the bones" (Proverbs 17:22) summarizes the power of belief in the experience of "Getting Well" for both of these visionaries.

This summarizes the integration of spirituality into the practice of medicine. This healing power, innately woven into the fabric of the spirit~mind~body, can become more powerful with a cheerful, optimistic outlook, generated from the experience of inner wholeness, the still small voice, otherwise described as the Physician Within. When the inner spirit is crushed by doubt, disappointment, and rejection, it can, and often does, decrease the healing power. The spirit can be crushed internally from your own thoughts, or externally from the words of the physician.

For many medical caregivers, it seems like superficial folly to try to be cheerful when there is nothing but bad news for the patient. There is too much scientific research about the power of prayer, meditation, faith, hope, love, and the effect of belief on the physical system not to pay attention to the inner spirit of each patient for whom care is provided.

We all know how powerful good news can be to restore energy and vitality, for a group of hikers lost on the trail, or a homesick child at summer camp who sees father and mother. Even if the patient has only moments to live, there can always be some "good news" shared and experienced by loving family and sensitive medical professionals. Creative caregivers can experience and offer legitimate, realistic, joyful cheer, even when the facts seem to call only for tearful despair. Fortunately for Wayne, Dr. Guyer is one of those caregivers who honors the power of faith to draw close to the Physician Within, and who also has knowledge to remove the obstacles for the cells and tissues to rejoice, thereby rejuvenating the spirit~mind~body.

Now, what about you? What will you do with this invitation from Wayne and Dale? Will you simply continue with old, limiting beliefs and knowledge? In his book *Scripts People Live*, author Claude Steiner shows that people develop early patterns of belief based on negative or positive influences of those around them. Thus, children decide, however unconsciously, whether they'll be happy or depressed, winners or failures, strong or dependent. Having decided, they spend the rest of their lives making the decision come true. For those who choose a negative script, the consequences can be disastrous.

If you're living a pattern that says that growing older means deterioration and limitations of your health and wealth resources, only a conscious decision to change the pattern will bring you positive results. You have a chance to change that pattern, and do whatever you can to maximize your chances of "Getting Well."

It's as if you've come to a fork in the road. The signpost on the right reads, "New Choices." The one on the left says, "Old Choices."

Let's consider the left fork first. Honestly examine any patterns, tendencies, and beliefs you have about the concept of aging and prospect of experiencing "Getting Well." Do you believe that your current medical problems worsen as you age, resulting in less energy and more limitations? See yourself five, ten, or twenty years from now, living those patterns. What do you think your life would be like? Are you afraid you might not have enough resources to sustain you? Will your lifestyle leave you de-energized and demoralized? Will you even be alive? What a frightening picture!

Now, envision the right-hand path. Suppose you make a new choice to believe that you can maximize your chances of "Getting Well," and that it is possible to *improve* with age. Imagine how your life would be if—starting today—you did everything in your power to create a reality of increasing health, energy, and possibilities. See yourself five, ten, or twenty years from now, living those new patterns. What would your life be like? What would you be doing that would result in a high quality and length of life, with all the resources necessary to sustain that vision? If

252

you like what you saw in the right-hand path, what new choices could you make today to invite an optimistic vision of your future?

Adorning my wall is a teakwood plaque with the words "Lead with vision: 'Where there is no vision, the people perish.'" This signpost reminds me daily how critical it is to have a vision—but not just any vision. Old, ineffective patterns invite a future just left to chance. Compelling, energizing, transformational visions are like signposts to a wonderful life. This exercise is about creating a new, empowering signpost. By taking a few minutes to write down your answers, you'll begin to experience energy, vitality, and renewed vigor. But, this is just a beginning.

If you take this book seriously, and commit yourself to a vision of "Getting Well," and then take responsibility courageously for your health-wealth energy, your vision would not adorn your wall, but would be etched upon your heart.

—Dr. Craig Overmyer

References

Listed are books that I have read or used as reference material that have helped to mold and guide my thinking, as I traveled down the road of "Getting Well"

Adolph, Harold Paul. *God's Prescription for Your Good Health.* 1991.

Anderson, Greg. *50 Essential Things to Do when the Doctor Says It's Cancer.* 1993.

Atkins, Robert C. *Dr. Atkins New Diet Revolution.* 1999.

Balch, James F., and Phyllis A. Balch. *Prescription for Nutritional Healing.* 2000.

Ballentine, Rudolph. *Radical Healing.* 1999.

Barefoot, Robert R. *Death by Diet.* 2002.

Barefoot, Robert R., and Carl J. Reich. *The Calcium Factor.* 2002.

Barnes, Broda O. and Charlotte W. *The Riddle of Heart Attacks.* 1992.

Baum, Seth J. *The Total Guide to a Healthy Heart.* 1999.

Brecher, Harold and Arline. *Forty Something Forever.* 1999.

Bridges, Jerry. *Trusting God Even when It Hurts.* 1988.

Brody, Jane E., and Denise Grady. New York Times *Guide to Alternative Health.* 2001.

Carper, Jean. Stop Aging Now! 1996.

———. *Miracle Cures.* 1997.

———. *The Miracle Heart.* 2000.

Carter, Mildred, and Tammy Weber. *Body Reflexology.* 1994.

Casdorph, H. Richard, and Morton Walker. *Toxic Metal Syndrome.* 1995.

Challem, Jack, and Victoria Dolby. *Homocysteine: The New "Cholesterol."* 1996.

Chopra, Deepak. *Alternative Medicine, the Definitive Guide.* 1994.

Clapp, Larry. *Prostate Health in 90 Days without Drugs or Surgery.* 1997.

Colbert, Don. *Toxic Relief.* 2001.

———. *What You Don't Know May Be Killing You.* 2004.

Cooke, John P. *The Cardiovascular Cure.* 2002.

Cranton, Elmer M. *Bypassing Bypass Surgery.* 2001.

Crook, William G. *The Yeast Connection.* 1994.

D'Adamo, Peter J., with Catherine Whitney. *Eat Right for Your Type.* 1996.

Diamond, John. *Your Body Doesn't Lie.* 1979.

Dillard, James, and Terra Ziporyn. *Alternative Medicine for Dummies.* 1998.

Eades, Mary Dan. *The Doctor's Complete Guide to Vitamins and Minerals.* 2000.

Elrod, Joe M. *Reversing Degenerative Disease.* 2003.

Enig, Mary. *Know Your Fats.* 1990.

Fallon, Sally. *Nourishing Traditions.* 1999.

Gills, James P. *Temple Maintenance.* 1989.

Graveline, Duane. *Lipitor: Thief of Memory.* 2004.

Hart, Kathleen. *Eating in the Dark.* 2002.

Hatherill, J. Robert. *Eat to Beat Cancer.* 1998.

Hawkins, David R. *Power vs Force.* 2002.

Jerome, Frank J. *Tooth Truth.* 2000.

Kaufmann, Doug A., and Beverly Thornhill Hunt. *The Germ that Causes Cancer.* 2002.

Kaufmann, Doug A., with David Holland. *The Fungus Link.* 2003.

Kemper, Donald W., and Diana Stilwell. *CIGNA Healthwise Handbook.* 1995.

Klatz, Ronald, with Carol Kahn. *Grow Young with GHT.* 1997.

Longacre Janzen, Doris. *Living More with Less.* 1980.

McCully, Kilmer. *The Heart Revolution.* 1969.

McMillen, S.I. *None of These Diseases.* 1984.

Miller, Judith, Stephen Engelberg, and William Broad. *Germs.* 2001.

Mindell, Earl L. *The MS Miracle.* 1997.

Moore, Pete. *Killer Germs.* 2001.

Morrison, Marsh. *Doctor Morrison's Miracle Body Tune-Up.* 1973.

O'Bannon Baldinger, Kathleen, and Larry Richards. *Health & Nutrition.* 1999.

Omartian, Stormie. *Greater Health God's Way.* 1996.

Overmyer, Craig. *Dynamic Health.* 2003.

Pfrimmer, Therese C. *Muscles—Your Invisible Bonds.* 1983.

Pierpali, Walter, and William Regelson. *The Melatonin Miracle.* 1995.

Prevention Health Books, Editors of. *Vitamin Cures.* 2000.

Rapp, Doris J. *Our Toxic World.* 2004.

Ravnskov, Uffe. *The Cholesterol Myth.* 1998.

Reisser, Paul C. *New Age Medicine.* 1983.

Rockwell, Sally J., with Louise Bondi. *Blood Sugar Blues.* 1995.

Rosch, Paul. *Dangers of Cholesterol Lowering Drugs.* 1999.

Rosenfeld, Isadore. *Power to the Patient.* 2002.

Rubin, Jordan S. *Patient Heal Thyself.* 2003.

Ruwart, Mary J. *Healing Our World.* 1993.

Salaman, Maureen. *Foods That Heal*. 1994.

Sears, Barry. *Mastering the Zone*. 1997.

Shimer, Porter. *New Hope for people with Diabetes*. 2001.

Siegel, Bernie S. *Love, Medicine & Miracles*. 1986.

———. *Peace, Love & Healing*. 1989.

Silverman, Harold M. *The Pill Book*. 2002.

Smith, Timothy J. *Renewal, The Anti-Aging Revolution*. 1998.

Stanek, Lou Willett. *Writing Your Life*. 1996.

———. *Death by Prescription*. 2003.

Steinman, David. *Diet for a Poisoned Planet*. 1990.

Stewart, David. *Healing Oils of the Bible*. 2002.

Strand, Ray D. *What Your Doctor Doesn't Know May Be Killing You*. 2002.

Thomas, John. *Young Again*. 1994.

Trowbridge, John Parks, and Morton Walker. *Chelation Therapy*. 1994.

Walker, Morton. *The Chelation Way*. 1990.

———. *Elements of Danger*. 2000.

Walker, Morton, and Hitendra Shah. Chelation Therapy. 1997.

Weil, Andrew. *Natural Health, Natural Medicine*. 1995.

Whitaker, Julian. *Dr. Whitaker's Guide To Natural Healing*. 1995.

Wright, Jonathan V. *Dr. Wright's Guide to Healing Nutrition*. 1990.

Valentine, Tom and Carole, with Douglas P. Hetrick. *Applied Kinesiology*. 1987.

Van Belle, M. Arlene. *A Journey of Healing*. 2002.

Ziff, Sam and Michael F. *The Missing Link*. 1991.

———. Dentistry without Mercury. 1995a.

———. Dental Mercury Detox. 1995b.

Publish Your Own Story

I have found that all of us love to read true stories about what has happened to other people. I have also noted that when we accomplish a goal, like "Getting Well" from a chronic illness, most of us like to share our experience, hoping to help others.

Having observed this, I have decided to make you, the readers of the book *Getting Well*, an offer:

#1 In 500 words or less, tell how you personally used the book *Getting Well* to improve your own health or to cure a chronic illness.

#2 Send your personal story to me, Wayne Cox:

   wbcox@msn.com   or   Cox Limited Publishing, LLC
                                                P.O. Box 253
                                                Brownsburg, Indiana 46112

#3 Your personal story will be read by the eight readers/critics or editors listed on the "Acknowledgments" page of this book. They will then pass on to me those stories they feel will most benefit other chronically ill people.

#4 Dr. Guyer and I, personally, will select the 100 best stories and will publish them, as soon as I have a good representation of examples, in a book titled *Getting Well, Too—By You*. Each of you, if your story is selected, will receive a free copy of the paperback book in which your personal story appears.

#5 For your story to be eligible for consideration for publication, **you must include a return mailing address** when you submit your personal story. Should your story be selected for publication, editing and small changes in the wording may be required, and then it would be necessary to submit to you the edited copy along with a legal release to publish, requiring your approval and signature.

#6 Personal stories received **without a return address will not be read and will be destroyed by shredding.**

On behalf of Dr. Dale Guyer and me, **We Thank You** for reading *Getting Well*, and we remain eager to hear from you!

—Wayne

About The Author

The person who discovered "The Four Basic Principles for Getting Well" is the author, Wayne Cox. His courageous journey begins and ends with faith and experience of the Physician Within. His amazing and unforgettable story will inspire and educate you. Dale Guyer, Wayne's physician and creator of the Advanced Medical Center, provides invaluable insight that should form the heart of all treatment plans designed to restore your body to complete wellness.

Wayne and Dr. Guyer use the forum of this book to inspire, educate, and challenge you or a loved one not to settle for anything less than complete wellness that will bring excitement and richness of vitality to your life.

Printed in the United States
24489LVS00003B/55-1008